Biller
1978

The Real Wealth of Nations

The Real Wealth of Nations

S. R. Eyre

Edward Arnold

First published 1978
by Edward Arnold (Publishers) Ltd
25 Hill Street, London W1X 8LL

British Library Cataloguing in Publication Data

Eyre, Samuel Robert
The real wealth of nations.
1. Wealth
I. Title
339.4'1 HC79.W4

ISBN 0 7131 5970 7

Set in 11 on 12 point Plantin by Computacomp (UK) Ltd., Fort William and printed in Great Britain by Richard Clay (The Chaucer Press) Ltd, Bungay, Suffolk.

Contents

Figures

Tables

Acknowledgements

I wish to express my sincere thanks to all those who have helped me in the preparation of this book. In particular I am most indebted to Professor Helmut Lieth, Professor P.J. Newbould, Professor J.P. Cooper, Professor S.J. McNaughton and Dr R. Andrews for their advice on primary productivity, to Dr E.B. Worthington and the staff of the Central Office of the International Biological Programme for giving me access to productivity data, to the Forestry Commission, the Institute of Petroleum, the Tin Research Institute and the Copper Development Association for their help in providing information, and to Dr R.W. Grimshaw for his advice and guidance on the subject of mineral production. Without this assistance the material included here could never have been assembled and digested. I am also very grateful to Mr T.G. Boaz and Dr D.R. Hodgson for reading parts of chapter 5 and for their most helpful comments, and to Mr J.R. Eyre and Mr N.J. Eyre for their opinions on the material in a number of the chapters. However, all the interpretations and expressions of opinion to be found here are entirely my own and are not necessarily shared by any of those who have so kindly assisted me.

For their advice and creative skills in devising and drafting the maps and diagrams I am deeply indebted to Mr G. Bryant and Mr T. Hadwin. I would also like to acknowledge the financial assistance provided by the Social Science Research Council and the University of Leeds Standing Committee on African Studies for travel and other expenses in Britain and East Africa.

Last and first, I am most grateful to my wife for her help and for her support in sharing a view of the future which demands a rare blend of apprehensiveness and equanimity.

Preface

Throughout the 'fifties and 'sixties we said little. Our training, our observations and the inferences we drew from them caused us to have serious reservations about the industrial juggernaut and all that followed in its train. At times we implored our students to pause and be objective, but we had no right to expect them to be convinced when we did not commit ourselves completely. In spite of the evidence, we still felt that those who spoke with authority in technology and government and social science could not all be wrong. But as the 1960s drew on and apprehensions began to be translated into reality, it became only too clear that they were wrong — fundamentally wrong — and that we too had been wrong for not having had the courage of our convictions. In mitigation one might perhaps plead that it was not until the later 1960s that massive evidence about resource depletion began to emerge — the kind of evidence which might reasonably be expected to make an impact on minds which are the product of half a dozen generations of Industrial Revolution. But this is not seriously offered as an excuse. The writing had long been on the wall and should have been interpreted even before intrepid anti-pollutionists like Rachel Carson made their first protests about resource destruction.

This, then, is not a book written only for geographers and other people professionally concerned with resources: it is a belated attempt to interpret the predicament of humanity for all those who are perplexed and disturbed by the present state of the world, with its seeming contradictions, perversities and injustices. Of necessity, it spans the entire field of human economy and, as a consequence, has obvious limitations. Complete systematic treatment of every field of investigation impinged upon is clearly beyond its scope. Aspects of plant ecology, petrology, demography and so on are the basic material from which the text is fashioned, and a great effort has been made to explain individual points clearly as they arise; but appropriate authorities must be consulted by those readers who require a more comprehensive introduction to the sciences involved. Furthermore, I am well aware that in these days of rigorous specialization, anyone who ranges widely through the sciences is open to accusations of superficiality, if not rank misconception. In prospect one cannot counter general strictures of this nature; all that can be said is that the author is only too conscious of his limitations but that, over the years, he has persistently sought the advice and opinions of many people whose knowledge and penetration could not reasonably be in question, and to whom he is greatly indebted.

The necessity of bringing together a wide range of scientific knowledge is obvious. Piecemeal assessment of the earth's resources is always liable to reach unrealistic conclusions: the specialist can so easily overlook the many urgent demands on land and materials other than those in which he is particularly interested. The industrial developer may forget that there are such essentials as food crops and forests. It is impossible to sustain any quantitative arguments about resources and the population pressure upon them without a comprehensive overview: demands on food, mineral fertilizer, energy and metals are inseparably related.

Finally, it is important that the reader should not be misled by my declared intention to present a quantitative study. No attempt is made here to create a new model of the world system after the manner of Jay Forrester and Dennis Meadows. An analysis can be incisively quantitative without resort to computer-based statistical models. Indeed there are some grounds for suspecting that formulation of the abstractions which are inherent in cybernetics may divert the mind a little too far from terrestrial realities. It would be both presumptuous and ungenerous to decry the outstanding contributions to thought that have originated from the Massachusetts Institute of Technology, and nothing could be further from my intentions; moreover, both Forrester and Meadows have made it abundantly clear to the initiated just what one may infer and what one should not infer from their models. Nevertheless, their projection of continuous smooth lines representing trends in the level of population, pollution and natural resources, up to the end of the twenty-first century, does tend to produce mental images which may not facilitate clear thinking.

If one may resort to analogies, it is as though they are likening our world system to an indestructible elephant in an unstable environment. During the rains it is fat and ebullient, but in the dry season it becomes weak and emaciated. Yet there is always *something* to eat and drink so that it is still alive to flourish again when the variables move in its favour. Its fortunes fluctuate, but life goes on. My own mental image is quite different. Our industrialized system is more like a defective machine which can be made to run at different speeds but which, over the centuries, has been made to go faster and faster and to process more and more material. It is still theoretically possible to slow it down, modify it, and give it less to do, but there is little sign yet that this is going to happen. Consequently, certain moving parts may shortly melt or shatter, and the whole construction fly to pieces. And although there may well be lots of fragments lying around after this has happened, it seems unrealistic to project graphs any further, suggesting that a "machine" is still in existence.

The inherent limitation of cybernetics is that it can indicate future occurrences which, in terms of any conceivable demographic and political realities, seem quite impossible. This can be illustrated very clearly from one of Forrester's simulations (1971, p.109) in which, because of a postulated pollution crisis, a population crash from seven billions to little more than one billion is shown to occur between 2025 and 2050 AD. This is accompanied by a spectacular rise in the "quality of life" and followed by a population recovery to a peak of three and a half billions by 2090 AD. The statistically initiated can appreciate the rationale of Forrester's diagram, but its usefulness must be in doubt: one cannot imagine any set of circumstances in which such a course of events could possibly happen in the real world.

My basic precept is that no manageable world model will ever be able to take account of political realities in all their complexity. It is partly for this reason that the present book has developed in the way it has: it sets out to take a quantitative look at trends in population growth and resource usage, trying at the same time to remember that there are such things as frontiers and other human institutions which, in one form or another, are inseparable from the physical existence of man on the earth.

S. R. EYRE

University of Leeds
November 1976

The green, flat earth lay infinite,
Its edge was out of mind,
We ate the fruit, we grubbed the root,
The forest closed behind.
And then it got all globular
And we could sail it round
'Twas ours to keep, we burrowed deep
To see what could be found.
That great big world is shrinking now,
It's getting very small,
Perchance we'll wake one morning and
It won't be there at all.

I

Introduction: Fundamental Reasons

Within little more than half a decade, a perceptible change has taken place in the general outlook of reflective people in many countries. As recently as 1965 it was rare to meet anyone who doubted that technology would inevitably ensure the continued and indefinite rise of the material standard of living of the peoples of the earth. This was "progress", and it was inconceivable that there could be any fundamental reason why "progress" should not go on for ever. The grey depression years between the wars were not permitted to dim the vision — they were merely a temporary setback the like of which could always be cured by a strong dose of Keynesian economics. The totalitarian spectre of the second world war, though seen by some to threaten another Mongol dark age, was quickly consigned to oblivion following military victory. And even "the bomb", which more than a small minority of marchers saw as casting doubt on man's ability to survive, was thought by the majority to be controllable, provided the leaders of the nations recognized the obvious and avoided the extremes of stupidity and turpitude. Even if the worst came to the worst, civilization would disappear in one glorious bang and most of us would not suffer for long. Throughout the thinking of all sections of the community there was no suggestion of any necessity to modify our way of life radically and to plan for a more austere future. The buoyant bubble of technological optimism thus swelled out apace with the onward march of the 'fifties and 'sixties.

This optimism still prevails as a basis for both public and private activity, but it has ceased to be implicit in the minds of many. In particular, an increasing number of those in public life seem to feel it incumbent upon them to express their *faith* in the possibility of continuing material advancement — so much so that it often seems, like the Player Queen in Hamlet, they do protest *too much*. There is now a persistent unease that something fundamental and all-pervasive is threatening almost every facet of existence. It is not just that semi-imponderables like overcrowding, congestion in public places and a decrease of social cohesion in the family and in the community are causing life to be more unpleasant: a multitude of specific trends and occurrences are giving the impression that the world has become a more unreliable place to live in. Even those in the less privileged sectors of society who had begun to feel that the relative improvement in their material fortunes over the past quarter of a century might presage a better world in perpetuity, are beginning to have doubts. Commodities such as sugar, petrol and toilet rolls have developed the tendency to disappear from the normal places of sale. And, most disturbing of all, there has been the progressive increase in the cost of nearly everything, with the concomitant that the savings worth £500 in January are worth no more than £400 by the end of December.

If society is to come to terms with these disturbing things, it seems essential that it should be given an explanation as to why they have arisen. Then, if there is a remedy, it can be pursued without undue delay; if there is no real remedy, the hardships involved are more likely to be tolerated with equanimity if the reasons for them are appreciated. Unfortunately, in the mid-1970s, there is a plethora of diverse, and often contradictory, explanations for our misfortunes. In the main, "explanation" takes the form of "blame" which, according to sectarian predelictions and particular cases, is laid at the door of communists, capitalist exploiters, coal miners, farmers, oil sheiks, gnomes in Zurich, and numerous other ill-intentioned categories of humanity. Indeed, sometimes the cause is seen to be non-human, and the weather is found to be the culprit. Presumably the blame must then rest squarely on the shoulders of the Almighty.

In a certain limited sense these diagnoses may be correct: a single pressure group or quirk of nature may well be the immediate reason why a difficulty descends upon us at a particular point of time. But if we go along with this kind of analysis we are permitting the statistical noise to obscure the really important underlying trends: what we should really be saying is that human organization has not allowed a sufficient margin of safety as a buffer against almost inevitable chance occurrences, errors and human perversities.

As every good historian knows, the explanation of complex social phenomena is never a simple matter: large-scale happenings can usually be explained on at least three levels. For example, at the shallowest level the first world war was "caused" by the assassination of Archduke Ferdinand but, although this probably did affect the actual date on which hostilities began, few would be inclined to accept the view that no war would have occurred if the fatal shot had not been fired in Sarajevo. At the second level of explanation are the long-term ambitions of political groups and individual potentates: in this context, the ambitions of the Kaiser and the long-term aspirations of a unified Germany would be examples. But thirdly we have "explanation" at its most fundamental level. This involves the analysis of underlying natural, economic and demographic pressures under whose constraints nations and empires have expanded or collapsed — constraints which make certain lines of development increasingly difficult, and others more obvious and more profitable.

The kind of history with which most of us are familiar confines itself almost exclusively to the first and second levels of explanation. (The marxist interpretation of history, which does seek explanations at the third, more profound, level, has been over-selective in the processes and pressures it has subjected to scrutiny.) This is unfortunate because, at the present critical stage in the history of mankind, it is all-important to have an analysis of the contemporary scene at the most profound level, otherwise factional recriminations will continue to be taken at their face value. Selfish sectional and commercial interests may well be the stuff of first-and second-level historical analysis, but when viewed in the light of more deep-seated environmental forces, both natural and social, gnomes in Zurich and reds-under-the-bed are nearly always found to be part of the statistical noise — mere ripples ruffling the surface of the massive groundswell which breaks against the sea-wall of our security. Nevertheless, society will continue to hold the ripples responsible unless the groundswell, and the strong winds out to sea which cause it, are identified.

In the early 1970s people perished in their thousands in the dry zone on the southern fringes of the Sahara. They died of starvation and malnutrition diseases during a period when the summer rains failed them. The drought was held responsible. But droughts such as this one have occurred before and the area is notorious for its variability in rainfall. Droughts must be regarded as the immediate reasons for disasters, not the fundamental ones. What men did not perceive was that the population had doubled several times since a drought of similar proportions last occurred.

In Britain in the 1970s the pound poses problems and threatens disasters. It fluctuates from day to day and a variety of reasons are offered, often contradictory, and usually implying factional blame. The long-term implications are disquieting in the extreme because the country imports so much of the food and industrial raw materials for its 57 million people, and all this must be bought with pounds.

The two cases just cited, and thousands of others the world over, trouble and puzzle humanity. They will continue to trouble us for a long time to come; they will also continue to puzzle us if we do not begin to ask the right questions about them. With regard to the sub-Saharan lands one obvious question is whether the recent famines would have been anywhere near so serious if the population had been no greater than it was in 1900. The answer is almost certainly in the negative. The same kind of question can be asked about the population and the pound in Britain (see chapter 8); perhaps even more pointed is whether the pound would be suffering as it is if Britain were more than self-sufficient in food and had a mining industry which produced great surpluses of copper, tin, lead, zinc, silver, high-grade iron ore and fossil fuels. In such a situation would not the countries of the world be falling over each other to get hold of pounds with which to obtain these precious materials? Would the pound, worth four dollars a generation ago, now be worth less than two? In such happy circumstances surely gnomes in Zurich, speculators and reds-under-the-bed would be impotent.

But the situation in Britain is almost the opposite of this. Mass imports of food and industrial raw materials are essential to maintain gastronomic standards and to support almost the whole of manufacturing industry, and manufactures are produced for exchange purposes. But similar manufactured articles are made by a large and ever-increasing number of other nations, some of which produce a much larger proportion of their own raw materials and food. Overwhelmingly therefore, the evidence indicates that the state of the pound is a reflection of far deeper ills than many seem inclined to admit.

There are powerful reasons for thinking that other growing problems also require a fundamentally different analysis. If this is the case, the implication is that the traditional economic analysis is leading us astray, and that the basic precepts of Adam Smith are no longer appropriate. It is for this reason, though not without feelings of deep humility and an abounding consciousness of my temerity, that I join issue with the illustrious progenitor of modern economic thought.

2

Wealth

During the past couple of centuries two very significant developments have taken place over the earth. First, there has been a rapid increase in the disparity in material standard of living between the industrialized countries on the one hand and most of those who did not profit early from the Industrial Revolution on the other. Secondly, there has been the gradual dissemination of Western ideas throughout nearly all human communities — including those concerned with the nature of Western democracy and the equality of opportunity for all men and women. No two developments could have been more explosively juxtaposed: as people in the countries with predominantly peasant and pastoral economies learned about their increasing deprivation relative to people in Western countries, so the news spread that every man, whether or not he is as good as the next, should at least be given the opportunity to prove it. That there can be no peaceful future for civilization in a world in which there is this great disparity is a recurrent theme in the chapters which follow.

The peoples of the world have been referred to here as "deprived" and "privileged" rather than as "poor" and "wealthy". This is not due to any particular kind of pedantry but because, in my view, the term "wealthy" as applied to nations has become increasingly ambiguous in recent times. In a sense, of course, the Western industrialized countries are "wealthy": the majority of their inhabitants can indulge themselves with food, drink and clothing and still have a large excess of income to spend on other things which, to underprivileged peoples, are inaccessible luxuries. Nevertheless, every man has his own conception of wealth. To many, particularly in the past, it was a strong-box, containing gold and silver, concealed somewhere under the floorboards. To others it is a collection of pictures or antiques. To the few, it has always been expansive acres, as a source of produce, rent, recreation and prestige. But these are all narrow and personal views of the concept of wealth and it has long been understood that, to assess the relative wealth of nations, much more sophisticated criteria are required.

It is true that, until the latter part of the eighteenth century, a large percentage of political economists, though by no means all (Johnson, 1937), held to the view that the wealth of a nation could be assessed in a very similar way to that of an individual merchant. Sixteenth- and seventeenth-century writers such as Hales, Malynes and Thomas Mun certainly subscribed to the "mercantilist" view of international economics — that the wealthiest nations were those which, by sale of their own materials or by the accumulation of profit from trading in other people's goods, had amassed the greatest amount of "treasure". It was not until the publication of Adam Smith's *The Wealth of Nations* (1776) than an alternative philosophy of national wealth was widely promulgated. In this great classic of economic and social philosophy Smith carefully developed the argument that the only fundamental way of assessing the wealth of a nation is by examining the manner in which it utilizes its labour. It appeared clear to him that "the annual labour of every nation is the fund which originally supplies it with all the necessaries and conveniences of life" (p.17) and that the wealth of a nation is solely the amount and quality of the labour it possesses and the efficiency with which it sets it to work. This view of economics, with its implications in the fields of agriculture and manufacturing, was subsequently accepted by nineteenth-century economists. In essence it has come through to the latter part of the twentieth century unchallenged. Although laissez-faire economists and businessmen of the present day might well wish to make some of Adam Smith's points in a rather different way, it is doubtful if they would have any fundamental reservations on the main issue. Furthermore, although their marxist counterparts would certainly denounce all the capitalist overtones to be found in *The Wealth of Nations*, the way in which labour and industry have been organized in socialist states over the past half century does not seem to indicate that they would wish to dissociate themselves from Smith's basic precept. It appears, therefore, that this view of economics remains the philosophical cornerstone of modern industrial society.

And indeed, up to a point, Adam Smith's thesis seems unassailable. Without labour there can be no wealth (indeed no income) for anyone. Even in the most primitive hunting and collecting society, the wild products of nature do not become "food" unless the men exert themselves in the hunt and the women labour with the collecting basket; and in the complex modern society, not only are the wheat harvest and the steel ingot the products of labour, but so are rents, dividends, pension funds and the salaries of prime ministers. Moreover, on the world scene, a superficial view of national economies seems to support Smith: by and large the countries with the highest average standard of living are those which use labour most productively; they are the ones which have the largest mean output per man-hour.

No, the point upon which Adam Smith's philosophy has so misled nineteenth- and twentieth-century society is that it attributes no inherent value whatsoever to the raw materials upon which agriculture and industry are founded: it assumes that these are the free gifts of nature and that they are

available in infinite quantities. The clear implication of his thesis (though he did not put it this way) is that if there are two countries with the same population and an equally low material standard of living, they must be regarded as equally "wealthy" even though one has enormous unused areas of potentially productive land and huge untapped reserves of iron, copper, tin and oil, whereas the other has none of these things.

There is a purely semantic point here, revolving around the definition of the word "wealth". According to the Oxford Dictionary we are at liberty to go along with Adam Smith or not: on the one hand "wealth" may be taken to mean "welfare" or "prosperity" while on the other it can mean "riches" and "abundance". Indeed, many who have written on the subject of natural resources have not held to Smith's narrower definition but have committed themselves to expressions such as "great wealth of *untapped* natural resources", though whether by design or inadvertently is not clear.

It seems to me, however, that the point of departure here is far from a purely semantic one. Adam Smith was obviously intending to present some means by which the *total economic well-being* of nations could be assessed and compared, and his choice of the term "wealth" can be regarded as both fortuitous and unimportant. Although much of his analysis is masterly and many of his major points, in their context, must be regarded as universal truths, some of his views are very clearly a reflection of his time. He was writing at the beginning of the Industrial Revolution when the vast majority of the population of the world, even in Western Europe, was still at the peasant and pastoral stages of cultural development, but when technological innovations and the division of labour were increasing rapidly and sparking off significant social changes. The "efficiency" of specialized labour and machines as compared to that of all-round competence and hand labour was being increasingly demonstrated by their relative economic successes. On the other hand vast areas of the earth were still unexplored by people of European origin, and the organic and inorganic resources of even larger areas were almost completely unexploited. One can appreciate why the possibility of land shortage and wholesale depletion of the earth's store of metal ore and mineral fuel seemed to Smith so remote as to be unworthy of serious consideration.

Yet it cannot be said that he completely overlooked the possibility. He specifically makes the point that "in a country fully peopled in proportion to what ... its territory can maintain ... the competition for employment would necessarily be so great as to reduce the wages of labour to what was barely sufficient to keep the number of labourers, and, the country being already fully peopled, that number could never be augmented" (p.88). However, he goes on to say that "perhaps no country has ever yet arrived at this degree of *opulence*" (my italics). He admits, of course, that starvation has occurred on a mass scale in places like Bengal and China, but he puts the blame for the former on the "mercantile companies" which control places like Bengal. In the case of China he feels that it "probably long ago acquired that full complement of *riches* [my italics] which is consistent with its laws and institutions. But this complement may be much inferior to what, with other laws and institutions, the nature of its soil, climate and situation might admit of." He thus admits that, in places, a population limit has already been reached in relation to *perceived* resources, but he feels that organizational and cultural limits are entirely responsible where this has occurred, and that the acquisition of different attitudes and a higher technology would increase the carrying capacity of the land immeasurably.

The subsequent flourishing of the Industrial Revolution demonstrated the soundness of this last point, and it is probably because of this that Adam Smith has continued to enjoy the reputation of being the father of modern economic thought. *The Wealth of Nations* was, however, written two centuries ago so that, although its author may have had some excuse for regarding the earth's resources as being virtually inexhaustible, humanity at the present time has ample evidence to indicate that it should take a very different view of things. All those who believe that we can continue to follow the expansionist philosophy of Smith should ponder two main points. First, the earth's population has doubled and then more than doubled again since the time when he was writing and, while doing so, it has consumed more than a hundred times as much mineral material as had been used up during the whole of previous history. Secondly, Adam Smith, though a compassionate and humane man for his times, was able to contemplate suffering and deprivation as a perfectly normal and expectable part of the order of things in a way which would be revolting to many people in the latter part of the twentieth century. He envisages (without further comment) the natural balance whereby the existence of too many labourers lowers wages, which increases child mortality, which in turn lowers numbers and, ultimately, causes a rise in wages again (pp.77–8). It is well to remember that this latter point must always have been at the back of Smith's mind: in his philosophy matters could never get completely out of hand because, if a nation actually managed to reach population saturation point (the point he refers to as that of maximum "opulence") and then continued to increase, starvation and child mortality would take care of the situation. At the present time it seems as though large numbers of people have reached that unrealistic state of mind where they wish to have the best of both worlds: they would like to retain Adam Smith's laissez-faire with regard to both resource exploitation and having children, and at the same time to build up an infallible system of social welfare to ensure that no one goes hungry or suffers an untimely end because of neglect or disease. In the final assessment, since the earth is of finite size, it is axiomatic that the two are incompatible.

It is also salutary to recollect that Adam Smith had a contemporary called Thomas Malthus. Their views about human existence on the earth have usually been regarded as almost antithetical, the former being portrayed as expansionist and optimistic, the latter as restrictive and gloomy. Smith argued that cultural and technological advances can increase the carrying capacity of the earth almost indefinitely. However, Malthus's main point was that, whereas population tends to increase in a geometrical progression, striving to double every generation, increase in food production is arithmetical, with roughly the same increment of production being added over equal periods of time. He inferred from this that the lot of man is, and always will be, deprived and precarious, particularly in the lower strata of society (Malthus, 1798). The general opinion seems to have been that the Industrial Revolution proved Adam Smith right and Thomas Malthus wrong. Certainly the latter was unfortunate in that the century and a half following the publication of his *Essay on the Principles of Population* (1798) was a period in which industrialization took place at a pace and on a scale utterly unprecedented in the history of mankind. This permitted wholesale urbanization to an extent which even Adam Smith might not have thought possible: even he might well have resisted the temptation to imagine that by the year 1970 it would be possible for only 2 per cent of the population of Britain to be directly engaged in agriculture.

As popularly presented we have then the contrast between Adam Smith, the successful interpreter of the laws of economics, and Thomas Malthus, the man who failed to anticipate the possibilities of the Industrial Revolution. But perhaps the intellectual and philosophical gulf between them is not so profound as is usually supposed. One of them wrote the following words:

> Every species of animals naturally multiplies in proportion to their means of subsistence, and no species can ever multiply beyond it.

If asked to guess which, most of us would probably say it was Malthus. But no, these words appear in *The Wealth of Nations* (p.76) and they demonstrate very clearly that Smith was just as convinced about the inevitable laws of nature as was Malthus. Also in numerous places Malthus indicates quite clearly that he is fully aware of the fact that cultural changes are capable of accelerating the agricultural productivity of a society. The difference between them is mainly one of outlook. They were both concerned about the condition of mankind, and were both sufficiently humane to give consideration to the possible ways of alleviating it. While Adam Smith devoted much of his effort to outlining an economic system in which he thought the general lot of mankind would be gradually improved into the indefinite future, he had no illusions regarding the inexorable controls under which humanity, like all other species, will always exist. And while Thomas Malthus devoted most of his attention to the nature of these natural controls, it is perfectly clear that he wished very much that things were different from the way he found them.

As so frequently happens, the motives of both these great men have been presented in a distorted fashion in subsequent popular commentary. Their basic contentions remain, however, and the time for a radical reassessment of the relative value of their contributions is overdue. For two hundred years the consensus has been in favour of Adam Smith. The main aim of the present work is to examine the population/resources equation to see whether there is a chance that Malthus will have the last laugh. Adam Smith unequivocally equated a high birth rate with prosperity while Malthus saw the carrying capacity of land inevitably being outrun by population growth. The Industrial Revolution seemed to refute Malthus but did it do any more than put off the evil day? The earth is now carrying an enormous "post-Malthusian" population, made possible by the industrialization and urbanization which he failed to visualize. Is it not likely that this population is a long-term impossibility because of a resources problem which Adam Smith's philosophy failed to take into account? In Britain today there are more than 50 million people where there were little more than five million at the beginning of the Industrial Revolution. Industrial growth made possible the accumulation of a vast empire which in turn supplied food and industrial raw materials when indigenous reserves were outgrown and, ultimately, depleted. What would both Adam Smith and Thomas Malthus have said regarding the chances of these 50 million people now that both indigenous resources and empire have evaporated?

Although the world of economics and business, capitalist and marxist, still holds firmly to the precepts of Adam Smith, our very survival seems to be dependent on a radical review of his conception of wealth. The world may seem to be a much "wealthier" place than when *The Wealth of Nations* was written, but we must ask ourselves whether appearances are not illusory.

3

Population Increase

Our educational system seems to have failed to engender a widespread and lively interest in the quantification of organic and mineral resources. This is surprising in view of the fact that the magic of quantification has triggered off new developments in almost every branch of learning, from limnology to linguistics, during the past two decades. The dichotomy between C.P. Snow's "two cultures" does not provide an explanation. The degree of educational over-specialization is still a matter for regret, but the assessment of world resources is not one of the things which has been permitted to slide into the ravine between the well tilled plateaux of artistic humanism and respectable science. Indeed the broadly based and thoroughly cultured young person may not be quite such a rarity as some have supposed. What is really surprising is that although a young scientist may be very knowledgeable about Beethoven and Van Gogh, and genuinely appreciative of their works, it is rare to find one who has a sound knowledge and understanding of the occurrence of phosphate deposits, copper ore and soil erosion. It is even more unusual to find one who knows a great deal about world supplies of rice, cotton and timber.

In large measure this may be due to the rather uninspiring ways in which education in "commodities" developed in the twentieth century. Up to the time of the second world war, teaching about "products"fell within the field of the old style commercial and economic geography (see chapter 10) where the student found himself involved in memorizing the amounts of commodities, country by country, often with no demands whatsoever on geological or ecological understanding. When this fell into disuse, little was done to fill the gap: only a very small number of economic geologists and agricultural economists have provided formal education in these fields and their audiences have been very small. Clearly a new and more stimultating approach to world resources is required. If this is not forthcoming young scientists will perhaps still be justified in viewing this field of knowledge as of no more intellectual worth than philately, and the only substantial group of people with a primary interest in commodity production figures will be those who stand to profit from them financially — manufacturers, commodity speculators and dealers in "futures".

One point in particular seems to have been overlooked by those who have sought to popularize resource studies as an intellectual pursuit, and the omission is probably vital. Quantitative study of commodity output and resource reserves cannot have much point unless closely linked to an assessment of the present and future populations dependent upon them. The fact that the world annual production of food grains between 1968 and 1970 averaged 1,113·6 million metric tons (Borgstrom, 1973) has little significance and makes very little impact on the mind unless one is told that the human population of the earth in the same period was about 3,500 millions. Similarly, the rate at which food production is increasing is a statistic of very limited importance unless one is told whether population is increasing at a faster or a slower rate over the same period of time. Any analysis of material standard of living must take into account the numbers of people involved. The material well-being of society can only be discussed meaningfully in the light of the equation which sets numbers of people against the quantities of materials which they consume.

One important reason why it is difficult to apply this equation to different communities arises from the contrasts in expectations. A group which has suffered declining fortunes, for instance, may bewail its deprivation even though its per capita consumption is enormously in excess of that of another group which accepts its condition without complaint because it has never experienced material emancipation and has no visions of it. The fact remains that average-sized individuals in all communities require similar amounts of calories and protein to keep them alive and healthy, along with clothes and housing to protect them against the elements. (Climatic differences do give rise to some differentials in requirements. Food, clothing and housing needs in cold, windy and wet environments are usually somewhat greater than elsewhere.) In general, therefore, *at a given technological level,* if annual resource production is static then population must be static in order that material well-being should not decline. Also, if resources are becoming scarcer, then population must decline to accommodate this. And even if the amount of available resource is increasing, material well-being will decline if population is increasing yet more quickly. Only if the whole range of resources required by the communities involved is increasing faster than population can there be an argument in favour of continued population increase; and only if it can be clearly demonstrated that the increase in resources can be sustained indefinitely, can this argument be regarded as sound.

This line of reasoning, though basically unassailable, does present the population/resources issue in its simplest terms: considerable qualification and refinement are necessary. Were it not so, all arguments in favour of economic growth and population increase would long since have been discredited and, indeed, population could never have increased to its present size. The main complication, as shown in the previous chapter, is that communities do not stay at the same technological level: over the past two centuries, in particular, they have continuously developed sophisticated methods of exploiting the environment so that more and more people could be supported. It is mainly for this reason and because it has hitherto been impossible to forecast the amounts of resource reserves that are going to be available in the future, that the assertions of technological optimists have so far been able to carry conviction.

In order to focus clearly on the balance between population and resources in the immediate future, it is necessary to review the changes that have taken place in human population since our species had its origin. It is now thought to be almost two million years since some kind of hominid, which can loosely be referred to as "man", first appeared on the earth (Leakey, 1965). Over the vast period from this time up to about 8000 BC, the average rate of population growth must have been very small; it may have been virtually static for long intervals. The evidence is scanty and very difficult to interpret, but it suggests that at the time of the neolithic revolution, when man first began to till the soil and to have domesticated flocks and herds (Hole and Flannery, 1969), the human population of the earth was probably about five millions (Deevey, 1960) — about half that of Greater London. Subsequently, because plant and animal foods were now being manipulated, they were more plentiful and more conveniently to hand, and a greater density of population became possible. At first, however, such nuclei of settled agriculture were of very restricted distribution in a few areas like Mesopotamia, Egypt and Palestine; diffusion over wider regions was slow and spasmodic. Britain was not reached until just before 3000 BC and much of the Great Plains of North America until 1870 AD. Consequently, although densely packed cities like Ur of the Chaldees and Jericho came into existence, they made only a small impact on the general picture of world population and the upward trend continued to be very slow. The interval over which world population doubled was still considerably more than 1,000 years: it was not until about 1820 that the one billion (1,000 million) mark was first reached.

In the light of this slow development over some two million years, the trend from the early nineteenth century onwards can only be regarded as startling. In the mere hundred years between 1820 and 1920 a second billion was added to the world's population. It then took only 40 years for the same thing to happen again, the three billion mark being achieved by about 1960. Then, after a mere 15 years, four billion was reached in 1975 (figure 3·1). Consequently, for the

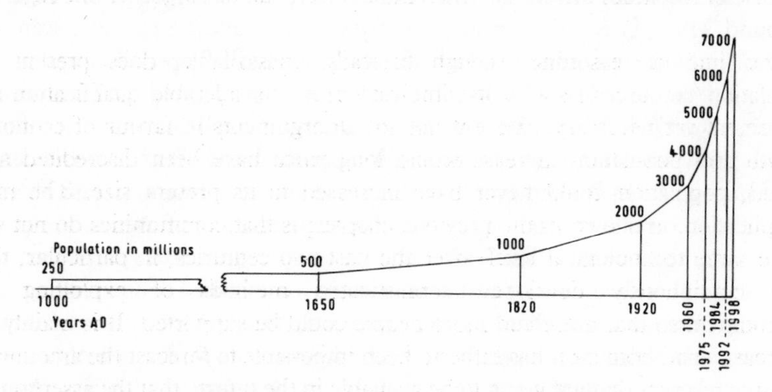

3·1 World population growth, 1000 to 2000 AD

first time in history, anyone who is more than 40 years old at the present time can truthfully say that the population of the world is more than twice what it was in the year in which he was born. And every morning, when we wake up, there are almost a quarter of a million more people on the earth than at the same moment on the previous day.

Such an exceptional event in the history of the world is a clear indicator of unusual circumstances. In that it was unprecedented (for the human species) it is small wonder that Malthus failed to detect its onset. Indeed, were it not for the accumulation of census data and the products of historical research over the past century, it is doubtful if we could bring ourselves to accept that it has really happened. In the light of the technological developments that have taken place since the beginning of the Industrial Revolution, however, an enormous acceleration in population growth might well have been anticipated. Throughout history in the average community, a hundred parents were rarely survived to adulthood by more than a hundred children. With a lower incidence of famine (McKeown, 1976), advances in medicine and better housing, the death rate decreased markedly without a commensurate lowering of the birth rate, so that within a generation or two the increase in population was dramatic. This took place first in technologically sophisticated countries in the nineteenth century; it was followed by a similar trend in the countries with predominantly peasant economies in the twentieth century, culminating in the wholesale suppression of malaria, cholera and yellow fever.

No attempt will be made here to discuss the multifarious factors which determine the rate of population change; clear and authoritative accounts are to be found elsewhere (see Clark, 1967) and should be consulted by those who seek a proper understanding of demographic trends. The only reason for touching on demographic issues is to explain why there are powerful reasons for concluding that, as yet, the earth has not felt the full impact of the demographic revolution. Probably the most significant demographic change which took place in Europe during the nineteenth and early twentieth centuries was the enormous reduction in infant mortality: infants survived the first year with increasing success. Thus, in Sweden, whereas between 1816 and 1840 there were 192 infant deaths per thousand live births in the cities and 163 per thousand in rural areas, by the decade 1881–90 this had fallen to 131 and 102 respectively (Clark, 1967). Furthermore, by the 1960s, the overall mortality rate for the whole of Sweden had fallen to a mere 13 per thousand (Population Reference Bureau, 1971). In Ireland in 1840, there was an infant mortality rate of 81 per thousand in rural areas and of 138 per thousand in towns of over 2,000 people, whereas by the 1960s, in the Irish Republic as a whole, it had fallen to 20·6 per thousand. There are now no countries in non-communist Europe with an infant mortality rate of more than 25 per thousand, with the exception of Austria, Portugal and Spain (see appendix III). On the other hand, in spite of the recent substantial increase in general life expectancy in the countries of Africa, Asia and Latin America, infant mortality rates remain very high — in some cases probably exceeding those in Europe at the beginning of the nineteenth century. Quite a large proportion of tropical countries do not record infant deaths, but of those which do, Zambia has 259 per thousand, Gabon 229, Guinea 216 and Niger 200. With the exception of Tunisia, Algeria and Mauritius, all African countries which record have more than 100 per thousand. In Asia, India has 139 and Indonesia 125 per thousand, while in Latin America, Brazil is outstanding with 170, and Chile comes next with 92 (Population Reference Bureau, 1971).

It is most thought-provoking to speculate on what the present social condition would be in these countries if, over the past ten years, they had had infant mortality rates similar to those prevailing in Western Europe — say 20 per thousand. The figures presented in table 3.1 (columns 5–10) are both approximate and theoretical. In the first place the births and infant deaths for all years of the decade in question have been calculated from the published values for 1971 (Population Reference Bureau, 1971). Secondly, the figures do not reflect accurately exactly what would have happened had infant survival rates been higher because, if more had survived, this would have affected other things. For instance, the survival of more babies in a particular year would inevitably have influenced the attitudes of some parents with regard to the number of children they had in subsequent years. The aim here is merely to give some impression of the enormous flood of extra people that would have accrued given European-type survival rates along with the existing fecundibility.

With all its limitations table 3.1 shows clearly that the present "population explosion" would already have had far more serious results if over the decade 1967–76 welfare and medicine in the more deprived countries had been as effective as in Europe. Far more people would have survived infancy, either to augment the pressure on land and other resources up to adulthood, or to die of starvation and disease during later childhood. An examination of columns 10 and 11 reveals that, as well as the 150 million added to the population of India during this period, an extra 28 million or so would have swelled the child population. (It is most important to understand that these "extra children" cannot just be added on to the 1976 population because, although the majority might well have survived to that date, a certain percentage which cannot be computed would not.)

Similarly Brazil would have acquired between five and six million extra children and Zambia more than half a million. A passing glance at the figures for the other countries in the table might seem to indicate that their cases are not quite so striking, but one should ponder carefully how a country like Niger, with its Saharan and sub-Saharan environments, could have coped with an extra 380,000 children surviving beyond the first year, over and above the 1,660,000 that it did acquire during this ten-year period. The significance of this point will be only too obvious in subsequent chapters. The figures presented for Africa as a whole are subject to a few more reservations, but their order of magnitude cannot seriously be questioned: over and above the population increase of between 80

Table 3.1 The effects of infant mortality on rates of population growth

	Population estimates for mid-1971 (Population Reference Bureau, 1971)				Population approximations for decade 1967–76 (in millions)						
	(1) Total population (millions)	(2) Annual rate of growth (per cent)	(3) Annual number of births (per 1000 of population)	(4) Annual infant mortality (deaths under one year per 1000 live births)	(5) Total live births	(6) Actual number of infant deaths	(7) Infant deaths if mortality rate had been only 20 per 1,000	(8) Actual number surviving infancy	(9) Number surviving infancy if mortality rate had been only 20 per 1,000	(10) Difference between columns (8) and (9)	(11) Actual population growth assuming the growth rate of mid-1971
India	569·5	2·6	42	139	239·19	33·25	4·78	205·94	234·41	28·47	150·40
Mali	5·2	2·4	50	120	2·60	0·31	0·05	2·29	2·55	0·26	1·26
Mauritania	1·2	2·2	45	187	0·54	0·10	0·01	0·44	0·53	0·09	0·27
Niger	4·0	2·9	52	200	2·08	0·42	0·04	1·66	2·04	0·38	1·18
Upper Volta	5·5	2·1	49	182	2·69	0·49	0·05	2·20	2·64	0·44	1·17
Zambia	4·4	3·0	50	259	2·20	0·57	0·04	1·63	2·16	0·53	1·34
Brazil	95·7	2·8	38	170	36·37	6·18	0·73	35·19	35·64	5·45	27·25
Africa	354·0	2·7	47	151*	166·38	25·12	3·33	141·26	163·05	21·79	86·23

* Average of 31 countries which record (16 do not record)

and 90 millions in this period, there would have been an extra child population of more than 20 millions.

It is thus incorrect to imagine that the "population explosion" has occurred because formerly deprived countries, during recent decades, have achieved Western standards of health and welfare. In particular, the chances of infant survival in these countries are still far less than those in the privileged countries, and one can reasonably infer from this that if equality of survival were achieved in all countries in the near future, without any lowering of fecundity, then the upward trend in world population would become even more dramatic.

In the light of these inescapable facts one can appreciate why an increasing number of people, particularly biologists, are reaching the conclusion that demographic disaster is imminent — that the explosion of numbers of mankind cannot be checked before it is too late. They make the point that any biologist who detected such an increase in growth rate as that depicted in figure 3.1 for any other species of animal would diagnose a "swarming stage" situation in which a culminating crash in numbers would be inevitable. The analogy of a laboratory culture of bacteria has sometimes been used (Taylor, 1970) where a population can be observed to mushroom outwards from an initial point of infestation until the whole of the nutrient medium is occupied. Subsequently, numbers fall off with increasing rapidity, partly through lack of food and partly because of the toxic effect of their own waste products. A crash to very low numbers is the best that can be expected.

Just how closely such a model can be applied to the present human situation is arguable. To say that the two cases must be very similar is obviously simplistic: on the other hand it is undeniable that some disturbing basic analogies are all too obvious. There is no more fundamental principle in ecology and evolution than that the numbers of all species are kept in check by a combination of controls such as food supply, predation, environmental stability and territoriality. If any one of these is relaxed, then the population tends to expand in a short-lived "swarming stage" until the particular control is re-established or until another one comes into operation. The way in which controls on human population have been relaxed has already been indicated; the point at issue is whether a new kind of control can be self-imposed and, if not, just when and by what means natural controls will again come into operation causing numbers to crash to pre-industrial (if not pre-neolithic) levels.

One of the favoured tenets of some social scientists is that population problems will produce their own solutions — that just as rural overpopulation in Western Europe stimulated influx into urban areas, followed by an enhanced material standard of living and ultimate fall-off in the rate of population increase, so the same kind of thing will happen elsewhere on the earth. There are certain aspects of this argument which demand careful scrutiny. In the first place, is it possible that such "automatic" demographic changes could occur quickly enough to prevent the massive population increases which seem to be presaged by straightforward extrapolation of present trends? Again it is important to recollect that the population of Britain was little more than five million at the beginning of the Industrial Revolution, but has increased to well over 50 million during the course of the industrialization and urbanization that has taken place. It is very doubtful if it has yet reached its peak. If the same general course of events were to occur in Africa, this would entail an increase from about 300 million in the mid-twentieth century to some 3,000 million in about 200 years and an increase for the whole of the non-industrialized peoples of the earth from about 2,000 million (two billion) to 20,000 million over the same period.

In other words, the evidence suggests that the "automatic" demographic changes that have accompanied industrialization in Western countries, far from providing an acceptable answer to the world's present problems, would be exactly what we seek to avoid. Nearly all the evidence presented in subsequent chapters demonstrates that the earth's resources cannot sustain increases of this order of magnitude, and that we must seek to ensure that trends in the rest of the world are very different from those which occurred in Europe.

One scans the present patterns in the hope of finding some indication that the rate of population increase will slow down in the near future. Unfortunately, in many parts of the world, exactly the opposite seems likely to occur. The very fact that massive disease control in the deprived countries has taken place so recently has resulted in an unbalanced age structure. In spite of the fact that infant mortality rates remain high, children account for a very large proportion of the total population in these countries. Whereas only 24 per cent of the people of Western Europe are under 15 years of age, in Africa as a whole the figure is 44 per cent (appendix III). For Asia as a whole the figure is 40 per cent and for Latin America, 42 per cent. Honduras seems to have held the record in the late 1960s with 51 per cent (Ehrlich and Ehrlich, 1970), but many countries were little far behind. One can infer from these figures that, by the late 1960s, about half the population of Africa was less than 17 years old.

The conclusion seems inescapable. Over the next ten or fifteen years, in the deprived countries, there are going to be far more (not fewer!) people in the age groups which produce families than has been the case in recent decades. The only ways in which this could fail to produce vast numbers of children are either by mass mortality or by an unprecedented reduction in the average number of births per family. Chances of the latter seem very remote, first because there is little or no evidence that such a trend has commenced, and secondly because all the social conditions that one can postulate as being favourable to such a trend are not materializing. Tendencies seem generally to be in the opposite direction. Under conditions of poverty (and even with slightly improved conditions of material welfare) the main sources of pleasure and pride for men and women are their families. It is only with a significant relaxation of the pressures of poverty that the intellect has a fair chance to expand a little and to find other outlets. But poverty remains the common lot of the great majority in the deprived countries. If religious and political leaders were to emphasize the moral importance of reduction in family size, and to encourage the propagation of sound practical advice about ways of achieving it, then some advances might be made quite rapidly. But wherever moral leadership in this field is apparent, it is all too often in the opposite direction.

Finally, it seems likely that the rapid diffusion of any philosophy which is new, alien, and possibly even repugnant, would be impossible without the wholesale commitment of efficient and adequately financed national educational systems, catering for both children and adults. But because of the increase in numbers which has already taken place, educational expenditure per head of population in the majority of deprived countries is falling rather than the reverse, and mass illiteracy persists. More than 80 per cent of the population in Africa is illiterate, more than 50 per cent in Asia, and between 30 and 40 per cent in Latin America (appendix III). Thoughtful and compassionate people the world over have long commented on the pitiably small amounts of credit and aid that have been made available to deprived countries by the more fortunate ones. The point that has not been emphasized sufficiently, however, is that if the volume of this aid rises no higher than what one might call the "survival threshold", then all it can do is keep alive large numbers of people in hunger and ignorance. Far, far more is required to ensure that sufficient funds are available to reduce the number of births to a point where people do not just come into existence to suffer malnutrition or even, ultimately, to die of hunger.

The population of Africa in 1971 was estimated at 354 millions, and was expanding at 2·7 per cent per annum. If this rate continued, the population would double by 1997 and would pass the billion mark by the year 2010. By 1971 the population of Asia was thought to have reached 2,104 millions and had a growth rate of 2·3 per cent; it would thus double by the year 2002 and would pass the five billion mark before 2010. Similarly, that of Latin America would double from 291 to 582 millions by 1995, and would be more than 887 millions by 2010. Although the population of Europe is increasing relatively slowly, it is still growing and, at 1971 rates, would double by the year 2059. The population of the earth as a whole probably reached four billions in 1975 and, with an annual increase of 2 per cent per annum, would double to eight billion by 2010. Looking even further into the future, the eight billion would then become 16 billion by 2045. This is not a forecast, of course, merely a projection. Although there are those who seem to think that such an occurrence is quite possible, the author is not to be numbered amongst them. The projection is presented here because it is necessary to give some impression of what present fertility rates could produce over the next two or three generations if controls did not come into operation.

4

The Organic Productivity of the Earth

During his occupation of nearly all the different types of terrestrial environment, man, as a species, has become as nearly omnivorous as almost any other creature. At one time or another the staple food of different tribes has included grass seeds, tree roots, shellfish, seals and bison; mesolithic Balts and seventeenth-century Caribs enjoyed major excursions into cannibalism. Like all the other animals, however, man remains almost completely dependent on terrestrial vegetation for his food — either directly or indirectly. As will be shown later, the possibility of supplementing terrestrial supplies from marine sources must be regarded as of very limited importance.

So long as the world was a place in which, for practical purposes, resources could be regarded as unlimited, the actual amount of organic material produced each year was a matter of purely academic interest. But in a world where this is no longer so, it is clearly important to attempt to compute annual production so that it can be viewed in relation to the numbers of people dependent upon it. In recent decades conflicting views have been expressed regarding the potential food-producing capacity of the earth. These have varied between the fears voiced by many ecologists that man's agricultural activities have already seriously overstrained the earth's productive capacity, and the optimistic statements of some economists and agriculturalists that the earth could support 47 billion people at North American standards of consumption or 157 billion if we all lived like the Japanese (Clark, 1967). More recently the spread of new, heavy yielding varieties of wheat, maize and rice in what has been called "the Green Revolution" has seemed to support the views of the latter, and to confirm many economists and politicians in their generally held belief that all present food shortages are organizational, not absolute. It seems clear, however, that no one is in a position to adjudicate between these extremes of opinion unless there is some notion, first of the productive capacity of the land masses under their original wild vegetation and second, of the amount of material they are producing at the present time now that most of their area has been profoundly affected by human activity.

To concentrate entirely on "food production" is to ignore the fact that we are dependent on vegetation for a great deal more than food: constructional timber, newsprint, packaging, furniture, clothing and toilet paper are all derived basically from the earth's plant communities. Moreover, realistic technologists who foresee an imminent shortage of mineral materials (chapter 6) are anticipating that other products will have to be used as substitutes. If sufficient metal is not available for gadgets and fittings or oil for nylon and polythene, then obviously a great range of plastics, mainly derived from vegetation, will be needed. Our technological society has now reached a stage where anything organic can be turned into almost anything else, the only important constraint being the economic one — that the product can be marketed at a price which a sufficient number of people are able and willing to pay. Colin Clark (1967) recognized the fact that man cannot live by bread alone, but unfortunately he limited himself to a consideration of the two categories of "cropland" and "forest land" and chose to ignore so many political, ecological and other fundamental realities in his assessment of their potential productivity that his subsequent arithmetic produced answers which some of us can only regard as fanciful (see below p.43).

PROBLEMS OF MEASUREMENT

The annual production of the earth's vegetation is a broad concept which, on brief consideration, seems simple and uncomplicated. Although it is easy to appreciate that there may well be practical difficulties in measuring the weight of the annual production in the form of stem, root, leaf and fruit, the fact that there are also perplexing theoretical and conceptual difficulties is not immediately apparent. However, it is important to obtain figures which will be meaningful and useful to those who have to operate the world economy. Consequently it is necessary to assess not only the actual production at the present time, but also the potential production under optimum conditions. Unless this is done, over-optimistic critics will always be in a position to assert that far more could be produced than has been calculated for the present time and that, in a carefully managed world, technology would find ways of doing this. The first important theoretical problem, therefore, is to decide on the kind of vegetation cover to postulate for the earth as an "experimental control" against which to assess present and future situations.

The original wild plant communities of the earth must have been extremely efficient and flexible. This is self-evident: were it not so, how could their component plants have survived countless millennia of competition and the fluctuating stresses of the physical environment? They must also have been very productive, capable of sufficiently luxuriant growth, both above and below ground, to outstrip the competitors which would constantly be evolving and attempting to displace them. More will be said later about their productivity in relation to that of possible alternatives but, at the outset, it seems reasonable to attempt to reconstruct the natural climatic climax vegetation of the continents and to assess its productivity. Such a reconstruction is far from simple since human activity has been almost all-pervading over wide areas for quite a long period. Nevertheless, enough evidence has now been made available by historical and prehistoric research for a world climatic climax map to be drawn up (Eyre, 1968), and there are surviving relics of this original cover to permit realistic assessments of its productivity.

A second conceptual problem arises when one begins to consider what actually constitutes the annual production of unit area of vegetation. The basic facts about green plant metabolism are well understood: carbon dioxide, water and mineral nutrients are absorbed from the environment via the stomata and the root hairs, and the whole complex of organic compounds of which the plant is constructed are formed from these chemically simple origins. The first main stage involves the synthesis of carbohydrates in the presence of chlorophyll in the green organs of the plant, using energy derived from part of the spectrum of the sun's radiation. With regard to productivity, however, complications arise from the fact that the organic materials which are originally synthesized by the plant are not all accumulated as net weight gain. A helpful analogy can be sought from the animal kingdom in the case of a man of known weight sitting down to consume a large meal. Even though the exact weight of the meal is known, it is nevertheless very difficult to compute the exact weight of the man when he rises from the table. Since he has continued to breathe, evaporate and possibly even perspire during the course of his gastronomic exertions, an increment of loss to the environment, mainly in the form of CO_2 and H_2O, has taken place, and it would have been very difficult to measure this without seriously inhibiting his activities. Similarly, during the whole of the period when it is extending, developing girth, producing flowers and fruit and storing up food materials, a plant is respiring and transpiring and losing quite a large percentage of the carbon and the water which it has absorbed. The production ecologist is therefore compelled to use sophisticated concepts and techniques. In particular, since different species of plant, and different organs on the same plant, contain different percentages of water, he must always deal in "dry weight" gains. Also he must be careful to distinguish between the total synthetic product of a plant community on the one hand and, on the other, that proportion of this total product which ultimately goes to increase the bulk of the plant. This latter concept of the "net primary productivity" of ecosystems (subsequently referred to as the NPP) is now generally accepted as the most useful one; it is defined as the dry weight gain per unit area of vegetation per unit time, usually stated in $g/m^2/day$ or in $mt/km^2/year$[1] (Westlake, 1963).

The purely practical difficulties of measuring NPP are great. One need only contemplate a luxuriant patch of woodland in the growing season to be intimidated by the problems involved. Quite apart from measuring the growth being made by herbaceous plants and shrubs, how does one begin to assess the amount of material which goes to increase the girth of the tree trunks, branches and twigs as well as that which goes into new green shoots and leaves? Even worse, how can one measure the simultaneous growth in the rooting systems underground? Another practical difficulty soon becomes apparent. Very few plants in a wild community are permitted completely uninhibited growth during

[1] For a list of all abbreviations see appendix I.

the course of a whole growing season: the entire herbivorous fauna is gnawing, nibbling and grazing away the new plant material even as it grows, and whatever is removed in this way must be taken into account along with that which remains. One cannot evade this difficulty by excluding the grazers (everything from insects to antelopes) and creating artificial exclosures in which to measure uninterrupted growth, because prevention of natural grazing can alter the productivity very considerably. At a site in northeast Colorado, for instance (Andrews *et al.*, 1974), the total NPP of an area of prairie was found to be only 855 g/m^2 during the growing season when it was left ungrazed, but rose to 960 g/m^2 if lightly grazed (one steer per 10·8 ha). Furthermore, if heavily grazed (one steer per 4·8 ha), productivity was as low as 819 g/m^2. Obviously the very presence of a small population of grazing animals, cropping away some of the herbage as it was produced, actually stimulated the plant community to greater productivity, whereas an increase in stocking constituted "over-grazing" because (presumably) it reduced the photosynthesizing potential of the grasses below the optimum level. On an area of tundra near Barrow Point in Alaska (Dennis and Johnson, 1970), whereas the productivity was as high as between 60 and 97 g/m^2 in years when there was a low lemming population, it fell to between three and 48 g/m^2 in a year when the lemming population was high. Two important decisions have to be made, therefore, before any valid assessments can be made of NPP in natural ecosystems — first, the intensity of grazing by the natural fauna that it is reasonable to assume and secondly, the number of years over which investigations must take place in order to ensure an adequate statistical sample of climatic and biological variation.

In the light of all these conceptual and practical difficulties it is easy to appreciate why progress in the evaluation of the earth's primary productivity has been slow. Indeed there is little doubt that some cautious production ecologists, with justification, would feel that general statements are still premature. Nevertheless, it seems to me that there is now a sufficient measure of agreement about the order of magnitude of productivity over a wide range of vegetation types for a sensible statement to be made. Four of the seven sections into which the activities of the International Biological Programme were divided were devoted to biological productivity (IBP, 1965), and one of them, the Productivity of Terrestrial Communities (PT), was concerned specifically with the productivity of terrestrial ecosystems. Thus, during the operation of phase two of the IBP (1967–72), a large number of projects were embarked upon which aimed to assess the biological productivity of all the world's main types of terrestrial ecosystem. From these, and from many independent projects, a mass of information is now available. Much of this material has been reviewed (Cooper, 1975; Lieth and Whittaker, 1975) and a number of independent efforts have already been made to compute the *actual* NPP of the land vegetation of the earth *at the present time*. One of the authors concerned (Lieth, 1973), is sufficiently confident about the factual basis of his calculations to feel that he is "not unjustified in suggesting that the major estimates offered ... of 100×10^9

metric tons of dry matter [per annum] ... net primary production for the land vegetation of the earth ... will be subject to refinement in detail but not to major revision." My own calculations, though carried out entirely independently and using a number of different criteria (appendix II), arrive at conclusions which are remarkably consistent with those of Helmut Lieth.

NET PRIMARY PRODUCTIVITY OF THE ORIGINAL WILD VEGETATION

The total land area of the earth, excluding the ice caps, is 128·2 million square kilometres ($128{\cdot}2 \times 10^6$ km^2), or approximately 50 million square miles. Over these land surfaces the original vegetation cover was very diverse: at one extreme there was the tropical rain forest of the wettest parts of the inter-tropical zone where neither moisture deficiency nor temperature conditions impose constraints on plant growth at any time of the year; at the other, there were the cold deserts and the hot dry deserts which were almost devoid of green plants. Between these two extremes lay a great variety of forest, scrub and grassy plant communities. These have been mapped on a scale of 1:16,000,000 according to all available information (Eyre, 1968), and a generalized impression of this world vegetation pattern can be obtained from figure 4.1. Using the original maps (see appendix II) the total area which was occupied by each vegetation type has been measured (table 4.1).

Any major plant formation-type, extending over large parts of several continents, must vary greatly in productivity from one place to another. Though each type is restricted to regions with the same general macro-climate, it will nevertheless embrace huge contrasts in local climate and soil characteristics. The macro-climatic extremes spanned by entities such as "the boreal forest" are so great that it has been found necessary to subdivide it regionally into northern, central and southern zones (Bazilevich and Rodin, 1971) with average NPPs of 500, 700 and 900 mt/km^2/year respectively. Arctic tundra, mid-latitude grassland, arid zone vegetation and tropical savanna have also been differentiated into sub-zones by various writers, and cognizance has been taken of these in calculating the various productivity values.

Even when this subdivision has been carried out, one still encounters the difficulty that different workers carrying out investigations in the same zone have arrived at different results. This is not necessarily because some are more "correct" than others but rather, for reasons already given, that significant contrasts do occur even in a set of communities which are very similar in almost every way. The fact remains that a decision has to be made on the figure to be used within the range of variation that the different workers have presented. Fortunately, as already stated, the results do not differ in order of magnitude so that, when a considerable number are available, it seems reasonable to use a figure which approximates to the average. On a few occasions, however, when only one or two reliable investigations have been completed, the decision has been more problematical and it has been necessary to consider carefully the innate environmental characteristics of the sites concerned and the degree to

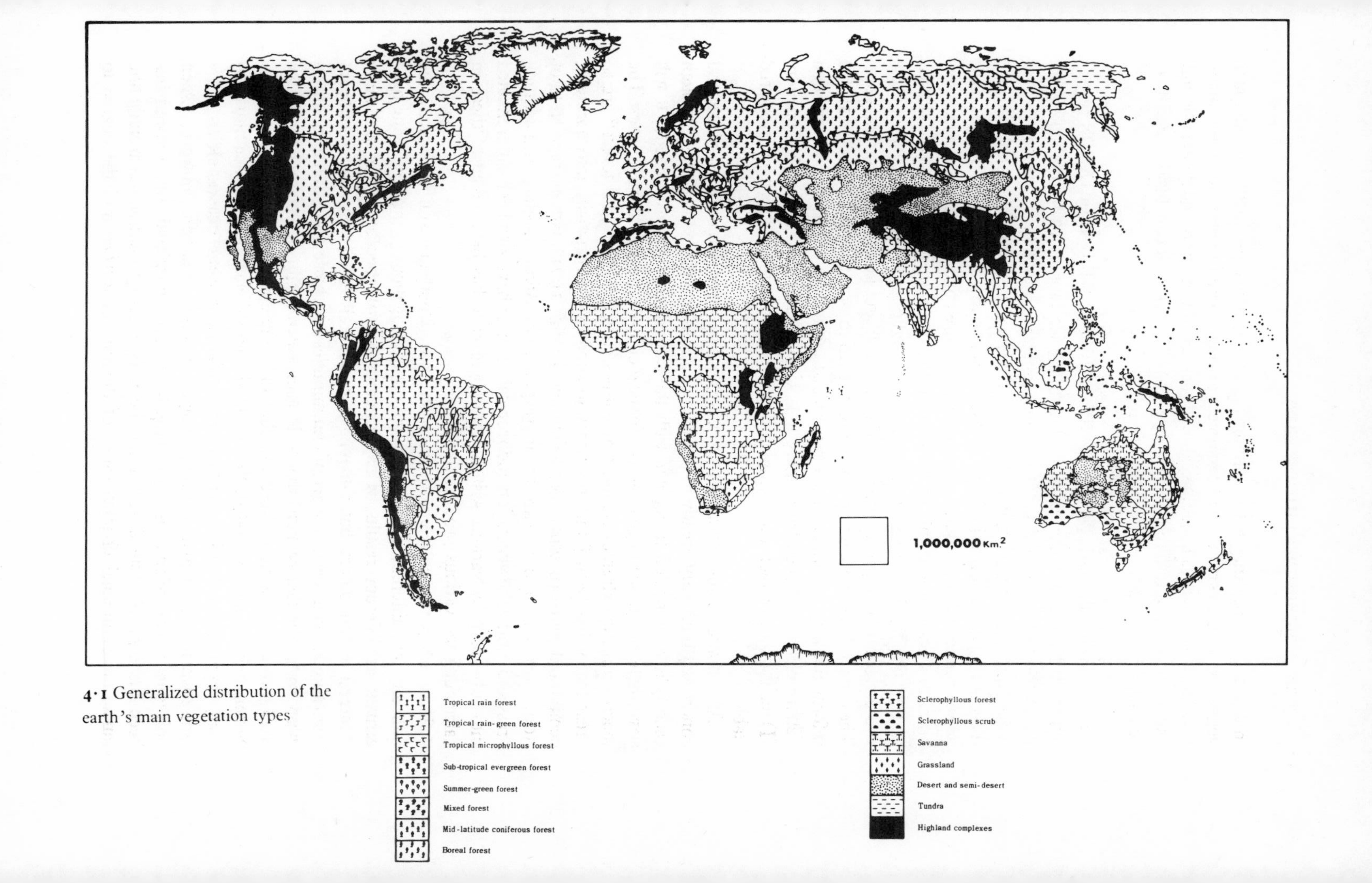

4·1 Generalized distribution of the earth's main vegetation types

Table 4.1 Potential productivity of wild vegetation

Vegetation type	Area (10^6km^2)	Mean NPP (m.t./km^2/yr)	Total NPP (10^6m.t./yr)
Tropical rain forest	12·8	2500	32025
Tropical rain-green forest	8·7	1500	13013
Tropical microphyllous forest	4·3	1000	4293
Tropical montane forest	2·7	1500	4078
Boreal forest	17·2	500 700 900 1300	12258
Sub-boreal aspen/birch forest	0·4	900	322
Mid-latitude coniferous forest	1·5	1800	2488
Mixed coniferous and summer-green forest	3·3	1500 1400 1100	3976
Summer-green forest	5·8	1300	7478
Broad-leaved and mixed evergreen forest	2·9	1800	5177
Sclerophyllous forest	0·9	1300	1225
TOTAL FOREST	**60·5**		**86333**
Mid-latitude "forest-steppe"	1·4	1250	1793
Sub-tropical savanna	0·5	1000	458
Tropical savanna	17·8	1500 1000 500	18193
TOTAL TREED GRASSLAND	**19·7**		**20444**
TOTAL GRASSLAND	**7·2**	1000 700	**6200**
TOTAL SCLEROPHYLLOUS SCRUB	**1·7**	700	**1165**
TOTAL DESERT AND SEMI-DESERT	**26·0**	500 150 50 3	**2807**
TOTAL TUNDRA AND ALPINE	**13·1**	75 175 325	**2132**
TOTAL	**128·2**		**119081**

which each one approaches or departs from the "average" in terms of the area covered by the plant formation-type as a whole. A case in point is the tropical rain forest. Because of its great luxuriance and complexity it has posed very obvious problems to production ecologists so that, as yet, relatively few computations have been made. Those which are available differ as widely as between about 1,000 mt/km^2/year (Lemon *et al.*, 1970) and 5,550 mt/km^2/year (Odum, 1970). One very comprehensive study in Thailand (Kira *et al.*, 1967) indicated something a little in excess of 3,000 mt/km^2/year. Lieth (1973) is of the opinion that 2,000 mt/km^2/year is probably not far from being a sound representative figure but, since in the present work I feel it would be undesirable to underestimate the productivity of any wild vegetation type,

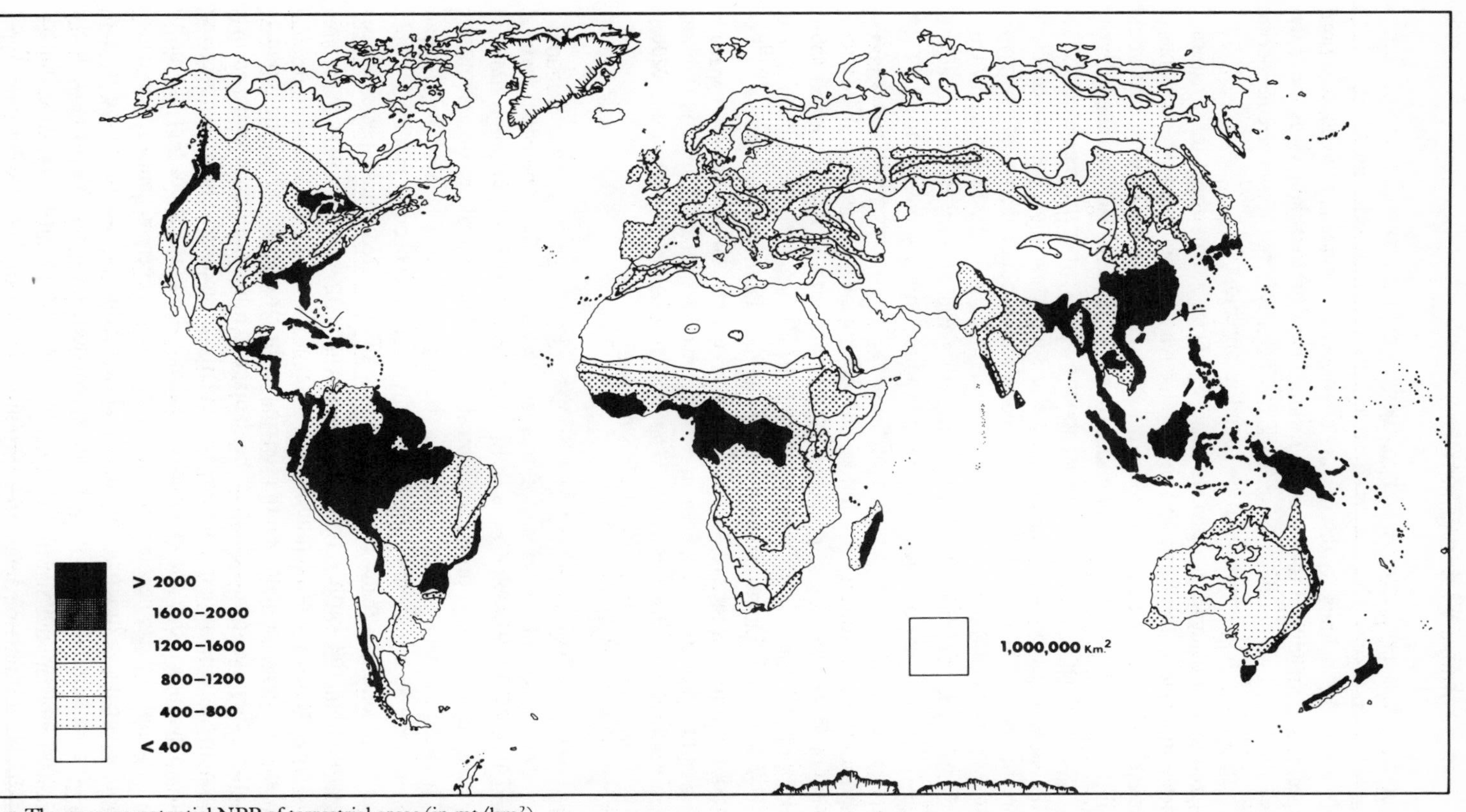

4·2 The average potential NPP of terrestrial areas (in mt/km²)

particularly this very extensive and productive one, the figure of 2,500 mt/km²/year has been taken. This may well err on the generous side, however.

It would be tedious to discuss at length all the evidence which has been considered in arriving at the mean NPP values used here (table 4.1). A list of the more important authorities whose work has been referred to when considering each major vegetation type is to be found in appendix II.

Examination of table 4.1 reveals some significant points about the "natural" vegetation cover of the earth and the productivity it would have were it able to reassert itself. Of the 128·2 million km², 60·5 million (over 47 per cent) would be forest, and another 19·6 million km² (over 15 per cent) falls into the category of "treed grassland". In other words, about 62 per cent of the vegetated surface of the earth must be regarded as capable of supporting some tree cover. Even more important is the fact that this area would produce 106·7 of the 119·1 billion (10^9) mt of the dry organic matter produced annually by the whole earth — some 89·6 per cent. By contrast, the 39·1 million km² of tundra, alpine, semi-desert and desert vegetation would produce only 4·9 billion mt — a mere 4·1 per cent from 30·5 per cent of the area. The grassy plant communities (steppe, prairie, pampas, veld and so on), occupying 5·6 per cent of the area, would produce about 5·2 per cent of the total dry weight. Probably most striking of all is the case of the tropical rain forest which is shown to occupy only 12·8 million km² (almost 10 per cent of the total land area) but, at an NPP of 2,500 mt/km² (see above), would yield 26·9 per cent of the total organic dry weight production of the earth — well over a quarter. If one is thinking scientifically about "organic wealth" (figure 4.2) it seems clear that the countries of the wet tropics have a great deal in the bank!

THE EXPLOITATION OF NATURAL ORGANIC PRODUCTION

The usefulness and relevance of this assessment of the "potential natural productivity" of the earth may well be challenged. First, even though the land areas may be capable of producing almost 120 billion tons of dry organic matter per annum, to what extent can this be regarded as available for human exploitation? Secondly, since the natural cover has now been so modified, would it not be much more realistic to use a sample of cultivated landscapes as a basis for computing the earth's potential to support population? These two basic issues require close consideration.

Many ecologists hesitate before referring to the "exploitation" of the products of nature; they are so conscious of the damage that has been done to the earth's ecosystems by human exploitation, particularly by industrial societies over the past two centuries, that the essentially mechanical, industrial concept of "using up raw material" has become distasteful. In a sense every organism "exploits" its environment, extracting organic and inorganic substances from it and releasing waste products to it, but the exploitation by *Homo sapiens* is far more wholesale and insidious than that of any other species that has ever existed. Nevertheless, no matter how hard mankind may try, it seems certain that it will never be economically and ecologically possible to utilize the whole of net primary production. In particular, that fraction of NPP which is produced below the soil surface, with only insignificant exceptions, decays *in situ*. The dry weight of all the roots and underground stems of land vegetation is now known to be a significant percentage of total production, though different plant communities distribute their mass very differently. Generally speaking, the main contrast is between herbaceous and arboreal communities: for instance, in the lightly grazed short grass prairie in Colorado already referred to (Andrews *et al.*, 1974) 75·1 per cent of the production was underground, and on the ungrazed site in the same area, 83·5 per cent; on the other hand, in stands of camphor (*Cinnamom camphora*) in Japan (Iwaki, 1974), only about 12 per cent of the NPP was underground.

One of the most resistant problems in studies of primary productivity has been the assessment of annual production below ground, particularly in the case of forest communities where increments of growth are added to pre-existing material year by year. There now seems to be a fair measure of agreement between authorities, however,[2] and the approximate percentage found below ground in each of the main vegetation types is presented in table 4.2. Given that these percentages are a fair reflection of actual productivity below ground, one can turn again to the productivity totals presented in table 4.1 and compute the proportion of the earth's total NPP produced above ground (table 4.3). This figure of 78,397 million mt is probably a fair indication of realities but, bearing in mind the number of approximations that have been used, it would be unrealistic to give credence to precise figures. However, in round numbers, 80 billion (80×10^9) mt would seem to be a figure which cannot be very wide of the mark. This was the dry weight production, above ground, of the earth's vegetation a few millennia ago. It is the theoretical amount which would be produced if wild vegetation were to reassert itself, given no major climatic or other environmental changes.

The really important practical question arising from this piece of quantification is just what proportion of the potential above-ground production

[2] Although it is a relatively simple matter to measure, fairly accurately, the proportion of the dry weight of a tree or a square metre of grassy sward which is to be found underground at any particular point in time, it is far more difficult to work out just how much is produced underground *in one growing season*. It is essential here to appreciate the difference between "total phytomass" or "standing crop" (which may be the product of many years' growth) and NPP (the total product of one year's growth). The basic problem stems from the relative rates of production (by the plants) and consumption (by the fauna), and these may be very different underground from above ground. To take a simple theoretical example, if a patch of forest produced twice as much above ground, over a period of years, as it produced in roots, then it would be perfectly true to say that two thirds of its NPP was produced above ground and one third below. In practice, however, it would be very difficult to know that this had happened. It is possible that losses to leaf fall, browsing and so on above ground might be twice as great as equivalent losses underground so that, at the end of the period, it would *appear* as though the vegetation had produced equally above and below the soil surface. Generalizing on the world scale is always hazardous but, in spite of what has just been said, the available evidence does indicate that there are no great systematic differences in the rate of loss of living material below ground as compared to above. It seems as though, by and large, the more that is produced, the more is consumed, whether it is in the daylight or in the soil. In a very general way therefore, and with many reservations, we may take it that the above/below ground ratio in the standing crop is a reflection of the realities of productivity.

could be regarded as "utilizable". This is such a complex question that no simple answer can reasonably be given. Quite apart from the fact that different types of vegetation have been exploited in different ways, human communities at different levels of technological attainment and of different social structure would use the same kind of vegetation in different ways. Perhaps the most useful and illuminating approach is to view vegetation productivity in the light of the attitudes of some of the kinds of people who have a profound effect on the earth's plant communities at the present time.

The lumberman and the businessman or politician who promotes the lumberman's activities come readily to mind. They are interested in forest communities or, more specifically, in the marketable timber to be found in these communities. The potential above-ground product of the forest lands of the earth (table 4.3) is something over 65 billion (65×10^9) mt. This is the dry weight of the material that would be produced annually by the natural forest cover if it were still present. At the present time detailed analyses of the proportion of merchantable timber in the total above-ground production of the earth's forest ecosystems are very rare, but a few careful studies have been made. One of these analysed in detail the total NPP of a stand of summer-green forest dominated by oak, hornbeam and beech in the Netherlands (Duvigneaud and Denaeyer-DeSmet, 1970). It concluded that, out of a total above-ground dry-weight production of 12·2 mt/ha/year, 3·5 mt (28·7 per cent) was in leaves, and 4·4 mt (36·1 per cent) was either in non-leaf litter or in bark, small twigs and branches; the bulk of this, at the present time, is rejected as unmerchantable by most lumbering and wood manufacturing concerns and either burned or left to decay. In other words, almost 65 per cent of the above-ground production of this particular stand would be either unavailable to, or rejected by, most

Table 4.2 Percentage of total phytomass in underground plant organs (Bazilevich and Rodin, 1968)

Vegetation type	Percentage of phytomass below ground
Discontinuous tundra	70
Continuous tundra	80–85
Boreal forest	21–25
Summer-green forest	15–33
Mid-latitude evergreen forest	20
Prairie and steppe	65–90
Mid-latitude semi-desert	80–90
Tropical semi-desert	40–75
Tropical rain forest	20
Tropical rain-green forest	30–40
Tropical savanna	35–50

Table 4.3 Above- and below-ground net primary productivity

Vegetation type	Annual production (10^6 mt/year)	Estimated percentage production below ground	Production below ground (10^6 mt/year)	Production above ground (10^6 mt/year)
Tropical rain forest	32025	20	6405	25620
Tropical rain-green forest	13013	35	4,555	8458
Tropical microphyllous forest	4293	35	1503	2790
Tropical montane forest	4078	20	816	3262
Boreal forest	12258	23	2819	9439
Sub-boreal aspen/birch forest	322	24	77	245
Mid-latitude coniferous forest	2488	20	498	1990
Mixed coniferous and summer-green forest	3976	20	795	3181
Summer-green forest	7478	24	1795	5683
Broad-leaved and mixed evergreen forest	5177	24	1242	3935
Sclerophyllous forest	1225	35	429	796
SUB-TOTAL				65399
Mid-latitude "forest-steppe"	1793	55	986	807
Savanna	18651	50	9325	9326
Prairie and steppe	6200	78	4836	1364
Sclerophyllous scrub	1165	80	932	233
Desert and semi-desert	2807	70	1965	842
Tundra and alpine	2132	80	1706	426
TOTAL	119081		40684	78397

lumbering operations. It is not possible to say how typical this particular stand of summer-green forest is of forests in general in respect of the proportion of "waste" products to merchantable timber, though the evidence does indicate that some other forest types produce a smaller percentage, by weight, of leaves, twigs and bark. But even if we take 50 per cent instead of 65 per cent as being a representative average, this still means that, from the point of view of the industrial and commercial interests concerned, the annual above-ground production of the world's potential forest cover should not be regarded as 65 billion tons but as not exceeding 32·5 billion.

The character of lumbering operations varies widely from one area to another so it is difficult to generalize about the ecological desirability of the attitudes and practices of timber merchants and foresters. Some leave behind them a denuded waste, devoid of seed parents for most of the tree species that have been extracted, so that natural regeneration back to the type of community that has been removed is, in the short term, impossible. Others ensure optimum conditions for natural regeneration, while others carry out wholesale replanting, often with exotic species. There can be no doubt that, in one respect, the attitudes and activities of the good forester are viewed relatively favourably by all who are ecologically minded: the fact that he assumes that around 40 per cent of the above-ground annual production is to be returned to the soil in the form of leaves and other debris is clearly ecologically desirable. On the other hand he does extract timber, and a considerable proportion of the nutrients which trees abstract from the soil becomes locked up in their wood. In the summer-green forest in the Netherlands already referred to (Duvigneaud and Denaeyer-DeSmet, 1970), it was discovered that for every 151 g of exchangeable magnesium in the soil, there were 70 g locked up in the trunks and branches of the three dominant species of tree. Even more striking, for every 157 g of exchangeable potassium in the soil, there were 159 g in the large timber. Indeed, extraction of all the large timber would have resulted in the removal of almost one third of the potassium present in the nutrient cycle of the whole ecosystem. (In one hectare there were 157 kg of exchangeable potassium in the soil and 342 kg somewhere in the plant community). True, there was plenty of potassium (and other nutrients) locked up in the rock particles of the soil and subsoil, but the rate at which these are released, by weathering, to become available as plant nutrients is extremely slow when viewed in the context of the life span of a generation of trees. It follows, therefore, that even enlightened forestry practices may not be sustainable in the long run unless plant nutrients, in some form, are applied to the areas from which the timber is removed. But a great deal remains to be said regarding the role of fertilizers in the general picture of resource problems (chapter 6).

Another group of people whose influence on the earth's vegetation is profound and widespread are the owners of flocks and herds of domesticated ungulates. Itinerant pastoralists such as the Masai and the Fulani in Africa have for many generations driven their herds to and fro over enormous tribal territories and, in more recent times, individual peasant herdsmen in countries such as Brazil, Madagascar and the Philippines in ever-increasing numbers have appropriated terrain in the wake of destructive lumbering operations (Denevan, 1973) or, by persistent nibbling at the forest edges, have themselves gradually transformed wooded land into some kind of pasture. Indeed, a body of ecological evidence now indicates that much of the land in the tropics traditionally referred to as "savanna" would today carry a great deal more timber were it not for the fact that, for many millennia, peoples such as these have been preventing the regeneration of trees by spreading fires and by their grazing practices.

In a sense the attitude of the pastoralist to the forest is the exact opposite to that of the forester. Whereas the latter is concerned solely with a forest product, the former is only what he is because the forest has been removed, and he will only survive as such if he succeeds in preventing it from reinvading. He is therefore instrumental in depriving the soil of the annual products of leaf fall, and of maintaining a vegetation which varies between an almost pure grassy sward and a mixture of grass and scrub. This kind of usage certainly permits the return of a certain amount of organic debris to the surface which, along with the droppings of the animals, maintains a nutrient cycle. But this cycle is impoverished as compared to that of the forest for one very important reason: the rooting systems of the grasses and shrubs are generally at much shallower depth and are thus incapable of bringing fresh mineral ions into the nutrient cycle when these are released from deep-seated rock minerals by weathering. Generally speaking, vegetation productivity will fall if the supply of mineral nutrients falls. It follows that pastoralists, although occupying potential forest land, do not manage it in a way which maintains a forest level of productivity; indeed, if they are persistently pushing back the forest margins, or reducing the number of trees in savanna land, they are automatically lowering the NPP of the territory they occupy. But since they are primarily interested in a degraded type of vegetation, and not in a forest flora, this loss in productivity, even if recognized as such, would be welcomed rather than deplored.

THE PRODUCTIVITY OF CROPLAND

Yet much of the land area of the earth is no longer occupied by wild vegetation in either a pristine or degraded state. To use an expression common to early nineteenth-century agriculturalists and twentieth-century developers, it has been "improved". In the case of land which has been appropriated for road surfaces, aircraft runways, car parks, factories and houses, this implies that its organic productivity has been reduced practically to zero. Of greater interest, however, are the much more extensive areas of cropland and improved pasture.

A first glance at assessments that have been made of the NPP of cropland, both in the tropics and in higher latitudes, suggests that conversion to agriculture really does constitute "improvement". Sugar cane has been reported with an NPP of 6,730 mt/km^2/year in Hawai (Burr *et al.*, 1957), Napier grass (*Pennisetum purpureum*) with more than 8,500 mt/km^2/year in both El

Salvador (Watkins *et al.*, 1971) and Puerto Rico (Vincente-Chandler *et al.*, 1959), and a hybrid sorghum × sudangrass with 4,660 mt/km^2/year in California (Worker and Marble, 1968). Tropical tree crops such as manioc (De Vries *et al.*, 1967) and cassava (Cooper, 1975) also seem capable of producing at a rate of around 4,000 mt/km^2/year. Cooper (1975) reports that some of the highest NPPs recorded for the common mid-latitude crops are as follows:

	mt/km^2/year	
maize	3,400	Turin, Italy
sugar beet	4,240	Salinas, California
alfalfa	2,970	Fresno, California
soyabean	1,040	Ames, Iowa
wheat	2,980	Pullman, Washington
rice	2,200	Peru

In case of misunderstanding it must be re-emphasized that these are not figures of productivity of marketable product, but of *total* dry weight. One set of observations has shown that of the total dry weight of a sample of crops of rice in Japan, only between 40 and 45 per cent was in the actual grain (Iwaki, 1974), and all the evidence suggests that good crops of wheat have a similar ratio of grain to straw and root. On the other hand, maize grain ratios are somewhat less.

A substantial number of other reports on crop productivity could be given, all seeming to indicate that the NPP of a cultivated plant cover equals, or even surpasses, that of the wild vegetation it has replaced. But one salient fact casts a very different light on this point. The vast majority of these reports of high crop productivity are from abnormally productive sites, indeed a large proportion are from experimental stations. Many are even referred to as reports on "experimental crops". This is not unexpected since the people who are most interested in crops are farmers and agricultural scientists, and careful work on the productivity of average or poor crops would make little sense to them under most circumstances. What little attention has been devoted to the general run of crop yields, however, puts a very different complexion on agricultural productivity. In 1972 a crop of wheat at Saitama Experimental Station in Japan produced 16·81 mt/ha (1,681 mt/km^2), whereas the average production of wheat for the whole of Japan in the same year was only 7·3 mt/ha (730 mt/km^2) (Iwaki, 1974). Similarly, it is estimated that although ladino clover swards in Japan can produce as much as 1,800 mt/km^2 under optimum conditions, the average for stands of moderate productivity is only about 1,200 mt, and the average yield for mixed pasture is no more than 1,000 mt. It seems, therefore, as though the most productive crops of both cereals and forage in Japan have an NPP not far short of that of the evergreen and summer-green forests which originally covered most of the country, but that average crops are probably less than half as productive as the natural forest cover. Moreover, one must bear in mind that Japan is a technologically advanced country where even the producers of moderate crops apply substantial dressings of mineral fertilizer to their land.

Statistics of consumption of mineral fertilizers demonstrate very clearly that this cannot possibly be true of the great majority of farmers belonging to the deprived nations of the world.

THE PRESENT PRODUCTIVITY OF HUMANIZED LANDSCAPES

Clearly the NPP of highly capitalized cropland does not provide us with an acceptable indication of the NPP of land under general agricultural and pastoral usage. The evidence seems to show that deforestation and pressure of human activity reduces productivity far below the level achieved under the original wild plant communities. It is not yet possible to say precisely by how much the overall world productivity has been reduced, partly because the actual extent of forest clearance and degradation is not accurately known and partly because far too few investigations into the productivity of intensively used areas have been carried out. Nevertheless, an examination of the evidence that is available does provide some indication of the order of magnitude of the reduction.

A number of preliminary investigations carried out in the eastern USA (Whigham, Lieth *et al.*, 1971; Stearns *et al.*, 1971; De Selm, 1971; Art *et al.*, 1971) have provided information on a county basis about the overall productivity of settled landscapes as a whole. Whigham and Lieth, for example, have arrived at an average productivity figure for each county in the state of North Carolina — an area originally covered by a patchwork of summer-green and coniferous forests. Their assessments were based on eleven crops and seven other land use categories. Over 94 counties the mean NPP was found to vary between 150 and 500 mt/km^2/year,[3] and their arithmetical average, in precise figures, was 299·4 — or almost exactly 300. My own assessment of the NPP of the original vegetation of North Carolina varies between 1,300 mt/km^2/year for the summer-green forest and 1,800 mt/km^2/year for the southern pine forest. There were also extensive areas where stands of the two types of tree were mingled in roughly equal proportions and consequently the average productivity would be approximately 1,500 mt/km^2/year. Since vegetation reconstruction indicates that the three forest types — summer-green, pine and mixed — occurred in roughly equal proportions over the state, the average productivity must have been about 1,500 mt/km^2/year.

The inescapable conclusion is that the average NPP of the cropland and grazing land of North Carolina is now only about one fifth what it was under forest cover some centuries ago. There seems no reason why the remainder of the formerly forested lands in eastern USA should not have suffered a similar reduction. The problem is whether or not conditions in the eastern USA are fairly representative of those in the settled lands of all the other countries for which no comparable data are available. Here it is only possible to reach conclusions by

[3] In 1972 these assessments were revised substantially upwards (Lieth and Whittaker, 1975). However, this was due in large measure to an increase in the estimate for the productivity of the remaining forest land, and not in that for cropland and grazing land, which was little modified.

way of analogy. North Carolina comprises a varied terrain of coastal lowland, river plain, upland plateau and Appalachian slope up to 6,000 feet above sea level. Its land use pattern is a patchwork of woodland, rough grazing and cropland, roughly analagous to that found in many parts of the world where former forest land has been appropriated by agricultural communities with their appurtenant urban service centres. Nevertheless, it is generally acknowledged that, in the USA, where capital-intensive (as opposed to labour-intensive) agriculture is more strikingly developed than in almost any other country, rough pasture and "waste land" tend to be more over-exploited and degraded than average. On the other hand, capitalization does imply a generally high level of fertilizer application on those lands which are under crop production, and this must ensure a much greater NPP for crops than is obtained (on soils of comparable inherent fertility) in deprived countries where the high cost of fertilizers prohibits their use by nearly all farmers. There can be no doubt that general productivity in the settled lands of Europe is greater than in the USA (Lieth, 1973) but, even in the case of Europe, it must not be imagined that the long-established agricultural communities have been successful in maintaining a high productivity over the whole of the terrain they have occupied. Although some croplands of exceptional fertility may have an average productivity which is not far short of that of the forests which were displaced, there are large areas which have been used as commons or community grazing lands for many centuries (Eyre, 1966 and 1973) where both soil and vegetation have been seriously degraded. The almost bare limestone slopes of much of the Mediterranean region, where once luxuriant forests of beech, evergreen oak and Aleppo pine flourished, are spectacular evidence of this. Also, the extensive peaty heaths and moorlands of northwestern Europe, now mainly used as rough pasture, must have been very much more productive before being denuded of their former cover of oak, pine and birch.

It seems generally true that over lands which have been extensively grazed for long periods, productivity has been much decreased, and that where this has taken place over former forest land, productivity may well be as little as one fifth its original value. On the other hand, the productivity of cropland seems to have decreased less; it may even be almost equal to that of the original forest cover on heavily fertilized farms, particularly in the tropics and sub-tropics where double- and treble-cropping is possible. However, the Japanese evidence indicates that, even in countries where capital has been plentiful, the average cropland NPP probably does not exceed half the original. And over the vast areas of cropland in the deprived countries, to which no mineral fertilizer is applied, average productivity is so low that it is unlikely to be greater than one quarter of the native forest and in places considerably less.

The Food and Agriculture Organization of the United Nations has produced a comprehensive set of land use figures for the countries of the world (FAO, 1970) which give, for each national territory, the areas of cropland and pasture in the 1960s. For these figures the FAO was dependent upon statistics provided by the individual countries concerned — no data were produced by unified authority. As a consequence the information from different countries is not directly comparable, and this is apparent after only a brief examination. The figures for cropland probably have a high degree of comparability, but it is clear that ideas as to what constituted "pasture" were very diverse in different countries. Whereas some administrations tried to include all "grazed land" in the pasture category, others included only that grazing land which was actually enclosed within farm units. For anyone trying to assess the proportion of national territories which, in any way, is "subject to grazing" by domesticated flocks and herds, the statistics of many African countries are particularly unhelpful. This is well illustrated by the entry for Niger. Here there are said to be 2·9 million ha of "permanent meadow and pasture" and 15·6 million ha of "forest", but a footnote to the "forest" statistic states that 15 of the 15·6 million ha are "used also for grazing". The inference is that there are vast areas in Niger which carry some trees (or which formerly did so) but that only a tiny proportion of this land can be regarded as protected forest, fenced against the depradations of grazing animals. The most disturbing aspect of this point is that other African states with similar environments, economies and social structures report large areas of "forest" but without any categorical statement that grazing takes place within them. For these reasons, it seems almost certain that the FAO statistics greatly understate the area which is subject to grazing pressures, and that our present dependence upon them must result in an underestimation of depletion caused by grazing.

The vegetation types that have been displaced to make way for crops and grazing in middle latitudes are mainly the southern boreal forest, summer-green forest, mixed forest, mid-latitude evergreen forest, long-grass prairie and short-grass prairie with mean productivities of 900, 1,300, 1,100, 1,800, 1,000 and 700 mt/km^2/year respectively (table 4.1). Bearing in mind the relative extents of each of these six types, it is unlikely that their mean NPP can have exceeded 1,000 mt/km^2/year. The vegetation that has been displaced in the tropics is mainly tropical rain forest, tropical rain-green forest, microphyllous forest, broad-leaved tree savanna and microphyllous tree savanna with mean productivities of 2,500, 1,500, 1,000, 1,500 and 1,000 respectively, and a conservative estimate of the mean productivity of all the area involved is 1,500 mt/km^2/year. Assuming that the productivity of all pasture land has been reduced to one fifth, and of all cropland to one half (in middle latitudes) and one quarter (in tropical areas), then one arrives at the conclusion that the annual NPP of the croplands and pasture lands of the earth has been reduced by 38·5 billion ($38·5 \times 10^9$) mt (table 4.4). If this is substracted from the potential of 119·1 billion mt (table 4.1), then the total is reduced to 80·6 billion. This seems to be a reasonable, though probably rather generous, estimate of total terrestrial NPP at the present time.

However, as already indicated (table 4.3), almost exactly one third of the potential NPP would be produced underground (some 40 billion mt of the 120 billion, in round figures). Although many arable crops, particularly those produced in moist and fertile soil, have no more than 10 to 15 per cent of their dry weight below ground (Lieth, 1973), crops grown in poorer and drier soils, tree crops, improved grasslands, and the grasses and shrubs of poor grazing land all produce a far larger percentage of their material below ground. Since most forests have 20–25 per cent below ground, it follows that the ratio of above-ground to below-ground production has not been increased by man's activities — probably very much the reverse; one can safely say that at least one third of the computed 80·6 billion tons NPP at the present time is subterranean — some 27 billion tons — and only some 54 billion tons is above-ground yield.

A MODEL OF THE FUTURE

At this point one can perhaps be excused a short excursion into futurism. Although I make no suggestion that civilization could possibly survive the complete removal of the earth's forests, it is salutory to reflect on the resulting level of primary productivity if, in a vain paroxism of attempted self-preservation, it succeeded in doing so. At the present time, of the 17·4 million km^2 in agricultural usage in middle latitudes, 7·2 million (41·4 per cent) is under crops and 10·2 million (58·6 per cent) is pasture (table 4.4). If all the remaining forests in these latitudes were converted to cultivation and pasture in the same ratio as at present, and assuming present levels of agricultural and forest productivity, then the NPP (potential 33 billion mt/year — see table 4.1) would be reduced to something like 10·6 billion mt/year of which only two thirds — about seven billion mt — would be above ground. Similarly, in tropical latitudes at the present time, of the 22·7 million km^2 in agricultural usage, 6·6 million (29 per cent) are cropland and 16·1 million (71 per cent) are pasture. If all the remaining tropical forest land became cultivation and pasture in the same ratio

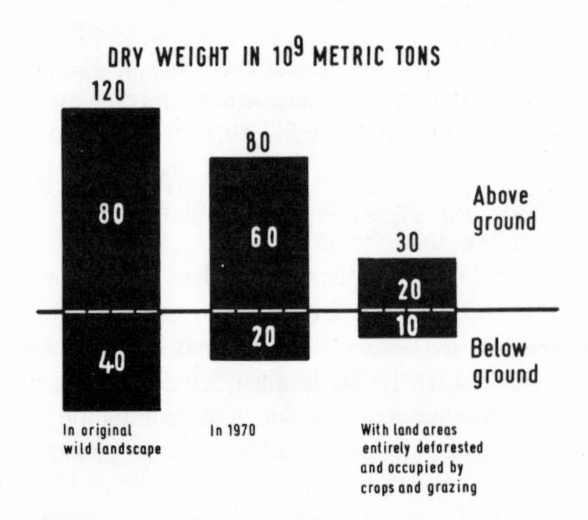

4·3 Depletion sequence in the total NPP of terrestrial areas.

as at present, assuming present agricultural productivity levels and a mean forest NPP of 1,870 mt/km²/year (computed from table 4.1), then the NPP (potential of 53·4 billion mt/year) would be reduced to about 11·4 billion mt/year of which about 7·6 billion would be above ground.

Table 4.4 The depletion of productivity in cropland and pasture (data from FAO, 1970)

	Cropland		Pasture and Meadow		
Region*	Area (10^6km²)	Depletion (10^9mt)†	Area (10^6km²)	Depletion (10^9mt)†	Total depletion (10^9mt)
Europe (without USSR)	1·5	0·75	1·9	1·52	2·27
USSR	2·3	1·15	3·7	2·96	4·11
Canada and USA	2·2	1·10	2·8	2·24	3·34
China and Japan	1·2	0·60	1·8	1·44	2·04
	7·2	3·60	10·2	8·16	11·76
Tropical and sub-tropical Asia	3·4	3·82	2·7	3·24	7·06
Latin America	1·2	1·35	5·0	6·00	7·35
Africa	2·0	2·25	8·4	10·08	12·33
	6·6	7·42	16·1	19·32	26·74
World total	13·8	11·02	26·3	27·48	38·50*

* Because of difficulty in assessing the Australian entry for "pasture", Oceania has been omitted. The world total is therefore a conservative one: it would probably be shown to be some two or three billion mt higher if Oceania could have been assessed on the same basis and included.

† The following assumptions have been made in this attempt to quantify depletion:
(a) that the mean NPP of all the original wild vegetation was 1,000 mt/km²/ year in middle latitudes, and 1,500 in tropical regions;
(b) that the productivity of all pasture land has been depleted to one fifth its original NPP;
(c) that the productivity of all mid-latitude cropland has been depleted to a half, and all tropical cropland to a quarter its original NPP.

The rather startling conclusion of this tentative computation is that whereas the above-ground potential NPP of the earth's forest land is about 65·4 billion mt (table 4.3), following the course of events just outlined the actual NPP would be no more than 14·6 billion. This would lower the overall above-ground NPP of terrestrial vegetation from its original 78·4 billion mt to 27·6 billion, even if one assumes that all savannas, prairies and scrublands remained unaltered. But since serious exploitation of all these other types of vegetation is already far advanced in many places (see Curry-Lindahl, 1974) this is not an acceptable assumption. If the whole of the vegetated land surface — grassland, scrubland and tundra as well as forest — were converted to agricultural usages in the same proportions and at the same levels of productivity as at present, this would reduce above-ground mean annual NPP to no more than 20 billion mt (figure 4.3) as compared to the potential of just under 80 billion mt (table 4.3). Those who have fixed beliefs about the supremacy of man and his beneficial role in changing the face of the earth would do well to ponder this point.

PRESENT TRENDS

Although one cannot imagine how our present economic system could survive the complete elimination of forests to make way for food production, there is no doubt that the development towards stage 3 (figure 4.3) is proceeding with frightening speed. At the present time the United Nations Environment Programme (UNEP), in consultation with other international bodies such as the International Union for the Conservation of Nature and Natural Resources (IUCN), is embarking on a programme in which one of the main aims is to "identify the extent of world forest cover" (IUCN, 1975), but as yet we have no clear idea about deforestation rates. Some technologically advanced countries such as those of Scandinavia are certainly ensuring that cut-over areas are efficiently reforested — their economic and demographic condition permits them to do so — but this is completely overshadowed by trends in many parts of the humid tropics. The world has changed so rapidly over the last quarter of a century that our atlases have not been capable of keeping up with events. Those broad expanses of dark green across the lands of the humid tropics can so easily give the impression that almost limitless pristine forests will always be part of the established order of things on earth! But, in reality, although wild forest on a regional scale remains in Amazonia, New Guinea and the Congo Basin, forest clearance on a sub-continental scale has taken place over the last few decades, and huge tracts in West Africa, Southeast Asia, Brazil, Central America, Indonesia, the Philippines and Madagascar have been utterly changed. So rapid is the present rate of forest removal that even though, as yet, the mean annual production of wood may just exceed mean annual consumption and destruction by man (and this is by no means certain), the time is not far distant when, given present trends, the area of forest will be so small that far less wood will be produced each year than is used up by human beings.

The world timber situation is critical and will remain so even if administrations begin to recognize the problem and to take action. It seems clear that there is going to be an increasing demand for alternative materials in the years ahead. One apparently obvious source is the remainder of the above-ground product of food plants such as cereals, straw often being produced in larger quantities than the grain itself. This byproduct of arable production could be used to manufacture vast quantities of paper, packaging, upholstery and even constructional board.

This kind of industrial development has been advocated and already materials like cereal straw and bagasse (sugar cane residue) are widely used. But this may well be one of the most critical instances where a partial or slanted view of the world resources situation could lead to large-scale technological developments which, in the long run, could not be sustained. The burning of straw in the field, after harvest, became a common feature of the autumn landscape in Britain during the 1960s. It arose with the development of the stall-fed beef industry and the demand that this created for home-produced barley. Enormous quantities of barley straw were thus produced in lowland Britain and, since there was also a great increase in the segregation of arable farming from stock farming, barley straw was often of little or no economic value in the places where it was produced. There were few stock requiring winter bedding in these areas, and barley straw has relatively low nutritional value; consequently, in the prevailing economic climate, there was no way in which its organic contents could be returned to the land. Although it might be contended that burning the straw on the land was a good thing because the mineral ash it contained was thereby returned to the nutrient cycle, this was really of minimal importance because the operation took place in the early autumn and was followed by six months of British winter weather before growth of crops could restart. Substances such as the very soluble potash salts were therefore leached away into the ground water before they could be absorbed and recirculated.

Straw burning was not only condemned by ecologists; it was also viewed with disquiet by some agriculturalists, and many good farmers looked on it as a bad practice which was excusable only because of overriding economic considerations. It was merely tolerated even then because farmers allowed themselves to be persuaded that mineral fertilizers "out of the bag" would maintain soil fertility, at the price of abandoning long-established good farming practice.

In fact the climate of opinion in the 1970s is changing rapidly — and not entirely for immediate financial reasons. True, the escalating cost of mineral fertilizer (chapter 6) is having a profound effect on farming economics, but also soil scientists are discovering that the optimism of the 1960s about the maintenance of soil fertility beneath a near-monoculture of barley was perhaps premature. It is becoming apparent that, on certain types of soil, basic fertility and soil structure are beginning to break down, and that one of the main reasons is the decline in humus content below a certain critical level (Ministry of Agriculture, 1970). Whereas in the 1960s it was confidently asserted that cereal roots and stubble would keep humus content sufficiently high to preserve the soil structure, this is already very doubtful. And if this is the case in a country like Britain, where the breakdown of humus is relatively slow and where plentiful mineral fertilizer has been available to stimulate growth, it is only too clear what can happen in many agricultural soils in the tropics if the return of organic material is inadequate.

One should not draw the conclusion, therefore, that straw burning in Britain was bad merely because it wasted a raw material which might well have been useful elsewhere. One should certainly not assume that agriculture all over the world should produce a large excess of straw and sell it off to industry. The point has already been made that the very clearance of the original forestland and its conversion to cropland deprives the soil of the products of leaf fall; furthermore, many arable crops produce only 10 to 15 per cent of their NPP below ground. It may well be necessary to ensure a much greater organic return to the soil than takes place at the present time, either by way of the cereal straw or, even better, by producing fewer grain crops and intercalating turf-forming forage crops which produce a very large percentage of their NPP at or below ground level. For this kind of reason one is forced back to the basic precept that a carefully maintained forest cover in the long run may be the only really substantial source of fibres for industry.

TERRESTRIAL PRODUCTION PER CAPITA

In 1975 world population reached four billion; a mean annual above-ground NPP of something over 50 billion mt thus gives us about 13 tons (dry weight) per head. Given that catastrophe does not intervene, and population increase continues to double at its present rate, by the year 2010 there will be eight billion people. If forest depletion continues, even at a reduced rate, it is probably optimistic to say that the 50 or so billion tons per annum will have been reduced to 40 billion by the same year. In 2010 AD there would then be a mere five tons per head.

What are the implications of an above-ground world dry-weight production of only five tons per head? As already indicated, something like half is returned to the soil even though men might prefer it otherwise. (It is probably worth reiterating that if human communities were reduced to such straits that they began, as a regular practice, to consume the leaves from the trees and to gather up every fallen fragment of twig and bark for fuel, then reduction in productivity would occur even more rapidly.) There remains a mere two and a half tons to be exploited. At the present time, the average person in North America and much of Europe eats the equivalent of one dry-weight ton per annum. (This is taking account of the fact that much vegetable "food" is literally wasted at both the manufacturing and domestic stages, and that a very large amount of vegetable material goes into the production of a relatively small quantity of meat. For information about vegetable-animal conversion ratios see chapter 5.) Apart from this, in Britain each of us consumes almost half a ton dry-weight equivalent of timber in the form of paper, packaging and various other products, and in the USA the per capita consumption is far greater. Add to this that, over much of the world, forest is being wantonly destroyed, grass is being burned and vegetation generally is suffering destructive usage. Precise data for much of what is happening is not available, but mere inspection of the world scene suggests that humanity is consuming or destroying more per head than will actually be available for each person in the year 2010.

Apart from being a very disturbing conclusion this is also a most surprising one when viewed against some of the more optimistic statements of relatively recent years (see Clark, 1967). At the outset it is difficult to see how one can begin to reconcile what has just been said with Colin Clark's assertion that the earth is capable of supporting not eight billion, but 47 billion people at American levels of food consumption. A closer examination suggests that the discrepancy arises mainly out of the fact that our underlying assumptions and precepts are very different. The reason why he was able to produce such unrealistic figures was because he chose to ignore so many realities which we regard as both inescapable and fundamental. Not only does he base all his productivity assessments on a broad world classification of climates, ignoring the multifarious contrasts in slope and innate soil fertility, but he also assumes that it is feasible to rectify natural infertility by the application of mineral fertilizer wherever this is needed. Indeed he states categorically that he has made no allowance "for poor soils, the description of which is largely a matter of opinion, and which, in any case, can be improved by fertilization, if we really need their output" (1967 p. 142). Quite apart from the fact that the supply of mineral fertilizers will probably pose very serious problems in the not too distant future (chapter 6), the sublime assumption that all countries are going to have sufficient excess wealth to be able to afford these expensive commodities in whatever quantities their soils require is little short of astounding. It is the immensity of the implied resource requirement which makes Colin Clark's vision of the future unacceptable. He assumes that the vast areas of relatively poor soil in humid and moist sub-humid regions, where natural NPP is low or where extensive pastoralism has already reduced productivity, can be made to produce abundantly. But to permit this, nutrient minerals would have to be available to replace those removed in crops and timber, water would have to be available in large quantities for irrigation in times of inordinately dry weather, and supplies of energy would have to be at the disposal of those who had to carry out the massive engineering works necessary to permit all these developments. This kind of thing has taken place to a certain extent over some of the relatively fertile terrestrial areas, but to suppose that resources could be made available to permit it over vast and much less responsive regions demands a disregard of too many solid realities.

It may well be that in the near future some of the countries now regarded as "poor" will be capable of purchasing fertilizers on a much more substantial scale than at present; a trend in this direction is already apparent. But to imagine that vast and increasing masses of people in the underprivileged countries as a whole are going to have an increased per capita consumption of the world's raw materials in the near future is surely unrealistic. Apart from the question of resource availability, the problems of organization and social reorientation are far too great to be solved quickly. Colin Clark's thesis seems to assume that the world can become a rational and well ordered place within a very short time — that capital and expertise can be applied in almost unlimited quantities so that soils produce at the maximum rate without depletion, erosion, salinization and all the other ills which can beset agriculture and forestry when they are not carried out with the utmost skill, care and ecological judgement. The evidence of history seems to indicate that technological applications and innovations, even when they are physically possible, can take place only gradually. Colin Clark's vision of the future, even if it were ecologically viable, is of little help to mankind unless our institutions are capable of such rapid modification that a doubling of world population can be accommodated over the next 35 years. Most present trends in forest destruction and expanding pastoralism run counter to any of the rational ordering of terrestrial resources that would be necessary to cope with this.

SALVATION FROM THE OCEANS?

The oceans have frequently been presented as an almost limitless source of food from which to supplement terrestrial production. On the face of it this is not surprising since some 360 million km^2 of the earth's surface (about 70 per cent) are oceanic and, throughout history, small boats fishing in relatively tiny areas have returned to port with enormous catches of fish. No attempt to quantify the total organic productivity of the earth could hope to carry conviction without taking into account the productivity of the sea.

In spite of its relatively large area, however, the sea seems to have a far smaller total NPP than the land. One estimate (Koblenz-Mishke, 1965) put it at about 130 billion mt (wet weight) per annum, while others (Rodin et al., 1974; Lieth, 1972) estimated it to be between 55 and 60 billion mt (dry weight) per annum. Thus there appears to be fairly close agreement that the NPP of the green phytoplankton of the oceans is something less than half that of the potential for terrestrial plant communities. But even this tends to give an exaggerated impression of the organic contents of the oceans. The rate of turnover is far more rapid in the oceans than on land, so that nowhere near 130 billion tons of green organic matter (60 billion tons dry weight) is actually in existence in the oceans at any one point of time. As Ricker (1969) has so clearly expressed it: "The plants die or are eaten ... and the minerals released are then available for a new cycle of production. Thus some of the same actual atoms take part in production many times over during the course of a year." Bogarov (1967) has estimated that the actual standing crop of phytoplankton, at any one point of time, is no more than 1·5 billion tons (wet weight), or not much more than one per cent of the annual production. The great contrast between a terrestrial forest and the plankton of an area of ocean is that, whereas the standing crop in the former greatly exceeds the NPP, exactly the opposite is true of the latter. We thus have the seemingly paradoxical situation in which, although the oceanic areas are so much more extensive than the land areas, at any point in time the dry weight of the living matter in the oceans is only about 0·13 per cent of that on land (Rodin *et al.*, 1974).

The higher trophic levels of marine life are dependent on the production of phytoplankton, and recent independent assessments seem to have achieved a fair measure of agreement regarding the annual production of the uppermost one —

that of the larger fish and the marine mammals. This has been calculated to be in the region of 300 to 320 million mt (Ricker, 1969) of which only about 150 to 160 million mt can be regarded as harvestable if yield is to be maintained.

Already, by 1966, the total world catch of marine products had reached 60 million mt (FAO, 1966), and although it may be theoretically possible to increase this to 100 or even 150 million mt, it is clear that the oceans cannot be regarded as a vast reservoir of readily available animal protein. The exploitation level of marine mammals at which sustained yield is assured has already been far surpassed, and catch limitation, both planned and involuntary, has been imposed. Those fishing grounds which remain little exploited are remote from the large populations of the earth and can be reached only with greater effort and capital outlay. Furthermore, of all the fish caught at the present time, between 80 and 90 per cent are taken at depths of less than 200 metres (Ricker, 1969). An extension of fishing is bound to entail greater exploitation of the deeper levels of the ocean, where only one third of the total number of fish are spread through a great depth of water, so that smaller catches per unit of time and effort will be inevitable. It is equally clear that any attempts to increase marine food supplies by mass harvesting of the lower trophic levels, such as the plankton and the small plankton feeders, would be much more costly per unit of production, quite apart from the fact that conventional fishing would become less profitable as the basis of fish subsistence was removed.

If the annual world catch is to be increased to around 100 million mt (an increase of between 60 and 70 per cent over 1966), this can probably only be achieved with a 200 per cent increase in investment. If an attempt is then to be made to push production to its probable limit of 150 million mt, an educated guess suggests that this could only be achieved by an investment in ships and equipment of about six times that in the 1960s (Ricker, 1969). A 500 per cent increase in investment to effect a 150 per cent increase in production may well be countenanced by industrialized countries during periods of economic boom; it seems an unlikely course of action for a technology-deficient country. This is obviously not an inexpensive way in which protein-deficient nations can improve or maintain the quality of their diet. The fact remains that, with a doubled world population in the year 2010, world production of fish would have to have risen to over 120 million mt in order to permit the same consumption per head as we have at the present time.

5

The Organic Productivity of Nations

Civilization is threatened if world consumption of plant material outruns production; but statements about the total world budget, and assessments of mean per capita production over the earth as a whole, obscure great diversities. A mere glance at the world productivity map (figure 4.2) reveals how great are the contrasts between hot and cold and between wet and dry regions. In fact about 60 per cent of potential phytomass production occurs in the tropics (42 per cent of the land area), something over 20 per cent in the sub-tropics (18 per cent of the land area), and less than 20 per cent over the whole of the sub-boreal, boreal and polar land masses (40 per cent of the land area). And whereas humid areas in the tropics could produce, on average, something like 2,500 mt/km^2/year, the most climatically favoured areas in the polar zone are not capable of producing more than 200.

Of even greater interest are the contrasts between the potential NPPs of national territories, particularly when these are expressed in terms of production per capita (see appendix IV). A first indication of the significance of this can be obtained from an examination of the most extensive and most heavily populated countries (figure 5.1). Eleven countries have an area of more than two million km^2 and, among these, it is intriguing to find that Australia, in spite of its generally arid character, has a potential to produce over 470 mt per head, placing it at the top of the table. Sparsely populated Canada also, despite its high latitude, occupies one of the top four places. More predictably, Zaire and Brazil with their moist tropical environments, are pre-eminent. On the other hand, in spite of their vast areas of tropical and sub-tropical forest land, India and China are dragged to the foot of the list by their enormous populations, India having a potential of only 6·9 mt per head. Of the 14 countries with over 50 million population, Brazil, with over 165 mt per head, has more than three times as much as any other nation, while the USSR (49·9 mt) and the USA (40·6 mt) occupy second and third places. Japan comes last with a mere 4·9 mt per head, but West Germany and the United Kingdom are only a little ahead with 5·2 and 5·5 mt respectively.

These figures demand closer scrutiny. Though they have an inherent significance, they are clearly underlain by diverse and complex realities which must be explored before one can feel assured that they reflect relative resource potential. The larger and more heavily populated countries already referred to have an obvious importance but it is necessary to review the per capita potential NPPs of the whole spectrum of nations (appendix IV) in order to appreciate the

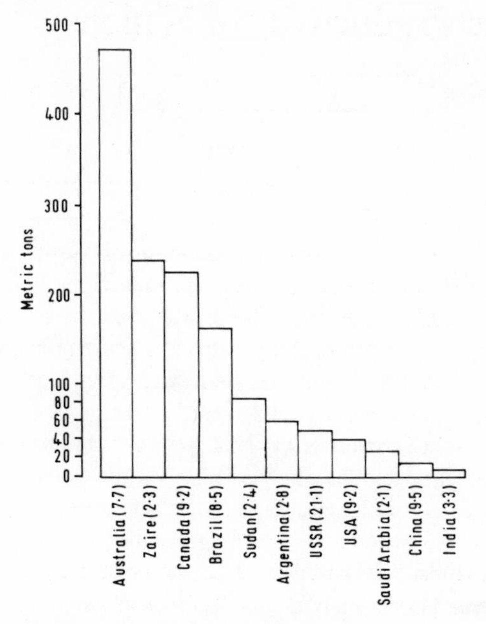

5·1a PPCNPP of countries with a land area exceeding $2 \times 10^6 km^2$ (figures in parenthesis indicate area in $10^6 km^2$)

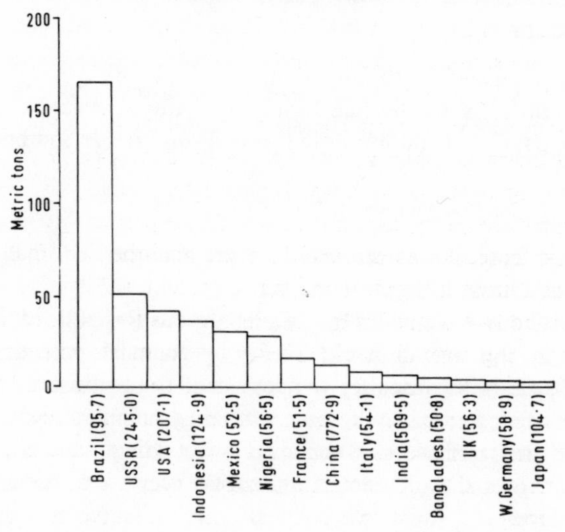

5·1b PPCNPP of countries with a population exceeding 50 millions (figures in parenthesis indicate population in millions)

complexity of the world organic share-out. Of the 147 countries (figure 5.2) whose potential NPP has been computed from the world vegetation map, 27 have a production of less than 10 mt per head and eight have less than 5 mt. At the other extreme, 23 countries have a potential production of more than 200 mt per head, three of them having more than 1,000.

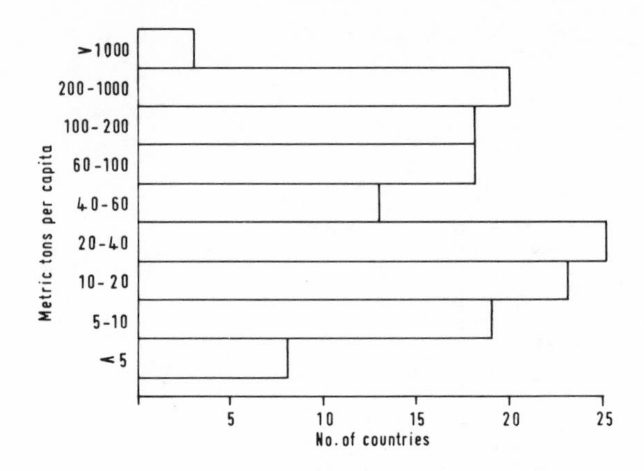

5·2 The range of PPCNPP over 147 countries

THE POORLY ENDOWED NATIONS

One encounters some fascinatingly diverse bedfellows when nations are grouped on the basis of per capita NPP (figure 5.3), but some interesting generalizations do emerge. Among the 27 most poorly endowed, for instance, the following groups predominate:

(a) heavily populated European countries;
(b) dry countries of the Middle East and southwest Asia;
(c) heavily populated and formerly forested countries in southern and eastern Asia;
(d) heavily populated islands in the West Indies

Indeed, outside these four categories, there are only the two small African states of Rwanda and Burundi (figure 5.4).

The British Crown Colony of Hong Kong and the Republic of Singapore were not included in the overall world survey of national potential productivity (appendix IV), partly because they were too small to be measured realistically on the map scale used, and partly because it seemed pointless to do so: so large a proportion of their territories is occupied by buildings and other biologically unproductive usages that it seemed unrealistic even to consider their organic productivity. However, these two political units can serve as a useful basis for comparison and deserve a little attention. They are now very urbanized territories with nearly 10,000 people per square mile (3,700 and 3,500/km^2 respectively) subsisting basically by means of manufacturing and commerce, and it is inconceivable that any technological miracle could ever permit them to survive on food and fibres raised from the land they occupy. On the basis of Colin Clark's optimistic assessments (1967), Hong Kong has nearly eight times

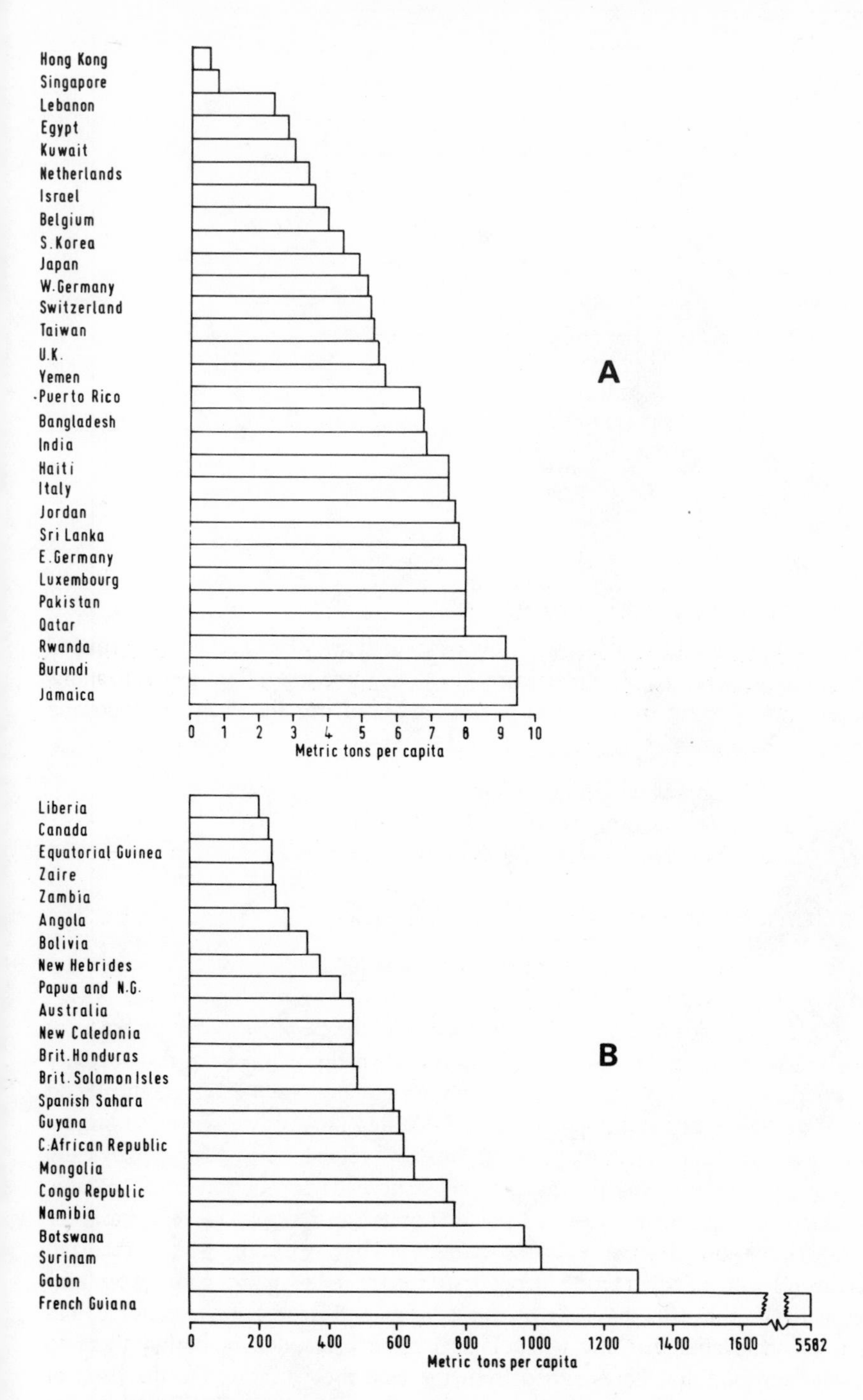

5·3 The PPCNPP of (**A**) the most poorly endowed, and (**B**) the best endowed nations

5·4 The PPCNPP of the nations (in mt)

as many people as its *total* area could support at American standards of eating (even assuming that their houses, roads and other constructions took up no room at all, and disregarding the fact that most of the territory which is not built upon is precipitous hillside where agriculture cannot possibly take place!).

Because there are two territories such as these, whose population has already far outstripped the productive capacity of the land they occupy, it is thought-provoking to view them in the same context as the 27 other poorly endowed nations (figure 5.3a). Hong Kong, with an area of 1,045·6 km^2, would have an annual NPP of about 1·9 million mt if covered by its original broad-leaved evergreen forest producing at the rate of 1,800 mt/km^2. Simple division of this figure by that of the 1971 population (3·95 million) produces an answer of just under 0·5 mt. Similarly, if the 581·5 km^2 of Singapore were covered with tropical rain forest with a mean productivity of 2,500 mt/km^2/year, it would produce 1·45 million mt per annum and, dividing this by the population of 2·07 million, one arrives at the answer of almost exactly 0·7 mt.

Given that these two territories could not conceivably be self-supporting in organic materials even if they were to attempt it, the tantalizing question arises as to whether this is not also true of other countries occupying lowly positions on the productivity table. There is certainly a considerable difference between the 5·5 mt for the United Kingdom (or even the 2·4 mt for Lebanon) and the 0·7 mt for Singapore but, as already shown, Singapore and Hong Kong have passed so far beyond the threshold of potential self-sufficiency that even countries with many times their per capita production may also have done so.

The main fascination about the geography of nations is that the resource potential of each country is unique and the selection of just one or two examples to demonstrate particular points is always hazardous. However, within the confines of the present work it is obviously not possible to scrutinize the resource complexities of all the countries whose cases might be critical, or even to embark on an exhaustive assessment of only a few of them. Hopefully in the near future, detailed national stock-takings will be carried out for all the countries of the world. All that can be attempted here is to pioneer methods by which the potential self-sufficiency of nations might be assessed, and to apply these methods to one country in particular. Then, since the 27 poorly endowed nations recognized here fall into four main regional groups, it seems a useful preliminary exercise to assess the resource position of some examples from each in order to discover whether or not there are grounds for concluding that low NPPs in different types of environment reflect similar resource predicaments.

In the European group are the Netherlands, Belgium, West Germany, Switzerland, the United Kingdom, Italy, East Germany and Luxembourg. They all feature here (figure 5.3a) not because of a relatively low potential NPP — over most of their territories summer-green forest was the original vegetation — but because of high population density. West Germany, the United Kingdom and Italy are particularly important because each has more than 50 million people, while the United Kingdom has been selected for more detailed examination because it has probably ventured further along the road of over-industrialization than any other large nation: only one person in 50 is now engaged directly in agriculture, with all that this implies in terms of economic flexibility, internal political pressures and national instability.

THE CASE OF THE UNITED KINGDOM

Under natural conditions, before the arrival of neolithic herdsmen and cultivators, the 241,000 km^2 of the United Kingdom were mainly occupied by summer-green forest, dominated particularly by oak and elm and interspersed especially over the flatter lands of eastern England with patches of swamp and fen. Forests of this nature probably covered some 220,000 km^2. Pine and birch certainly occupied large tracts in the Highlands of Scotland (probably less than 20,000 km^2) while the higher mountains and some upland plateaux could only support alpine vegetation and peat bog (Eyre, 1968); but these were minor contributors to the total NPP. If one ascribes a mean NPP of 1,300 mt/km^2 to the summer-green forest areas (see chapter 4), 1,100 to the pine and birch forests, and 200 to the tracts of alpine and bog vegetation, then the whole country was producing just over 308 million mt per annum. This is probably a fairly generous assessment since, in many parts of the west and northwest, the natural forests of the British Isles were close to their climatic limits and, in consequence, must have been producing at a rate well below the average for their respective plant formations. However, it seems reasonable to take this approximation as the natural dry weight productivity of the United Kingdom — the productivity which could eventually be achieved were the country permitted to return to a pristine state of nature. If this figure is divided by the human population — 56·3 million in 1971 — the "national per capita potential NPP" is found to be 5·5 mt.

The fact that this is a purely theoretical figure does not detract from its significance, and one can certainly profit from subjecting it to closer examination. The 308 million mt (dry weight) of organic material would not all be contained in what we would now regard as merchantable timber — the "roundwood" of the timber trade. If production were distributed as in the stand of trees already referred to (chapter 4) in the Netherlands (Duvigneaud and Denaeyer-DeSmet, 1970), roughly 15 per cent would be underground, more than 65 per cent would be in leaves, twigs, smaller branches, bark, shrubs and herbaceous undergrowth, and something less than 20 per cent (18·3 per cent in precise figures) in solid roundwood. On a fairly optimistic assessment, therefore, production of what is now regarded as usable timber would be about 62 million mt (dry weight) — 1·1 mt per head. Since much of the wood we use comprises about 15 per cent water, 1·1 mt dry weight is equivalent to approximately 1·25 mt of commercial timber.

If one requires an expression to characterize this figure, it seems appropriate to refer to it as "the natural economic NPP per capita" of the United Kingdom. Apart from a relatively small amount of upland and mountain pasture, the original landscape carried no other living organic assets which would be regarded today as items of economic importance. Wild game, blackberries, bilberries, crab-apples and the wherewithal to make dandelion-and-burdock were doubtless very important to the small populations of mesolithic times, but the amounts in which these were produced were tiny when viewed in the context of the present population, quite apart from the fact that tastes have changed.

THE POTENTIAL PRODUCTIVITY OF FORESTRY AND AGRICULTURE IN THE UNITED KINGDOM

The present landscape is not shrouded in summer-green forest: this has been almost completely removed to meet some of the economic demands of the twentieth century. About 12 per cent of the area is occupied by houses, factories, roads and other urban features so that, with the exception of some gardens, it produces no food or vegetable fibres to support the economic system. Of the remainder about 8 per cent was forest land in the early 1970s (predominantly under conifers), about 30 per cent is regularly ploughed for arable crops and temporary grass, a little over 20 per cent is improved long-term grassland, and almost 30 per cent is heath, moor and fell used mainly as rough pasture.[1]

Although some of these changes in the landscape have traditionally been referred to as "improvements", they have not brought about an overall increase in the total NPP or even maintained it. Some of the species of conifer planted during the past half century such as the Monterrey pine (*Pinus radiata*) and the Corsican pine (*P. nigra*) are certainly capable of producing more than 1,300 mt/km^2/year (total NPP) if managed carefully on climatically-favoured and fertile sites; they are also capable of distributing their production more advantageously for the timber merchant, so that more than 20 per cent goes into the commercial roundwood. But such a large proportion of British forestry has now been relegated to higher, less favoured sites that it would be unrealistic to expect the average NPP greatly to exceed the 1,300 mt/km^2/year achieved by the original wild forest communities even when the relatively recent Forestry Commission forests have had sufficient time to reach equilibrium production. Probably 1,500 mt/km^2/year is a realistic (if rather optimistic) figure, this being roughly equivalent to 8·5 m^3 of timber per ha (see below, p.55). It would, however, be unreasonably optimistic to postulate an *average* productivity of more than 1,000 mt/km^2/year for croplands and improved grasslands, and an average of 500 mt from the rough grazing lands cannot be an underestimate bearing in mind the nature of their physical environment (see below, p.54). When these postulates are assembled (table 5.1) one arrives at the conclusion that the transformation of the national landscape has lowered total NPP from the order of 308 mmt to 184·5 mmt — a reduction of the order of 40 per cent.

[1]For more comprehensive and precise data see Stamp (1962) and National Farmers' Union (1975).

Table 5.1 Theoretical productive capacity of the United Kingdom given the present land use pattern

Usage	Approximate area in km² (and percentage of total)	Average production in mt/km²/yr (dry weight)	Total production in mmt (dry weight)	Usable production in mmt (dry weight)	Final product in mmt (actual weight)
Forest	19000 (8%)	1500	28·5	7·1 (dry roundwood)	8·36 (roundwood at 15% water content)
Arable	72000 (30%)	1000	72·0	28·8 (dry grain)	33·9 (grain at 15% water content)
Long-term grassland	48000 (20%)	1000	48·0	14·4 (dry grass)	30–1 1·07 (butcher's meat at 55% water content)
Rough grazing	72000 (30%)	500	36·0	5·4 (dry edible component)	60–1 0·20 (butcher's meat at 55% water content)
Urbanized land	29000 (12%)	?	?	?	?
TOTAL	240000		184·5	55·7	

Before one can assess the implications of an actual NPP of 184·5 mmt (3·3 mt per capita) in terms of the possibilities of national self-sufficiency in organic products, it is necessary to convert units of total production into units of usable production (table 5.1). In the case of the 19,000 km^2 of forest, the total NPP of 28·5 mmt (dry weight), given an average usable content of 25 per cent (mainly in dry roundwood), would yield 7·1 mmt (dry weight) of usable wood product; and since timber is often assessed at 15 per cent moisture content, this is equivalent to 8·36 mmt of merchantable product.[2] Secondly, if the 72,000 km^2 of arable land were entirely devoted to high-yielding grain crops with 40 per cent of the total NPP in the form of grain, then 28·8 mmt of dry grain would be produced — 33·9 mmt at 15 per cent moisture content. Finally, assessment of the end product of the improved grasslands and the rough grazings is more problematical, but if one postulates that they were devoted solely to the production of beef, mutton and lamb it is possible to arrive at a reasoned statement of their potential meat-producing capacity given standards of efficiency and productivity similar to those obtaining at the present time. The 48,000 km^2 of long-term (permanent) grassland, yielding an average of 30 per cent of their total NPP above ground (see chapter 4) would produce 14·4 mmt of grass (dry weight). At an average conversion ratio of 30 to 1 (3·3 per cent)[3] this would produce 0·48 mmt of dry meat, or approximately 1·07 mmt butchers' meat (55 per cent moisture). Also, the 72,000 km^2 of rough grazing land, assuming a mean NPP of 500 $mt/km^2/year$, and yielding 30 per cent of its product above ground only half of which was edible, would produce 5·4 mmt of dry edible component. With an average conversion ratio of 60 to 1 (1·6 per cent) this would produce 0·09 mmt of dry meat or 0·2 mmt butchers' meat.[4] The remaining 12 per cent of the country, at the present time, produces very little per km^2 and, indeed, much of the greenery to be found there is for appearance and

[2] This is based on the assumption that average forest in the United Kingdom yields at 8·5 $m^3/ha/year$ of roundwood with an average specific gravity of 0·5 at 15 per cent moisture content.

[3] This may seem a very poor ratio but it is probably an optimistic estimate given the production levels of the present time. It is based on the published figures of Leitch and Godden (1953), Holmes (1971) and National Farmers' Union (1975). There is no doubt that the productivity of the permanent grasslands could be raised, but this would require much greater capitalization in the form of fertilizer and labour input.

[4] The productivity of rough grazings is highly problematical (Eadie and Cunningham, 1971) but again, this is probably a very optimistic estimate. Bearing in mind that plants such as mat grass (*Nardus stricta*), cotton sedge (*Eriophorum* spp), ling (*Calluna vulgaris*), bracken (*Pteridium aquilinum*) and bog moss (*Sphagnum* spp.) are widespread dominants, it can be no exaggeration to postulate that half the above-ground production is inedible. Furthermore, since the animal devotes much of its time to walking around in search of food in windy and cool conditions, most of its energy intake must be expended in the maintenance of weight already achieved. Indeed a mature ewe, apart from growing a fleece, has no net weight-gain at all from year end to year end: all her energy intake is expended in maintaining her own weight and producing a lamb. These points must not in any way be taken as denigration of upland stock farming: if we are to remain meat eaters, then the raising of healthy lambs and calves on the rough pastures (for fattening elsewhere) obviates the necessity of using up large areas of more productive land for this purpose.

amenity rather than for food and industrial purposes; its potential, however, is an interesting field for speculation.

Given a land use pattern approximating to the one existing in the 1970s, therefore, one can postulate a potential national production of 8·36 mmt of usable wood product, 33·9 mmt of grain and 1·27 mmt of meat from 88 per cent of the land area. Moreover as will be seen later, it is doubtful if the actual volume of this theoretical product could be enlarged by the application of any credible technological or economic improvements, with the possible exception of that from the permanent grasslands. However, the model that has been constructed is an artificial one, particularly with regard to the usage of arable land, because in reality this is not and cannot be used solely for the production of cereals. The reason for presenting a figure which can usefully be thought of as the "grain equivalent" for the production of the whole arable area of the country will become clear later, but it is important first to view these quantities in the light of present levels of consumption.

PRODUCTION IN RELATION TO CONSUMPTION IN THE UNITED KINGDOM

In the early 1970s the United Kingdom was consuming the equivalent of about 21·6 mmt of wood per annum (Forestry Commission, 1976)[5] — some 13·3 mmt in excess of the potential production. Given present levels of consumption and population, it is apparent that the country could not become self-supporting in timber products without increasing its forested area by something over 150 per cent. Similarly, in 1972, 3·98 mmt of meat and meat products were consumed (United Nations, 1973b) — 2·71 mmt in excess of the potential production from the grasslands as calculated above. The deficit is so great that even if an attempt to raise the productivity of all the rough grazings to that of the improved grassland were successful, the United Kingdom would still not be able to meet its present demand for meat in the form of beef and lamb from the 50 per cent of the country concerned. And, in passing, one must add that any such effort would be at colossal expense and could not possibly succeed in face of the shorter growing season and other adverse physical factors on the uplands. The only item on table 5.1 which matches up to the present demand is the 33·9 mmt of grain from the arable land: in the early 1970s the country consumed, either as human food and drink or as stockfeed, an average of just short of 20 mmt of cereals per annum (Ministry of Agriculture, Fisheries and Food, 1974; UN, 1973b; UN, 1973a). There is thus an apparent surplus of about 14 mmt of grain in the model that has been presented.

But man does not live by bread alone. Nor, indeed, is the present population of Britain and Northern Ireland content to subsist exclusively on wheat bread,

[5] This figure assumes air-dry wood (15 per cent water content) with a specific gravity of 0·5. It is derived from the Forestry Commission's figure of 43·24 × 10^6 m^3 WRME (average for 1970–74). The WRME (wood raw material equivalent) is the standard unit of measurement now used to bring the whole range of wood products (sawn wood, pulp, newsprint, chipboard and so on) to a common basis so that total annual consumption can be assessed.

barley beer and the meat that can be raised on home-produced grain and grass. Vast quantities of dairy produce, sugar, fruit and vegetables, and almost countless other organic products are now regarded as part of the normal and rightful diet of the people. A very large percentage of this food is now imported,[6]

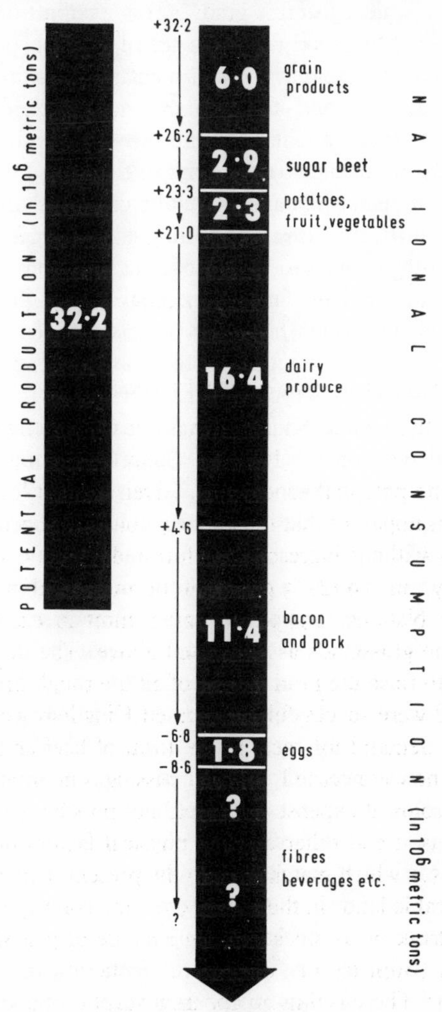

5·5 The potential production (in grain equivalents) of the present area of arable land in the United Kingdom, compared to national consumption in the early 1970s

[6] In the year 1972–3 the United Kingdom imported the following percentages of its consumption:

Wheat	49	Beef and veal	17	Butter	78
Other grains	22	Mutton and lamb	56	Cheese	44
Sugar	65	Bacon and ham	56		

and one way of assessing the possibility of producing it all at home is to determine how much of the grain-growing potential of 33·9 mmt each item is equivalent to (figure 5.5).

Before considering individual crops, however, it is important to look carefully at the area of the so-called "arable land". This has been presented as 72,000 km^2 — a figure which is merely a statement of the total map area devoted to arable farming practices. In point of fact a substantial fraction of this is occupied by walls, hedges, ditches and farm roads and, of necessity, the strips of unploughed land which border them. In the early part of this century these may well have occupied approaching 10 per cent of the total "arable" area, but this has been very much reduced mainly because of the enlargement of fields by fence removal. Nevertheless, anyone who has studied recent aerial photographs of different parts of the country is very conscious of the fact that the area of this "non-productive" land is still far from negligible and probably accounts for almost 5 per cent of the total. This being the case, a total area of 72,000 km^2 given over to arable farming practices would contain some 3,600 km^2 of non-producing land. If the actual crop area is 5 per cent less than the arable area shown on the map, it is necessary also to reduce our assessment of the potential grain-producing capacity by 5 per cent — from 33·9 mmt to 32·2 mmt. This latter should be the starting point for our calculations.

In 1973 the population of the United Kingdom ate an average of 72·6 kg (160·1 lb) of cereal products per head — a total of 4·09 mmt (Allaby *et al.*, 1975). In the same year 2·349 mmt of barley were consumed in beer production along with a much smaller amount by whisky distilleries. While a small proportion of the drink was exported, it is clear that over six million mt of cereals were directly consumed at home as human food. Subtracting this from the available 32·2 mmt grain equivalents leaves in the region of 26·2 mmt (figure 5.5). Also in 1973 the United Kingdom consumed just over three million mt of sugar (Ministry of Agriculture, Fisheries and Food, 1974); assuming a potential production of 500 mt/km^2/year, the country would need to occupy some 6,071 km^2 with sugar beet in a self-sufficient economy. This is equivalent to 2·9 mmt of grain so that the remaining grain equivalents are reduced from 26·2 to 23·3 mmt. 5·487 mmt of potatoes were also consumed in 1973 and, at a productivity of 3,000 mt/km^2 (fresh weight), these would have occupied an area of 1,829 km^2, corresponding to a grain equivalent of 0·9 mmt. In the same year 7·3 mmt of fruit and vegetables were consumed. The production of marketable material per unit area varies so enormously with market garden produce that it is very difficult to postulate an acreage equivalent; indeed, whatever figure is taken must be notional since achievement of self-sufficiency in fruit and vegetables would inevitably entail the substitution of temperate crops for tropical and sub-tropical ones. At one end of the spectrum there are crops such as cherries, blackcurrants and nuts with very low comparative productivities in terms of weight, and at the other there is the 20 tons or more per ha of crops like cabbages, and even 100 mt/ha for glasshouse tomatoes. In the light of quantities at present produced, an average of 25 mt/ha (2,500 mt/km^2) probably lies somewhere between the realistic and the somewhat optimistic, and this implies an area requirement of something over 2,900 km^2 (1·4 mmt grain equivalent). The requirements of potatoes, other vegetables and fruits thus reduces the total from 23·3 to 21·0 grain equivalents (figure 5.5).

The final and most important set of products are those derived from the dairy industry, and the land requirements of dairying can be considered conveniently along with the problem of the meat deficit. Fundamentally the production of animal products revolves around the amount of rotational grass incorporated into the arable systems. As already made clear, the total area of permanent grass and rough grazing is capable of producing only a proportion of the nation's meat demands, so that all the dairying requirement would have to come from the arable rotations. Working on the assumption that the average water content of milk is 87·5 per cent, and the average water content of all butter and margarine is 20 per cent, the United Kingdom consumption of milk solids and milk-substitute solids in 1973 was approximately 2·1 mmt. Leitch and Godden (1953) calculated that the average conversion ratio of feed solids to milk solids in Britain was 7·5 per cent (13·3 to 1), taking into account the consumption of the cow throughout the whole of its life from birth to the end of the third lactation. This was assuming a predominance of grassland feed — hay in winter and grass in summer — along with a ration of more concentrated food. Since the average milk yield has probably risen about 50 per cent since the 1950s, now standing at between 800 and 900 gallons per annum (National Farmers' Union, 1975) the average conversion ratio must have improved, though not in direct proportion to yield. It would probably be unrealistic to visualize an average "whole life" conversion ratio of better than 10 to 1 in the near future. If, therefore, one postulates an average NPP of 1,200 mt/km^2/year for all rotational grassland, with 50 per cent of production above ground,[7] this would imply an annual dry-weight yield of 600 mt/km^2 in grass and hay.[8] The problem remains as to the proportion of the required quantity of milk solids which should be produced from grass. Cattle are ruminants and thus have the admirable ability of being able to convert cellulose into animal product; they are also adapted to subsisting primarily on the leaves and stems of grass and other herbaceous plants. But in spite of this adaptation, it was demonstrated long ago that production, in terms of both milk and meat, is improved by a supplementary ration which is richer in carbohydrates and fats.

[7] Temporary grassland produces a far larger proportion of its NPP above ground than do the grasses of wild or long-established grassland. Clearly the percentage differs widely on different soils, but 50 per cent seems a reasonable average.

[8] This is probably realistic in the light of recent estimates. Eadie and Cunningham (1971) cite yields of 224 to 336 mt/km^2/year for unfertilized lowland grassland, 560 to 847 for fertilized grassland, and between 1,000 and 1,500 for heavily fertilized grassland. One of the most frequent commentaries on modern British farming is the continued low-productivity of grassland because of low fertilization rates (National Farmers' Union, 1975).

The classical Norfolk rotation of crops involved putting arable land under a temporary crop of grass and clover every fourth year; this was felt necessary to keep up the organic status of the soil and to help control the weeds of cultivation. Even today, temporary grass remains important, as in the "long ley" mixed farming systems of eastern Scotland. Indeed, in 1974, 32 per cent (some 23,000 km^2) of the total arable acreage was under temporary grass (National Farmers' Union, 1975) in spite of the depradations of barley and "barley beef" on the farming economy. Even if the present intensity of grain production can be maintained, it seems reasonable to suppose that an acreage of this order of magnitude will remain as temporary grass. 23,000 km^2 yielding at the rate of 600 mt/km^2/year is sufficient dry weight to produce 1·38 mmt of milk solids, and this is 0·72 mmt short of the 2·1 mmt consumed at present. This balance would have to be made up by grain from the remainder of the arable land[9] — some 7·2 mmt of grain being required. Since the 23,000 km^2 of temporary grass are equivalent to 9·2 mmt of grain, on the basis of the stated criteria the present consumption of dairy produce is thus equivalent to 16·4 mmt of grain — a little more than half the total potential production (figure 5.5). One should add that this dairying requirement can be altered slightly by varying the proportions of grass and grain (or other crops) fed to the cattle, but the long-term advantages and disadvantages of giving cattle more grain, reducing the amount of grass, and many other considerations are very problematical and, in any case, the basic issue is little affected.

The dairy requirement thus reduces the spare grain equivalents to a mere 4·6 mmt, and still the deficit of 2·71 mmt in meat production has not been met. There is certainly a meat spin-off from dairying, but a total of 2·1 mmt of milk solids would be produced by a little over four million milking cows if each were producing half a metric ton of milk solids annually (between 850 and 900 gallons). Something over a million animals would thus be sold off as fat cows each year, producing approximately 0·5 mmt of butchers' meat. We are therefore still some 2·2 mmt of meat below requirements, and to meet this by one of the most efficient methods, that of producing pork and bacon, would require some 11·4 mmt of corn (assuming a dry-weight conversion ratio of 10 to 1,[10] from corn with a 15 per cent moisture content, to butchers' meat with 55

[9] It is appropriate to mention here that small amounts of brewers' grains and beet molasses are used in stockfeed, and that a certain percentage of cereal straw can also be used for this purpose. Such materials can certainly be fed to dairy cattle. The amounts that would be available and the value of such bi-products in terms of "grain equivalents" is difficult to compute, but the overall potential of 32·2 mmt (figure 5.5) would be only slightly affected by taking these things into account.

[10] Leitch and Godden (1953) calculated conversion ratios of between 8·2 to 1 and 10·3 to 1 for bacon and pork production, their calculations only taking into account the pig's life between 18 kg (live weight) and final weight. If one also takes into account the feed consumed by breeding sows and by piglets in earlier stages of growth, even though great improvements in productivity have taken place since 1953, a conversion ratio of 10 to 1 at the present time is probably somewhat better than average.

per cent moisture). This corn requirement could not be met by the 4·6 mmt remaining (figure 5.5) and a deficit of 6·8 mmt arises.

There is one further important item of diet which could be produced at home. In 1972–3, 1,247 million dozens of eggs were consumed in the United Kingdom — some 0·21 mmt of egg solids. At a conversion ratio of 10 to 1 the production of this quantity of egg would take 1·8 mmt of grain (at 15 per cent moisture content) and this must be added to the deficit. Again, there would be an annual spin-off of about 50 million old hens for the meat market, but, at an average weight of just over two kg per bird, this would amount to about 100,000 mt of marketable carcass, and this does not materially affect the picture.

This protracted calculation seems to demonstrate that, despite all the technological advantages they posses and given the optimum economic climate, the foresters and farmers of the United Kingdom could not possibly produce sufficient wood and food: even assuming that the population accepted temperate fruits and vegetables instead of tropical ones and went without luxuries such as tea, coffee, chocolate and spices, organic self-sufficiency at present levels of living would be out of the question. Furthermore, it will have been noted that hardly any allowance has been made for fibres. Although there would be a modest production of wool and hides from the sheep and cattle on the grasslands, these would be nowhere near sufficient to provide clothes, shoes, blankets, furnishings and so on for more than 56 million people. The amounts of rubber, cotton, sisal and jute at present imported, along with the beverages already referred to, occupy immense acreages abroad. They could not be grown here and no attempt has been made to calculate the areas under flax and other substitutes that would be necessary to compensate for their loss.

The objection might be raised that the allocations of land made for the various usages are arbitrary. Up to a point this is true, but a brief consideration of the model presented will show that reasonable alternatives or rearrangements make very little difference; indeed they might even be less productive. For instance, by taking a few more thousand acres from the better parts of the rough grazing lands, the forests could be expanded to bring potential production a little nearer to our timber requirements.[11] Such an operation would inevitably be at the expense of the stock-rearing capacity of the country, and would put the remaining grazing land under greater pressure. Even with the existing areas of rough grazing, the arrangements and the intensity of production that have been postulated here would demand a very substantial intensification of upland and lowland grass farming. Although mountain sheep can survive at a high altitude throughout the winter, the vast majority of the animals that the uplands would have to carry in summer could stay for only five or six months and would have to be supported by hay or grass from the improved grasslands during the rest of the year. Hay and silage from the improved grasslands would have to be produced in

[11] To maintain contact with actualities, it is important to emphasize that the annual production of roundwood over recent years of around 3 mmt is nowhere near my calculated potential production of 8·36 mmt. The Forestry Commission only came into existence in 1919 and most of its forests, as yet, have not had time to reach equilibrium production.

greater quantity than at present during the summer, and this would entail a smaller area for grazing; the grazing pressure on the uplands would therefore have to be much more intense than at present. One is forced to reflect on the attitudes of urban water authorities, foresters and the strong protagonists of outdoor amenity in face of such a development (see chapter 11).

Some doubt might also be expressed regarding the productivity values that have been used for the different crops. In most cases it must be admitted that these are suspiciously "round figures", but they have been selected quite deliberately to allow for increases in average yield which might conceivably occur in the near future. In other words, the totals of production are well above the average for recent years, and the basis upon which figure 5.5 is constructed (400 mt/km^2/year of grain) is highly optimistic in the light of existing realities. For example, although between 1966 and 1970 annual wheat yield in the United Kingdom averaged 395 mt/km^2, the yield of barley was only 353, and that of oats was less than 330 mt/km^2. In 1970 the average for cereals as a whole was only 355 mt/km^2. If this figure is taken as the basis for figure 5.5 instead of 400 mt/km^2, then the total potential production in grain equivalents becomes 28·6 instead of 32·2 mmt, and the deficit becomes 12·2 and not 8·6 mmt. Indeed, although grain yields have risen steadily over the past thirty years (Ministry of Agriculture, Fisheries and Food, 1968), there was an ominous levelling off during the late 1960s which may well have been due to soil deterioration arising from cereal over-production and modern farming practices generally (Ministry of Agriculture, Fisheries and Food, 1970). (This is not to say that, in years of particularly favourable weather, very high yields will not continue to be recorded. In 1974, for instance, the average yield of grain for the United Kingdom as a whole was a record.) The evidence suggests that it may not be possible to achieve, let alone sustain, a mean annual yield of 400 mt/km^2.

There are other productivity figures here which may be over-optimistic. Annual potato production has been calculated on the basis of 3,000 mt/km^2 (fresh weight) but, in fact, an average as high as this has not yet been achieved. In 1970, for instance, it was only 2,420 mt/km^2 (FAO, 1970). (And indeed, although at the time of writing figures are not yet available, in 1975 yield was far, far below this. Potato production is notoriously dependent on the weather and an increase in national dependence upon it would lead to an even more precarious situation than the present one.) Also, the postulated area requirement for self-sufficiency in fruit and vegetables was 2,900 km^2; but, in the 1960s, the area already covered by orchards, small fruit and vegetables (excluding potatoes) in Britain alone (i.e. excluding Northern Ireland) was well over 2,400 km^2 (Ministry of Agriculture, Fisheries and Food, 1968). My suggestion, therefore, is that intensification, along with an increase of a mere 500 km^2 (20·8 per cent) could compensate for the loss of all imports of tropical fruits, early vegetables, tomatoes, peanuts and so on. There seems to be no room for the accusation that the potentialities of the horticultural industry for ingenuity and increased efficiency are being underestimated.

The final reservation regarding the potential productivity of the United

Kingdom is almost certainly the most important of all. During the past century average yields of wheat, barley and oats have doubled, those of potatoes have increased by between 60 and 70 per cent, and those of sugar beet, since it became an important crop around 1920, have also doubled (Ministry of Agriculture, Fisheries and Food, 1968). The most striking point about this increase in productivity, however, is that it has nearly all occurred since 1945. For this reason it has usually been attributed to the great increase in the use of mineral fertilizers, biocides and more productive varieties that has taken place over the period since the second world war. This general correlation is so striking that there can be little doubt about the causal relationship inferred, but there would not be universal concurrence about the relative importance of the three main factors involved. However, all farmers and agronomists would agree that a complete termination in the use of balanced mineral fertilizers would cause a crash in production. Discussions about the nature of the so-called "Green Revolution" on the world scene show quite clearly that the use of potentially more productive varieties may convey very little advantage without a high fertilizer input; indeed the relative susceptibility of these new varieties to disease in the absence of such fertilization might, of itself, cancel out any possible advantage. Although the advent of home-produced supplies from Cleveland now seems to have ensured Britain's self-sufficiency in potash for the foreseeable future, supplies of nitrogenous and phosphatic fertilizers are both problematical. Manufacture of the former is a very energy-intensive process (now mainly dependent on gas and oil), while almost all of the half million tons of phosphate (P_2O_5 content) has to be imported. Phosphates must be regarded as the crucial fertilizer requirement, not merely because the phosphorus atom is an essential component of protoplasm, but also because of the spectacular way in which it stimulates luxuriant growth in leguminous plants which, in turn, bring increased amounts of atmospheric nitrogen into the nutrient cycle (thus reducing the nitrogenous fertilizer requirement). Without phosphatic fertilizers it would be impossible to approach the present level of productivity, much less to envisage any advance towards self-sufficiency. Given a population of over 56 millions, even with the present level of food imports, a situation in which phosphates could not be imported would be most alarming. The full significance of the world phosphate situation will be discussed in the next chapter.

THE SIGNIFICANCE OF THE UNITED KINGDOM PREDICAMENT

The conclusion is inescapable. Without food imports the present population, even with an all-out food-producing effort, could not be fed at present standards, and the deficit might well be more than 12 mmt of grain or its equivalent in other foodstuffs. Even if the annual average productivity of cereals could be raised to 400 mt/km^2, the deficit would still be more than 8 mmt. Furthermore, this takes no account of the loss of imported beverages and numerous other gastronomic luxuries which, in toto, contribute little to energy and protein intake. Nor is it making any allowance for huge deficiencies in fibres, rubber and many other non-food industrial raw materials. The salient point is that, in the case of the United Kingdom with its high standard of living, material expectations and wastefulness, a "national average per capita potential NPP" of 5·5 mt is indicative of a country incapable of self-sufficiency in organic resources.

In order to present their cases convincingly, it would be necessary to examine, in turn the organic resources and agricultural practices of all the other 26 countries with low per capita potential NPP, and to do this in the same way and in just the same detail as has been done for the United Kingdom. One could then view these resources and practices against the background of the standard of living and the economic expectations of the population of each of the countries concerned. Such an exhaustive examination is not possible here: all that can be attempted is a review of certain aspects of some of their economies in an attempt to gauge whether or not their situation is significantly better or worse than that of the United Kingdom.

COUNTRIES IN EUROPE

Since the loss of the British Empire the financial and social problems of the United Kingdom have received much publicity, and one might be excused for inferring that its fundamental difficulties are far greater than those of its continental neighbours. It is therefore interesting to find that the Netherlands, Belgium, West Germany and Switzerland all have lower potential per capita NPP (PPCNPPs), and that Italy, East Germany and Luxembourg are only a little more fortunate (figure 5.3a). As all these countries originally carried a similar vegetation to that of the United Kingdom, it seems reasonable to suppose that the relationship between potential NPP and potential crop production will also be similar, and the available evidence seems to bear this out.

The Netherlands, with even less cropland, grassland and forest per head than the United Kingdom (table 5.2), imports almost as much stockfeed. Although some of this is re-exported, the fact is nevertheless most surprising since the United Kingdom has a population nearly four times as great. Moreover, in spite of this huge import of feeding stuffs, the Netherlands still imported 164,000 mt of meat in 1973 (UN, 1974a). In the same year it also imported 738,000 mt of sugar (a little more per head than the United Kingdom) and 2,265,000 mt of fruit and vegetables (more than three times as much). Belgium has less arable land per head than the United Kingdom and less than half as much grassland, but with twice as much forest, she must more nearly approach potential self-sufficiency in wood products. Switzerland is relatively well endowed with forest and grassland, but much of it is so steep or so elevated that it could not be converted to arable. But in spite of having about 20 per cent more grassland than the United Kingdom, she still imported over 60,000 mt of meat in 1974 and almost the same weight of dairy produce. Compared to the United Kingdom, Switzerland has little more than half the area of cropland per head, and it comes as no surprise that she imported about 1·75 mmt of cereals in 1974 — more than twice the per capita import of the United Kingdom.

A comparison of the present position of these three countries with that of the United Kingdom suggests that their populations are no better endowed than hers. Indeed, in several important respects, their potential resources per capita appear to be even more limited.

The cases of West Germany and Italy are different in a number of ways. The former has four times as much forest land as the United Kingdom and produces more than her timber requirements. On the other hand, the amount of land under rough and improved grazing in West Germany is less than half that in the United Kingdom — 56,000 as compared to 121,000 km^2 (FAO, 1970). Over the centuries there was an essential difference between the two countries in the evolution of their land use patterns: in Germany cut-over land, when left derelict or under-grazed, tended to revert to forest quite rapidly, while in the moister climate and cooler summers of Britain and Northern Ireland podzolisation and peat formation occurred relatively quickly when forest was removed, so that the minimum of grazing and firing maintained it as bog and heath. West Germany, with 82,000 km^2, has about 10,000 km^2 more cropland than the United Kingdom. In any attempt at self-sufficiency however, the former, having less grazing land, would have to devote more of its cultivated area to the growth of stockfeed if it were to produce the same amount of animal products as the latter. By weight, West Germany imports only about 65 per cent as much meat, 95 per cent as much dairy produce, 68 per cent as much cereals and 16 per cent as much sugar as the United Kingdom; indeed it even exports substantial quantities of processed food such as dairy produce to Italy and elsewhere. On the other hand it imports a surprising amount of fruit and vegetables — more than twice the quantity (by weight) imported into the United Kingdom. On balance the evidence suggests that if a careful calculation of its NPP were made, assuming its present land use pattern, population and level of consumption, West Germany would be found to be much nearer to a capability for self-sufficiency than the United Kingdom. Indeed, were it not for a very large deficit in fibres, it might well approach the potential self-sufficiency threshold very closely. At the present time however, despite the undoubted efficiency of its agriculture, its net import of food and fibres is very large. One should also take careful note of the fact that West Germany's import of phosphate is almost twice that of the United Kingdom — 902,600 as compared to 469,500 mt (P_2O_5 content) in 1972–3.

An assessment of Italy's NPP, given the present land use pattern, poses more difficult problems because the reduction in overall productivity here has probably been much greater than in central and northwestern Europe. The exploitation that has taken place from classical times onwards in the Italian environment, with its somewhat different sub-tropical climatic regimes, seems to have had lasting effect. For instance, the annual Italian wheat crop between 1966 and 1970 averaged only 229 mt/km^2 — far below that of the United Kingdom for the same period (395 mt/km^2), but just how much this difference is due to the reduced innate fertility of Italian soils and how much to present agricultural practices is not obvious. After all, wheat is sown on relatively well fertilized land, and Italy does import considerably more phosphate per head (though *not* per unit of cultivated land) than does the United Kingdom — 583,200 as compared to 469,500 mt in 1972–3. Italy has just over twice as much land under crops as the United Kingdom, almost exactly 150,000 km^2 being in cultivation in the 1960s, but the average quality of this land requires careful consideration. Certainly 15 per cent of it is permanently occupied by olive grove and vineyard, and most of this is steep, rocky land with little soil and unsuitable for the production of other crops. Furthermore, although Italy has a temperature advantage over northwest European countries and is thus able to grow maize as a grain crop (producing an average of some 4·8 mmt per annum) the average yield of the Italian maize crop in the five years 1966–70 was hardly greater than that of the wheat crop in the United Kingdom — 407 as compared to 395 mt/km^2 respectively — and far below the 441 mt/km^2 of the wheat crop of the Netherlands.

Only a meticulous examination of Italy's land use pattern in relation to the innate potentialities of her soils at the present time could provide the basis for a satisfactory comparison of her position with that of the United Kingdom; but a review of her imports does seem to indicate that, in a number of ways, their situations are similar. Although Italy does export a considerable quantity of fruit, this seems to be more than offset by her enormous import of cereals: in 1973 she imported 8·9 mmt as compared to the 7·9 imported by the United Kingdom (UN, 1974a). And despite the lower per capita sugar consumption of the Italians, and the fact that they devote much of the best land in the Po Basin to sugar beet production, Italy still had to import 754,000 mt of sugar in 1973 — almost a quarter of the amount imported by the United Kingdom. She also imported 876,000 mt of dairy produce as compared to only 532,000 mt imported into Britain. Italy approaches self-sufficiency in wood products, producing about five times as much as the United Kingdom, but her general position with regard to organic resources is far from favourable. Her large area of cropland, as compared to the United Kingdom, suggests that she ought to be capable of achieving self-sufficiency, particularly in view of the magnitude of her fertilizer imports; on the other hand, the available evidence about crop yields and imports indicates the reverse. In face of this evidence it seems unlikely, even if a considerable increase in productivity could be achieved, that Italy could support her present population in organic materials at their present standard of living.

COUNTRIES IN MONSOON ASIA

There are seven countries in Monsoon Asia within the same range of PPCNPP as the European ones just reviewed. South Korea, Japan and Taiwan are all lower in the table than the United Kingdom (figure 5.3a) while Bangladesh, India, Sri Lanka and Pakistan are all a little higher with values not very different from that of Italy. Table 5.2 reveals some other interesting parallels: South Korea has the same area of cropland per head as the Netherlands, while Japan and Taiwan have substantially less; Sri Lanka has just a little more per head than the United Kingdom, Bangladesh a little more again, while India and Pakistan have a great deal more — the former exactly the same amount as Italy.

Table 5.2 Areas of land per head in a selection of countries in Europe, Monsoon Asia, the West Indies and the Middle East (in hectares)

	All land	Cropland	Forest	Permanent grassland and rough grazing
United Kingdom	0·43	0·13	0·03	0·22
Netherlands	0·26	0·07	0·02	0·10
Belgium	0·31	0·09	0·06	0·08
West Germany	0·41	0·14	0·12	0·10
Switzerland	0·62	0·06	0·15	0·27
Italy	0·54	0·28	0·11	0·10
East Germany	0·65	0·30	0·18	0·09
Luxembourg	0·64	0·17	0·21	0·17
South Korea	0·30	0·07	0·20	
Japan	0·35	0·05	0·24	
Taiwan	0·25	0·06	0·16	
Bangladesh	0·28	0·18	0·04	
India	0·54	0·28	0·11	
Sri Lanka	0·50	0·15	0·22	
Pakistan	1·86	0·49	0·06	
Haiti	0·50	0·07	0·13	
Jamaica	0·54	0·12	0·10	
Puerto Rico	0·31	0·08	0·04	
Israel	0·67	0·14	0·04	
Jordan	4·07	0·54	0·05	
Kuwait	2·00	negligible	negligible	
Lebanon	0·34	0·11	0·03	
Qatar	13·76	negligible	none	
Yemen	3·31	—	—	
Egypt	2·87	0·08	negligible	

It would be premature to infer from this that the potentialities for self-sufficiency of these Asian countries are the same as those of their apparent European counterparts; environmental and social conditions on the two continents are so very different that a closer examination is necessary. Of the seven, the case of Japan is most comparable to those of the European countries. Japan is now heavily industrialized with less than 20 per cent of its employed population in agriculture, and it has a higher material standard of living than the other Asian countries. On the credit side Japan is remarkably productive: although she has only a small amount of arable land per head, at least one third of it is double-cropped and a great deal is under very productive paddy rice. Furthermore, she has about eight times as much forest per head as the United Kingdom and actually produces about 15 times as much roundwood per annum. Indeed, of all the heavily populated countries of the world, Japan probably has an actual NPP most nearly approaching its potential. Another point which must not be overlooked is that Japan exports substantial quantities of organic materials in manufactured form.

On the other hand, Japan's resource deficiencies are only too obvious. Five sixths of the country, if not actually mountainous, is deeply dissected with steep slopes predominating, so that very little land not already under productive cultivation could actually be converted to it. Over the past half century, almost one eighth of its area, much of it lowland, has been encroached upon by factories, roads, housing and other urban development. But probably the most significant point of all is that, in spite of the intensity with which the Japanese exploit all available land, their import requirement is still enormous. In 1974 Japan imported (by weight) 25 per cent as much meat, 32 per cent as much dairy produce, 246 per cent as much cereals, 47 per cent as much fruit and vegetables, and 150 per cent as much sugar as the United Kingdom (UN, 1975). She also imported huge quantities of fibres and other organic industrial raw materials, much of which was for home consumption. And not least, in 1972 she imported 717,000 mt of phosphates (P_2O_5 content) — much more than half as much again as the United Kingdom. There can be little doubt that without imports of organic materials, Japan could not sustain her present population at the present standard of living.

South Korea makes an interesting comparison. With a slightly smaller total amount of land and a little less forest per head, she nevertheless has about 40 per cent more cropland per head than Japan (table 5.2). Almost exactly half the employed population of South Korea is engaged in agriculture — a reflection of the fact that this is a country where the peasant way of life is still important and the material standard of living is much lower than in Japan. As in so many peasant countries during recent decades, emphasis has been placed on industrial development; but the five-year plan of 1962–6 had as one of its declared aims the achievement of a self-sufficient agricultural economy. It is not without significance, therefore, that in 1971 and 1972 South Korea was still importing almost as much sugar per head (475,801 mt in 1971) and almost as much grain per head (3·03 mmt in 1971 and 3·35 mmt in 1972) as Japan. It is also noteworthy that, for a country with a peasant economy, South Korea imports an inordinately large quantity of agricultural fertility. In 1972 this included 170,900 mt of phosphate (P_2O_5 content) — almost two thirds as much per head as the United Kingdom.

India, with a population more than ten times that of the United Kingdom, provides the most striking example of a country trapped between a desire to improve agricultural productivity and a shortage of the means by which to achieve it. On the one hand she needs more food and on the other, having few inorganic resources or manufactured goods with which to trade, she has to use up large areas of agricultural land to produce cash crops of tea, coffee and cotton to exchange for fertilizers and agricultural machinery. In effect she falls between two stools, using quite a large amount of fertilizer to produce the cash crops but still requiring large imports of cereals for food. It is not possible to summarize briefly the productivity problems of so large and varied a country, but two points are so obvious as to be inescapable. First, India has vast areas of degraded scrub and poor cropland: in this respect she can be regarded as the antithesis of Japan. Land under wheat, in general, probably receives as much fertilizer as any other type of land, but the average productivity of wheat in the year 1969–70 was only 121 mt/km^2 — less than a third of that in the United Kingdom. The actual NPP of India must be further below the potential than in almost any other country. Secondly, malnutrition is endemic and actual famine is so frequently recurrent as to indicate that the country could not support the present population even at their present low standard of living without large imports of fertilizer. Although some extension of irrigation beyond the present 275,000 km^2 (19 per cent of the cultivated area) could doubtless produce a marginal improvement in productive capacity, there seems to be every reason to think that self-sufficiency, if not already beyond reach, is rapidly approaching this point.

COUNTRIES IN THE WEST INDIES

The most crowded islands around the Caribbean have much in common with countries like South Korea and Taiwan (table 5.2). In a sense they are also microcosms of India in that they export organic materials such as sugar, coffee and cocoa in order to import, among other things, substantial quantities of food and fertilizer. The fundamental issue as to whether or not cash crop production could be diminished to a point where enough land for self-sufficiency in food, clothing and housing requirements would be available, is not easy to resolve. However, the fact remains that in Puerto Rico, Haiti and Jamaica the amount of cropland per head is so small (in the case of Puerto Rico it is the same as in South Korea and the Netherlands) that it is hard to believe that a large percentage of it is occupied by cash crops. Were it not for the capability of producing several food crops per annum from the same piece of land, the present density of agricultural population could not have been achieved even with the present level of imports. Furthermore, since the hilly or even mountainous terrain of these islands forbids the spread of permanent agriculture on to what is now steeply sloping forest or grazing land, there is little scope for the expansion of permanent cultivation from the coastal plains, river valleys and colluvial hollows to which it is largely confined at the present time. The evidence suggests that, even at the present low standard of living, the absolute productive capacity of these countries has been reached, and it would require an increase in imported food and fertility to permit further population growth.

COUNTRIES IN THE MIDDLE EAST

A nation whose territory lies within the arid and semi-arid zones of the earth has problems of a somewhat different nature when its PPCNPP falls to a low level. On the other hand, the possession of a fairly high PPCNPP by a dry country may be very misleading by comparison with countries in forested regions. This is mainly because a large area of semi-desert, even though its total organic productivity might be substantial, nevertheless may be unfit for any kind of agriculture or pastoral activity if it is level plateau with no access to a permanent supply of fresh drinking water. Thus, although the 65,000 people of Spanish Sahara have a PPCNPP of 595·4 mt/year (appendix IV), this must not be taken to imply that they are more than twice as well endowed as the 17·8 million people of Zaire with only 238·4 mt per head. The former lead a tenuous existence on the fringes of a near waterless terrain, whereas the latter have at their disposal a huge area of rain forest and relatively lush savanna, less exploited by man than most parts of the earth. How much more critical, therefore, must be the predicament of a semi-arid country whose PPCNPP is low!

Most arresting of all are the cases of the million or so people who inhabit the oil sheikdoms of Kuwait and Qatar. These rapidly expanding populations are now dependent almost entirely on the revenue from oil production: the food production of the land they occupy is practically nil so that nearly all that is consumed must be imported. Only a large scale development of irrigation could permit organic self-sufficiency, and since procuring water for drinking and industrial processes already poses difficult problems, its widespread use in agriculture cannot reasonably be envisaged. The ultimate fate of rapidly expanding populations almost completely dependent upon oil or other types of mineral extraction is a subject which will be broached again in later chapters.

In dry regions the percentage of the cultivable land which is irrigable is of primary importance. Dry-farming crops such as millet can be grown in localities where there is a fairly reliable seasonal rainfall, but in areas with very low mean annual totals, rainfall is generally so unreliable that to depend upon it is to court disaster, and irrigation is the only sound basis for permanent agricultural settlement. Assessment of rainfall *in situ* thus becomes unimportant: rather, the amount of water reliably available in watercourses, often derived from rain which has fallen in distant places, determines the size of the area that can be maintained in cultivation. This is the basis on which one must assess the actual productivity of countries like Egypt, the Yemen and Jordan and, to a certain extent, Lebanon and Israel.

The extreme case is furnished by Egypt where the NPP of most of the national territory has no relevance whatsoever to the subsistence of the people. With the exception of a few oases, all the arable acreage is dependent on rain which falls outside the country. Egypt relies almost entirely on some 2·83 million ha of irrigated land (FAO, 1970), nearly all of which is in the valley of the Nile, and it is from this river that effectively the whole of the irrigation water is drawn. By impounding it more efficiently with huge dams such as the one at Aswan, it has become possible to disperse it over wider areas and to extend its use over longer periods. By proliferation and extension of increasingly ambitious schemes it has thus been possible to support more and more cultivation, so that at the present time the population of Egypt has passed 35 millions and continues to grow at the rate of 2·8 per cent per annum — a doubling rate of only 25 years. Clearly there is still some scope for irrigation expansion, but there are absolute limits beyond which no benefit can be gained. Nor are these set merely by the actual amount of water coming down the Nile: another important consideration is the low gradient of the valley itself. A point can be reached where the loss of level alluvial land owing to inundation by impounded water cancels out any advantage elsewhere.

With as little as 0·8 ha of irrigated land per head, Egypt was already importing nearly two mmt of cereals in 1973 (UN, 1974a). But again, it must be noted that over a quarter of the irrigated acreage is under cotton, much of which is exported and, with the exchange capacity so gained, Egypt imports large quantities of fertilizer. This included 87,700 mt of phosphate (P_2O_5 content) in 1972–3 — almost one third as much per head as the United Kingdom and more than two and a half times as much per head as India.

Israel has nearly twice as much cultivated land per head as Egypt, and the Lebanon about one and a half times as much (table 5.2). But whereas Egypt's cultivated land is virtually all irrigated, this applies to only about 40 per cent of that of Israel and only about 20 per cent that of the Lebanon. Both these countries export large quantities of citrus fruit, indeed Israel devotes about one fifth of her cultivated acreage to this purpose. On the other hand, both countries import more cereals per head than the United Kingdom — Israel more than twice as much. Of the two countries, Israel has the more ambitious plans for the expansion of agricultural production, and a land use survey carried out recently noted that the amount of land which is suitable for irrigated cultivation is more than double the area which is actually irrigated. Statements such as this, though probably true in terms of the stated criteria, should nevertheless be viewed critically. That 23 per cent of the country is thought "suitable" for irrigation does not automatically guarantee that sufficient water could be made available for such an expansion. It is also interesting to note that, in the same assessment, about 52 per cent of the country is designated as land unfit for anything more productive than rough grazing (Stateman's Year Book, 1972–3).

STATE OF THE NATIONS

There are strong grounds for concluding that these 27 nations, along with Hong Kong and Singapore, have already reached a point where, if not actually incapable of organic self-sufficiency, they are on the threshold of it. If supplies of organic materials from outside were cut off and, more particularly, if imports of fertilizers were also denied, it is doubtful if any of them could maintain present standards of living, no matter how efficiently they set about trying to do so. In the cases where average standards are already near subsistence level, or where large sections of the population are divorced from sources of food production, or where land use practices are overspecialized and inflexible, the result could be widespread starvation. Population estimates for 1971 (appendix III) indicate that

1,117·4 million people were living in these 29 countries — more than a quarter of the earth's population.

The world picture takes on an even more startling appearance if one notes the present condition of China. In spite of the fact that she includes the sparsely populated provinces of Yunnan, Tibet, Sinkiang and Inner Mongolia within her frontiers, China has a PPCNPP of only 10·8 mt — just above the value of 10 mt which was rather arbitrarily selected as the upper limit for the analysis which has just been carried out. If one adds to the population of China those of Denmark, France, Austria, Portugal, Albania, Poland, Czechoslovakia, Yugoslavia, Hungary, Romania, Bulgaria, Syria, Iran, Afghanistan, Nepal, North Korea, Vietnam, the Philippines, Morocco, Tunisia and El Salvador — all the countries with PPCNPPs of between 10 and 20 mt, again one has more than a quarter of the earth's population (1,141·0 million in 1971). Although the European members of this second group have populations which are growing only slowly, China and the remainder have rapidly increasing ones which will, within a decade or two, reduce their PPCNPPs to less than 10 mt. It seems inescapable that by the year 2000 AD, given a continuance of present trends, more than half the population of the earth will be living in political units which are incapable, no matter how they might try, of being self-sufficient in the amount of organic materials which they would require to maintain a standard of living equal to the one they enjoy at the present time.

6

Reserves of Non-renewable Resources

Those who are swept along by the currents of conventional wisdom may feel it unrealistic to the point of silliness even to contemplate the possibility of national self-sufficiency in organic materials. The ruling assumption seems to be that nations are not self-sufficient in food and fibres because they do not set out to be and, even if a point has now been reached where a substantial number of political units are physically incapable of growing all the plant and animal products they require, this is of small account because the nexus of international trade which allowed such a state of affairs to arise will permit it to persist. Furthermore, in the minds of the privileged it is unthinkable that the enjoyment of anything grown or manufactured anywhere on the earth should be denied them, and those who have not already profited from this emancipation look forward to doing so in the future.

The history of the present world pattern is well known. The nineteenth-century centres of empire and higher technology drew food and raw materials from the rest of the world, to which they exported the excess of their manufacturing capacity. A complex trading system thus developed in which the countries and territories of the world all participated to a greater or lesser degree. Indeed, by the twentieth century, they could be arranged in a kind of trading spectrum with states such as the United Kingdom at the ultra-violet and those such as Jamaica at the infra-red. Both extremes now import food for their abundant populations because of the very specialized economies they have developed.

Unfortunately an understanding of the development of the present system does not necessarily imply an ability to perpetuate it. The development of mass trading during the Industrial Revolution was due to the production of industrial goods and an increasing number of machines to manufacture them; it was also dependent upon a transport system whose size, speed of operation and energy consumption were formerly undreamed of. All those who envisage the continuance and perpetual expansion of this system must assume, among other things, that the inorganic materials necessary to sustain it are going to be available in constantly increasing quantities.

The viability of the world trade nexus is dependent upon two sets of inorganic resources: first, there are those which sustain or promote high productivity in food crops and cash crops and secondly, those which are essential for the existence of sophisticated metallurgical and chemical industries. The availability of the former has often been taken for granted in discussions about the achievement or perpetuation of high productivity in agriculture: one might readily have been excused for inferring that, provided technical assistance and a non-recurrent injection of capital were made available to peasant farmers, then production would rise spectacularly and remain at high levels in perpetuity. The "Green Revolution" was heralded in a way which caused one to forget about the high continuing input of mineral fertilizer as a prerequisite for realizing the potential of the new varieties of wheat, rice and maize. On the other hand, in most of the urgent political and economic discussions about the continuance of industrial expansion and economic growth, all the essential mineral materials are assumed to be available (with the exception of oil, where the possibility of its not being available in substantial quantities beyond the immediate future does seem to have impinged upon political and economic consciousness since 1970). It is necessary to examine the degree of justification for these assumptions.

Fertilizer Resources

In addition to carbon, hydrogen and oxygen, three other nutrient elements are required in substantial quantities by plants. These are nitrogen, potassium and phosphorus, and all have to be abailable to the roots in an acceptable form. Nitrogen is absorbed as (NH_4^+) and nitrate (NO_3^-) ions, potassium as monatomic cations (K^+), and phosphorus as phosphate ions (PO_4^{3-}). The agriculturalist who wishes to replace or supplement natural fertility with mineral fertilizers must present the three elements in these chemical forms.

NITROGEN

Nitrogen in mineral fertilizer was first used in quantity in the middle of the nineteenth century, and since nitrate occurred naturally only in the Atacama Desert, this gave Chile a monopoly up to the time of the first world war. The importance of this naturally occurring sodium nitrate or "Chile saltpetre" would probably have been more prolonged but for the fact that it was used in the manufacture of explosives as well as fertilizer. Consequently, since some European countries were cut off from Chilean supplies between 1914 and 1918, there was a strong incentive to devise an alternative means of supply. A method of producing ammonia from atmospheric nitrogen was successfully commercialized and, from then onwards, the Chilean trade suffered rapid decline. At the present time almost the whole world production of nitrogenous fertilizer is based on atmospheric nitrogen.

This serves to emphasize the point that agriculture is not dependent for its nitrogen on any finite source of mineral material: the constraints on the production of substances such as ammonium sulphate, ammonium nitrate and nitro-chalk are those of energy availability. At the present time much of the ammonia required for fertilizer is produced by linking atmospheric nitrogen to hydrogen derived from mineral oil. With a developing oil scarcity and consequent escalation of prices, nitrogenous fertilizers have now become very costly in comparison with the 1960s. Even if oil and natural gas have to be abandoned as raw materials this will permit of no escape; the alternative method of obtaining hydrogen by the electrolysis of water, though using a cheap raw material, requires an even greater consumption of energy. The cost of nitrogenous fertilizer is thus linked inescapably to the world energy problem; if rising prices make the exploitation of Chile saltpetre economic again, one cannot imagine that the reserves would be sufficient to meet more than a small proportion of the increase in demand. In the decade 1963–73 world consumption of nitrogenous fertilizers increased from 15 to 36 mmt (UN, 1973b).

POTASH

Most of the world's supply of potash is obtained from silvite, carnallite and related minerals in evaporites, mainly of Permo-Triassic age, though there is a smaller production from more recent evaporites in localities such as those by the Dead Sea in Israel and Jordan. World reserves are very great and the static world reserve index has been put as high as 5,000 years (Flawn, 1966). Even if world demand were to rise to a point where all the nations were to apply potash at levels similar to those now reached in Europe, North America and Australasia, there would still be sufficient to last for several centuries. In fact world consumption almost doubled between 1964 and 1973 (from 10·3 to 18·7 mmt).

From the point of view of the peoples of Africa, Asia and Latin America, however, the world distribution of reserves is very unfortunate. With the exception of those already mentioned around the Dead Sea, all the large deposits are concentrated in relatively prosperous countries in the northern hemisphere. The largest known reserves are in the USSR, Canada, East Germany, West Germany, the USA, France, Spain and in the recently exploited British deposits in northeast Yorkshire.

As with nitrogenous fertilizer, therefore, it would seem that potash supply problems over the next few decades will not stem from a world dearth of the element concerned in its economically exploitable form: the difficulties that could arise would be those of transport, exchange and political discrimination. However, the fact that shortages are organizational rather than absolute will not make them any less real for the countries who do not possess deposits or who have trading difficulties.

PHOSPHATE

Most of the world's reserves of phosphate occur either as phosphate rock (calcium fluorophosphate) in sedimentary deposits, or as apatite in igneous intrusions, though there are some economically exploitable deposits of guano and of phosphatized rock derived by leaching from overlying guano. An inventory of production sites at the present time gives the impression that sources of phosphate are plentiful and well distributed over the earth: the USA, Morocco, the USSR, Nauru Island and Tunisia are all major producers (see appendix V), while smaller quantities are produced by Brazil, Egypt, China, Vietnam, Christmas Island, Jordan, Senegal, Algeria, Togo, Israel, South Africa, Namibia, Australia, France, Poland, Belgium, Spain, Peru and India. Production and reserves are small in these minor producers and in a number of cases actually insufficient to satisfy demand in the country where they occur. Indeed all the major reserves are very localized, more than 70 per cent occurring in the USA and Morocco alone (Flawn, 1966), and probably more than 90 in these two countries along with the USSR and Tunisia. Known terrestrial reserves (i.e. taking no account of deposits of phosphorite nodules on the sea bed) amount to something over 130×10^9 mt of phosphate ore which, at an estimated average content of 25 per cent,[1] implies a P_2O_5 reserve of about 33×10^9 mt.

In the light of the 1973 world consumption of 22·6 mmt of P_2O_5, this world reserve seems enormous, and in 1966 Peter Flawn calculated the world static reserve index to be about 2,500 years. As in the case of potash, therefore, it would appear that no world shortage could occur in the foreseeable future. However, in view of the rate of world population increase, it is important to look very critically at concepts such as the "world static reserve index": world consumption rates are not going to remain static and it is salutory to reflect on the depletion rates that occur when demand goes on increasing exponentially. In a sense most of the world already experiences a phosphate "shortage". In the year 1972–3 New Zealand consumed 45·3 mt of P_2O_5 for every km^2 of her cultivated area, the Netherlands consumed 11·7 mt, Japan 12·8 and the United Kingdom 6·5. By comparison India consumed 0·36 mt/km^2, Mali 0·08, Nigeria 0·03, Ghana 0·03 and Chad 0·014. In other words if a P_2O_5 input of 12 mt/km^2 (roughly the average of the Dutch and Japanese consumption rates) is regarded as normal for a very productive agricultural country, then for every ton of P_2O_5 that Nigeria applied to its cultivations in 1973, very productive countries applied 375 tons.

It follows from this that if the earth's 14·24 million km^2 of cultivated land were given an input of 12 mt/km^2/year, world consumption of P_2O_5 would be 170·88 mmt per annum as compared to the 1973 figure of 22·6 mmt. And if, having achieved that, consumption continued to increase at 3 per cent per annum to keep pace with a population rate of increase of around the same figure, the world reserve of 33 billion mt of P_2O_5 would disappear, not in 2,500 years, but in between 60 and 70 years.

It is not suggested that there is any possibility of this occurring during the coming decades: the above point is made in order to emphasize the near irrelevance of statements about the world static reserve index and to underline the fact that world consumption of phosphates is increasing at a very rapid rate. Between 1964 and 1973 it increased steadily at about 6 per cent per annum, and indeed the rate of increase in the majority of deprived countries was far greater than that in the economically emancipated ones. In Burma it increased six times, in

[1] Although the phosphate rock being mined in the USA at the present time has an average P_2O_5 content of well over 30 per cent, seven eighths of the reserves are stated to have less than 25 per cent (Lewis, 1965).

Albania 6·5, in Brazil 8·25, in Angola 13, in Afghanistan 52, and in Botswana 60 times (UN, 1974b). In spite of these great increases, the deprived countries still have a very low phosphate input as compared to Europe and Japan and if, in the medium term, any development can reasonably be postulated as a means of surviving the population explosion, it is surely a massive increase in the availability of mineral fertility in those places where it is now almost lacking. But if this occurs it must be regarded as merely a temporary expedient, because mineral phosphates will not be available in large quantities for very long.

Reserves of Metals

Men have been collecting metal ore and making metal objects for at least 8,000 years, and by 3,000 BC relatively sophisticated metallurgy was being practised in Anatolia, Mesopotamia and Egypt. Lead, copper, silver and tin were all being smelted and alloyed at this time, and man-made iron (as opposed to meteoric iron) was certainly coming into use in the Hittite Empire round about 1500 BC (Smith, 1965). In the light of this long period in which metal consumption has taken place, it comes as something of a shock when one is told that, since 1940, technology has consumed more primary metal than during the whole of previous history (Lovering, 1969). Probably no other single fact emphasizes so graphically the significance of exponential growth in the industrial exploitation of resources. During the 1960s, averaging over the whole range of industrial metals, production increased at the rate of more than 6 per cent per annum.

A further significant point is that most of this increase is attributable to growth in the technologically developed countries. In 1965, out of a world production of less than 7·5 mmt of aluminium, the industries of Europe, North America and the USSR consumed about 7 mmt and those of Japan a further 0·3 (US Bureau of Mines, 1965). Indeed, during the 1960s, the industries of the USA alone were consuming about 50 per cent of the world production of aluminium, 40 per cent of the lead, over 35 per cent of the nickel and zinc, 30 per cent of the chromium and 25 per cent of the smelted copper. The industries of the Netherlands (population 13 million) in 1967, consumed more tin than those of the whole Indian sub-continent (population 600 million). If the deprived peoples of the world are to seek increased economic emancipation through industrial development along conventional Western lines, as is so frequently envisaged, it seems important to give some consideration to the amounts of raw materials that would be required in order to achieve this.

During the century from 1860 to 1960, during which its population grew from 31 to 180 million, the USA consumed about 45 million tons of primary copper. If the population of the Indian sub-continent, given no increase whatsoever, were to use primary copper at the same rate per capita as did that of the USA in the 1960s, during the coming century it would consume 450 million tons. And if the remainder of the technology-deficient countries were to do the same thing, they would consume about 1,250 million tons. Inevitably the question arises as to whether there is so much copper available in the earth's crust.

In 1970 one authority (US Bureau of Mines, 1970a) calculated the amount of copper in proved ore reserves to be 308 million tons. Another one (Flawn, 1966), assessing on a somewhat different basis, had previously put it at only 212 million tons. Regardless of these differences between authorities, it seems very

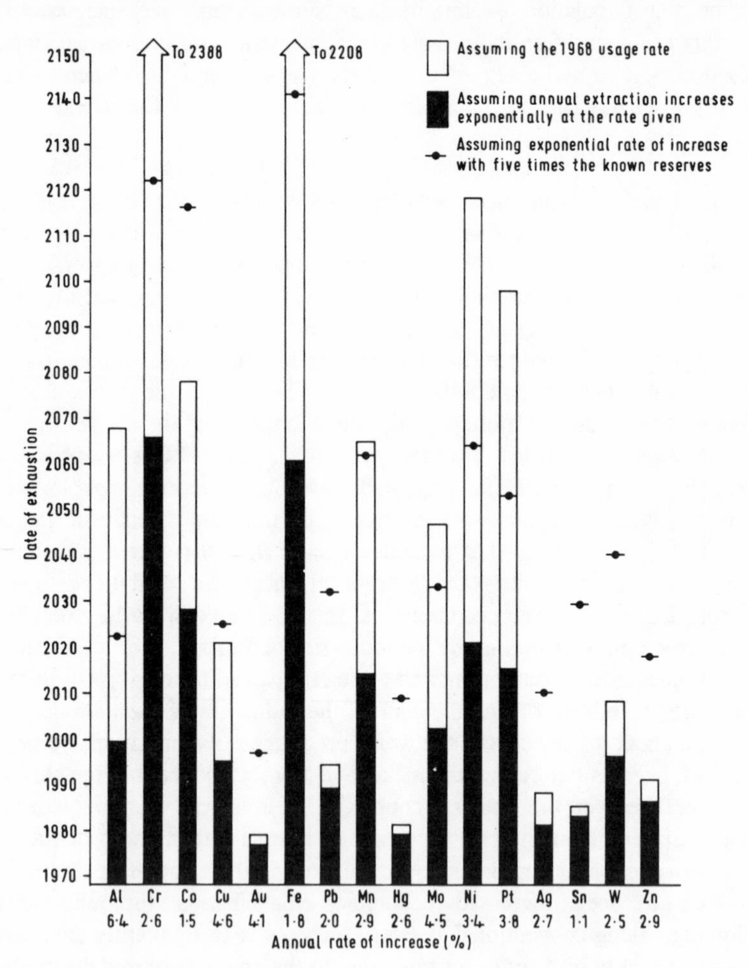

6·1 The date of exhaustion of world metal reserves on the basis of three different assumptions

clear that world reserves of copper in what, at present, are regarded as economically exploitable ores, are almost insignificant as compared to the potential demand from an "underdeveloped" world which found it possible to "develop" on anything like Western lines.

Copper is not alone among the industrial metals: the great majority of those consumed in any considerable quantity appear to have very unsubstantial proved reserves when viewed in the light of an expanding world demand (table 6.1).

Table 6.1 World reserves of metals*

	Quantity † (10^6 mt)	Projected annual rate of increase in extraction (%)‡	Static reserve index (years)	Exponential reserve index (years)	Exponential reserve index given five times known reserves (years)
Aluminium	1170	6·4	100	31	55
Chromium	775	2·6	420	98	154
Cobalt	2·18	1·5	110	60	148
Copper	308	4·6	53	27	57
Gold	0·010	4·1	11	9	29
Iron	100000	1·8	240	93	173
Lead	91	2·0	26	21	64
Manganese	800	2·9	97	46	94
Mercury	0·115	2·6	13	11	41
Molybdenum	4·90	4·5	79	34	65
Nickel	66·7	3·4	150	53	96
Platinum group	0·012	3·8	130	47	85
Silver	0·156	2·7	20	13	42
Tin	4·3	1·1	17	15	61
Tungsten	1·32	2·5	40	28	72
Zinc	123	2·9	23	18	50

* Quantities and rates of growth from US Bureau of Mines (1970a).

† Proved reserves in ores with a metal content which was economically extractable in 1968.

‡ This is an average of high and low forecasts, taking into account not only trends over the preceding decade but also a variety of technological and economic projections.

Forecasting demand for each individual metal over the coming decades is, of course, very problematical, but if one takes the arithmetical average of the high and low estimates of the rate of increase in demand that were made in 1968 (US Bureau of Mines, 1970a), then the proved economic reserves (in 1968) of 11 of the 16 most important metals will have been exhausted before 2000 AD (figure 6.1). Only iron and chromium appear to be in sufficient abundance for the proved reserves to last to the middle of next century. It should also be noted that the majority of the projected rates of increase upon which the depletion rates are based, are substantially less than those which have occurred over the past two decades. Consequently, those who have more faith in historical trends and the forces of inertia than in techno-economic prediction, will suspect that depletion will occur at an even greater rate than indicated here.

This last point may be far more important than is usually conceded by those technologists who concern themselves with resources. As technology has advanced over the past century, a number of metals not previously used (as such) have certainly come into importance. It is rarely stressed, however, that these innovations have not resulted in traditional raw materials coming to be regarded as "old fashioned" and falling into disuse. All the eight metals which were important in ancient Egypt and the classical world — gold, silver, copper, tin, zinc, lead, iron and mercury — continue to be sought and exploited with increasing intensity. With resource problems receiving greater publicity in recent years, the argument has often been advanced that, as shortages of specific materials develop, others will be found to substitute for them. There can be no question that this kind of development does take place — aluminium for tin, for instance, in the linings of metal containers; nevertheless, exactly the opposite stress can be placed on recent technological trends: as technology becomes more sophisticated, more and more uses are found for individual chemical elements and the compounds which contain them. Indeed, since all chemical elements are unique in their chemical and physical properties, technologists might be expected to view the unavailability of any one of them with some disquiet. And yet this loss appears to be imminent, at any rate for all but those few nations whose bargaining position is very strong (see chapter 8).

FUTURE DISCOVERIES

Before concluding that the dearth of proved reserves is a clear indication of a serious state of affairs, two points require closer scrutiny. First, can one be assured that large quantities of ore, of acceptable grade, do not remain to be discovered, and secondly, will a constantly improving technology not make it possible to exploit much leaner ores than are used at the present time? With regard to the first point it must be admitted that, despite the mobility of modern man, the surface of the earth is extensive and exploration of its underlying geology is still far from complete. There can be little doubt that substantial new discoveries will be made. Unfortunately geological strata and the igneous materials that have been intruded into them are notoriously complex and varied, so that the precepts of statistical probability cannot be applied to them in any simple or precise way. In one locality an emplacement of granite may be associated with rich deposits of cassiterite (tin oxide), whereas an apparently similar granite in another place may have no segregations of tin ore whatsoever. Also, some ultrabasic dykes are very rich in platinum whereas others contain a negligible amount.

Nevertheless, all who interest themselves in mineral resources, particularly those who might be tempted for any reason to take refuge behind our present ignorance, would do well to reflect on the statistical implications of one particular aspect of mining history. If undiscovered rich ore deposits within mineable depth still abound in the earth's crust, one might reasonably expect that these would continue to be discovered at fairly frequent and regular intervals. In particular, since mineral exploration techniques have progressively become more scientific and sophisticated, and the search for metal deposits has become more and more intensive, it might follow that a substantial proportion of the more productive metal-producing localities would be ones which have been discovered over the last two decades. The realities are not at all like this. A list has been compiled of all the sites (mines or groups of mines) in non-communist countries, which were the twelve major producers of each of eleven non-ferrous metals in 1973. An effort has then been made to discover the date at which each of these came into production. The work is incomplete but, at the time of writing, the dates[2] of 49 sites have been collected. These include the 12 most productive copper mines and the 10 most productive tin mining localities, along with some of the main

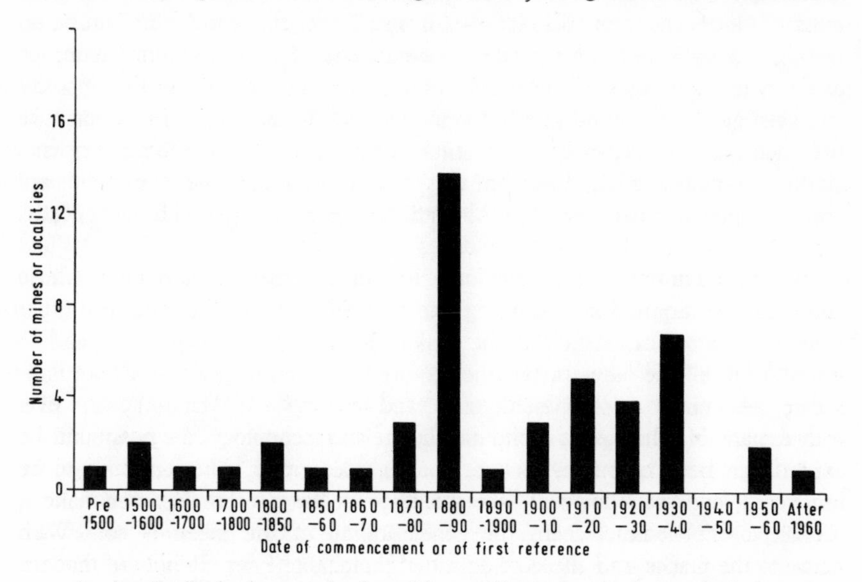

6·2 Age distribution in a sample of 49 of the world's most productive metal mines

[2]These are not always the dates at which production actually started. A number of sites were exploited long ago in prehistoric or early historic times, and in these cases the dates of the earliest references to production have been used.

sites of lead (6), zinc (2), nickel (2), cobalt (1), platinum (1), molybdenum (2), mercury (1), gold (7) and silver (5) extraction. Inclusion of sites of the last nine metals is entirely random as regards date: each site has been included merely because information came to hand and for no other reason.

The results of this simple exercise are quite arresting (figure 6.2). Of these 49 sites 55 per cent were in production before 1900, and a further 39 per cent had come into production before 1940. Well over 90 per cent were thus producers before the second world war. If these 49 sites are a representative sample of the earth's large metal mines (and there is no reason whatsoever to suspect that they are not), the conclusion is inescapable: the intensive prospecting of the last three decades has been singularly unsuccessful so far as the discovery of new, major ore emplacements is concerned. The evidence seems to make nonsense of so many optimistic generalizations which maintain that " ... the surface of the earth has hardly been scratched" (UN, 1970, p.12).

EXTRACTION FROM LEANER ORES

The second and rather more contentious issue revolves around the question as to what, in the future, will constitute a metallic ore body. Nearly all metals are present in nearly all rocks but usually in such tiny quantities that, until recently, they could not be detected, let alone extracted. With twentieth-century techniques however, it is possible to determine exactly how much gold or copper is present in a rock sample, even when the concentration is less than one part per million. On the basis of rock samples from all over the world it has thus been possible to work out the average concentration of each metallic element in ordinary granite, dolerite, shale and so on. From this information the "clarke" or "average crustal abundance" of individual metals has been worked out. Only two metals can be regarded as plentiful in the earth's crust: aluminium has a clarke of 8·13 per cent and iron one of 5·0 per cent. Manganese comes next with approximately one part per thousand, and the remainder are much scarcer (table 6.2).

At the present time it is not economic to mine any metal at clarke grade; even aluminium is required at something like four times the clarke, and iron (apart from exceptional cases such as the United Kingdom) at between five and six times. With all the other metals the required concentration above clarke is far greater — copper 140 times, tin 250, and lead 2,500 (Mason, 1952). Even with remarkable changes in economic climate and technology, the possibilities of exploiting a metal in country rock, at clarke grade, appear to be very remote. Far more problematical, however, are the large volumes of rock, often fringing economic ore bodies, where the concentration of the metal is somewhere between the clarke and the economically exploitable limit. It is here that one encounters the marked divergencies of opinion between those who view the future of technology with great optimism and those who do not.

During the 1960s over-generalization and sheer misconception led to exaggerated estimates of the extent of sub-marginal metal reserves. These arose mainly from a misapplication of what came to be known as the "arithmetic-

Table 6.2 Concentration clarkes for some industrial metals (after Flawn, 1966 and Lovering, 1969)

Metal	Clarke (in parts per billion)
Chromium	200000
Zinc	130000
Nickel	80000
Copper	70000
Tin	40000
Lead	16000
Tungsten	2000
Mercury	400

geometric", "A/G" or "Lasky's" ratio (Lasky, 1950). Lasky noted that, averaging over eight major porphyry copper deposits in the USA, as one proceeded from ore at 2 per cent content to ore at 0·6 per cent, there was an approximately logarithmic increase in volume. He concluded from this that, in such a deposit, for every million tons of ore at 2 per cent copper, there would be 10 million tons at 0·6 per cent copper, and that the ore tonnage would go on increasing at a rate of about 18 per cent for every 0·1 per cent decrement in grade (table 6.3). Unfortunately Lasky's work was used uncritically in an effort to demonstrate that there exist vast deposits of metaliferous rocks with a metal content not too far below the present level of economic exploitability. This is now known to be mainly fallacious: not only is the A/G ratio inapplicable to emplacements of metals other than copper, it does not even apply to other types of copper ore deposit. Indeed, it does not even apply exactly to porphyry copper deposits above and below the grades to which Lasky devoted particular attention (Lovering, 1969). This point requires no further emphasis: amateur geologists who have inspected old lead mines are often impressed by the way in which veins of almost pure galena give way abruptly to a very pure limestone carrying no more than 30 parts per million of lead. Most ore bodies are very distinct and a more or less sharp cut-off occurs between them and the rocks into which they have been emplaced.

Even where large deposits do occur with a metal concentration which is below currently exploitable grade but well above that of the clarke, it seems only prudent to have more reservations about their future value than have often been expressed. Copper ore with a copper content of 0·5 per cent is now being mined, but even if contiguous deposits down to 0·25 per cent and below exist, the rise in costs involved in moving on to them would be very great. Given the same technological processes, the cost of moving from 0·7 per cent ore to 0·5 per cent are far less than those which would have to be sustained in moving from 0·5 per cent to 0·3 per cent. As grade diminishes, more and more rock material has to be mined, transported, crushed and processed, and more waste has to be coped with; given a Lasky-type situation (table 6.3), although millions of tons of copper still remain when all the 0·5 per cent grade ore has been extracted, this residue is encased in an uncomfortably large volume of rock. Even if the

Table 6.3 Quantitative illustration of Lasky's (A/G) ratio in a porphyry copper deposit (assuming an orebody with an 18% increase in weight of ore for every decrement of 0.1% in grade)

Copper content (%)	Weight of ore (10^6 tons)		Weight of copper (10^6 tons)		Ore/copper ratio
2·0	428	60	1·2	7·55	50
1·9		71	1·35		52·5
1·8		83	1·5		55·5
1·7		98	1·65		59
1·6		116	1·85		62·5
1·5	980	136	2·05	12·4	66·5
1·4		161	2·25		71·5
1·3		192	2·5		77
1·2		225	2·7		83·5
1·1		266	2·9		91
1·0	2,244	314	3·15	17·2	100
0·9		370	3·3		111
0·8		437	3·5		125
0·7		515	3·6		143
0·6		608	3·65		166·5
0·5	5,150	720	3·6	13·76	200
0·4		850	3·4		250
0·3		1000	3·0		333
0·2		1180	2·36		500
0·1		1400	1·4		1000

relationship between bulk and cost is linear (and this is by no means axiomatic), whereas a decrease in grade from 0·7 per cent to 0·5 per cent (143 to 200 tons of ore for one ton of metal) will give an increase in cost of 39 per cent, a decrease from 0·5 per cent to 0·3 per cent (200 to 333 tons of ore for a ton of metal) amounts to an increase of 66·5 per cent. And extraction of metal from 0·1 per cent ore (1,000 tons for every ton of metal) would be five times as expensive as extraction from 0·5 per cent ore.

Technological literature abounds in optimistic statements which assume that advance in technology will continue to keep pace with this cost problem — or even get ahead of it. Apart from the fact that by the end of the 1960s it was already failing to do so (Lovering, 1969), it should also be noted that much of this optimism is to be found in writings which predate 1970. Thus, in 1966, an enlightened authority could write:

> Although potential reserves of a marginal nature most surely will constitute the domestic mineral sources of tomorrow, they will not come easily to the bin or the tank ... The world in which Granite Mountain is exploited for base metals, or a pipe in the sea produces quicksilver, is a more distant world with different economics and a different technology. We may be approaching it but we are not there yet (Flawn, 1966).

Even with all its caution and reservations, this statement does not have the ring of 1975! So many statements of the 1950s and 1960s seem to have been based on the assumption that cheap energy would continue to be available indefinitely. To misquote the Scriptures: "by faith and with cheap energy ye shall move mountains." Cheap energy now seems to be a thing of the past and technologists, quite rightly, have some hesitation in asserting that faith alone will keep down their costs.

METALS IN SEAWATER

The extraction of metals from seawater is subject to similar practical and economic limitations. Sixty of the 92 naturally occurring elements have been detected in seawater, amounting to some 5×10^{16} tons of dissolved material throughout the oceans as a whole (Cloud, 1969). Indeed a prospector's pulse might well beat a little faster when, for the first time, he is told that there are about 10 billion tons of gold in the ocean. Doubtless it would soon return to normal, however, when he contemplated the implications of its being dispersed homogeneously through 330 million cubic miles of water — about 0·14 g (0·005 oz) in every million gallons. Although water may have the advantage of being easier to transport than rock waste, this is outweighed by the fact that the occurrence of all metals in seawater is round about or below their clarke value.

Table 6.4 The concentration and value of selected elements in seawater (after Cloud, 1969)

Element	Concentration ($kg/10^6gal$)	1965 value as	1965 value in $\$/10^6gal$
Chlorine	75300·0	NaCl	924
Sodium	41700·0	Na_2CO_3	378
Magnesium	5350·0	Mg	4130
Bromine	260·0	Br_2	190
Phosphorus	0·27	$CaHPO_4$	0·08
Iodine	0·23	I_2	1·0
Zinc	0·04	Zn	0·013
Iron	0·04	Fe_2O_3	0·001
Aluminium	0·04	Al	0·04
Molybdenum	0·04	Mo	0·004
Tin	0·014	Sn	0·05
Copper	0·014	Cu	0·01
Nickel	0·009	Ni	0·02
Manganese	0·009	Mn	0·006
Cobalt	0·0018	Co	0·006
Silver	0·0014	Ag	0·02
Tungsten	0·0004	W	0·002
Chromium	0·00018	Cr_2O_3	0·00001
Lead	0·00014	Pb	0·00004
Mercury	0·00014	Hg	0·002
Gold	0·00002	Au	0·02

So far it has been found economic to extract salt (NaCl), magnesium and bromine from seawater. Whereas there are 117 mt of salt, 5·35 mt of magnesium and 0·26 mt of bromine in every million gallons (4,535 mt) of water, there is a far, far smaller quantity of all the main industrial metals (table 6·4). According to Preston Cloud (1969), the amount of gold in a million gallons was worth only two cents at 1965 prices — hardly an economic proposition! Of course, there is some substance in the contention that, if the exploitation of seawater for minerals were to take place, then gold would not be the only product and all the elements present could be extracted and used. A quantitative view of the substances involved, however, makes it clear that this does not materially affect the issue. At 1965 prices the total value of the mineral contents of a million gallons was just over $6,139 and, of this, magnesium accounts for $4,130 — more than two thirds of the total. The nine most plentiful elements (chlorine, sodium, magnesium, sulphur, calcium, bromine, potassium, lithium and rubidium) account for $6,125 — 99·77 per cent of the total. In fact, without the magnesium, the quantity of all the leading industrial metals present in a million gallons weighs about 200 g (less than half a pound) and was worth less than 20 cents at 1965 prices.

The price of metals has escalated since 1965, but so also have the costs of labour and energy. Despite the wizardry of which modern technology is capable, one must doubt its ability to extract metals at an economic price when many millions of gallons of seawater would have to be processed in order to obtain sufficient metal to pay a day's wages for one semi-skilled labourer.

Energy Resources

Again, we must remind ourselves that classical economists, in the mould of Adam Smith, have held that a continuing increase in "wealth", or the maintenance of a nation's place among the "wealthy", is dependent upon the efficient use of labour. But, even at the end of the eighteenth century, this already implied a supplementation of muscle power with mechanical energy derived from flowing water, charcoal and fossil hydrocarbon. This trend has been gathering momentum ever since and now, in many places, mechanical energy has almost supplanted muscular effort: in some occupations a raising of the hand or foot or, indeed, the mere switching on of a computerized control at the beginning of the shift, is the total physical effort required. Even where this has not yet been achieved, the technical know-how is often available to bring it about. The "efficient use of labour" in the context of the latter part of the twentieth century thus implies an enormous consumption of mechanical energy by almost every employed person in the privileged countries (see chapter 8). Our way of life and our aspirations are based on the assumption that such energy will continue to be available in ever-increasing quantities. This view of the economic system has implications for trading activity as well as manufacturing: it assumes that the transport of vast amounts of material around the globe will continue to be possible.

In the nineteenth century this way of life was given expression in the form of European and North American manufactures and transport facilities based on coal; in the twentieth century the same general pattern has persisted but with an accelerating trend towards mineral oil and natural gas, with hydro-electricity featuring but to a much smaller extent. The massive populations of the technologically deprived nations now aspire to follow Europe and North America along the technological road, using indigenous energy resources where they are available but, much more commonly, leaning heavily on imported oil, this being a fuel which is so eminently transportable and which, in the 1950s and 1960s, was available at a price which made it economically attractive.

Those who continue to insist that it is the efficiency of labour which determines the "wealth of nations" must admit that, if this efficiency in its turn has become dependent on mechanical energy, it is clearly essential to determine whether supplies of the materials from which the energy is derived are sustainable.

OIL RESERVES

Ever since the fateful day in 1859 when oil began to flow from Colonel Drake's first well near Titusville, Pennsylvania, this mineral has played an increasingly dominant role in the affairs of men. From the 1880s onwards, extraction has consistently doubled every decade. In 1950 annual production had reached $3{\cdot}947 \times 10^9$ barrels, by 1960 it had become $7{\cdot}995 \times 10^9$ barrels (BP, 1973), and by 1970 it was $17{\cdot}219 \times 10^9$ barrels (Institute of Petroleum, 1972).

With a world technological machine so intimately bound up with the exploitation of such a convenient source of energy, it will be extremely difficult to modify such a trend, let alone stabilize or reverse it. It is clear that reserves will soon disappear, regardless of their volume, unless the trend is changed quite radically. Assessment of oil reserves is problematical, but because the techniques for exploiting oil are fairly standard, and because its mode of geological occurrence is rather more predictable and regular than that of metal ores, it has been found possible to employ sophisticated statistical procedures with more confidence than in the case of most economic minerals. Prediction of the total exploitable oil reserves of the earth depends basically on an assessment of the changing success of prospecting over recent decades. The underlying precept is that if there were huge areas of oilfield still awaiting discovery, one might expect that prospecting would be as successful now as previously; a case can be made that it should be even more successful because geological information and prospecting techniques are now so much better. Success in oil prospecting is more easily measured than in other types of mineral exploitation in that, for any given period, a fairly exact statement can be made of the amount of oil recovered per foot of hole drilled. In the case of the USA, this has fallen from 276 barrels per foot in the decade 1928–37 to a mere 35 barrels per foot in the 1960s (Hubbert, 1969); in other words the success rate has declined to little more than one eighth of what it was. Reductions of the same order of magnitude have occurred elsewhere in the petroliferous areas of the world (Lovins, 1975).

Because of this declining success, a dramatic change in the trend of annual statements of proved reserves has taken place during the past decade. Whereas before 1967 the quantity of proved reserves in the ground increased steadily year by year (425×10^9 barrels in 1955 to nearly 650×10^9 barrels in 1967), since that year the rate of extraction has overtaken the rate of discovery so that by 1973 *proved* reserves had fallen to about 635×10^9 barrels (BP, 1973).

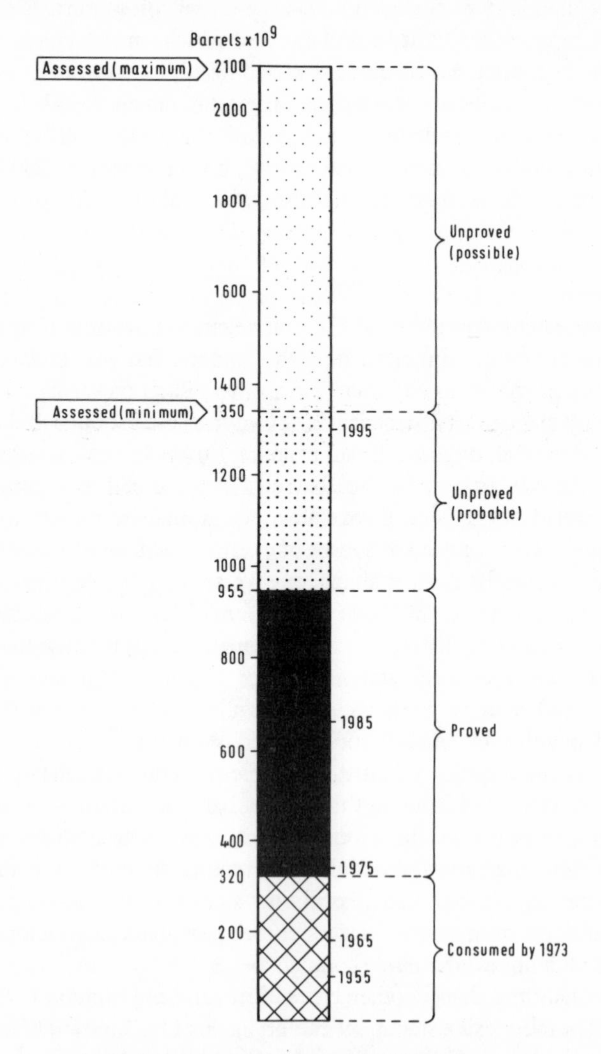

6·3 Projected rate of depletion of world oil reserves

Statistical analysis of this information has permitted assessments of the *total recoverable* oil reserves and it is felt that, within limits, these are sufficiently reliable to be viewed with confidence. The lower limit has been put at $1,350 \times 10^9$ barrels and the upper one at $2,100 \times 10^9$ barrels (figure 6.3; Hubbert, 1969). The total amount of crude oil available to man probably lies somewhere between the two. About 320×10^9 barrels had been extracted by 1973 — less than a quarter of the total available on the basis of the most conservative statistical assessments, and less than one sixth on the basis of the most generous ones.

From the standpoint of the mid–1970s therefore, there is still plenty of oil to go at! And, unfortunately, this is exactly the spirit in which our technological society seems to approach the situation. But if this spirit continues to prevail — in frenzied efforts to retain the automobile, to maintain Britain's balance of payments, to give underprivileged peoples in the oil-producing countries a material standard of living in the Western style, or to maintain a rate of growth of several per cent — then there can be no escape from the pattern whereby the level of consumption doubles every decade. This trend will ensure that more than half the established reserves will be gone by 1985, all "probable" unproved reserves will have been consumed by 1995 (figure 6.3) and, even if the most optimistic assessments of unproved reserves are found to be correct, that there cannot be sufficient oil to see us beyond the first year or two of the next century.

One might add that this is perhaps the most optimistic way of viewing present trends: it assumes that oil is going to be equally available to all nations at similar prices, and that no friction will arise because powerful or irresponsible or strategically situated nations feel that they are being denied their "fair share" of an increasingly scarce and vital commodity. The inescapable fact remains that about 55 per cent of the earth's reserves lie around the Persian Gulf, and a further 10 per cent or so in Africa (BP, 1973). The USA (including Alaska) probably has little more than 6 per cent and, despite a disproportionate publicity, probably less than 2 per cent lies beneath the North Sea (Lovins, 1975).

ALTERNATIVE SOURCES OF GAS AND PETROLEUM

If humanity is irrevocably caught up in the petroleum syndrome, it has only twenty-five years in which to find alternative sources of supply and to mass-produce petrol and gas from them at a rate which, by the turn of the century, will have to be at least five times the annual consumption in 1975. It is important to have this rate of consumption clearly in focus: it amounts to an annual consumption of more than 100×10^9 barrels, or about as much per week as was consumed in the whole of 1960.

A variety of alternative sources of motor fuel has been proposed, some clearly more promising than others and some verging on the ludicrous. In the latter category was a suggestion during the 1973 petrol crisis that Britain's cars should be adapted to gas consumption, and that the whole of this could be obtained in the form of methane by the fermentation of hen manure. Quite apart from the fact that this was yet another blatant example of a technologically minded person taking a partial view of the overall resources problem, and that the place for all hen manure is in the soil, a quantitative assessment of the amount of raw material that would be necessary to run several million cars an annual average of about 10,000 miles each, conjures up visions of a rather more poultricentric society than the one we live in.

More promising sources of car fuel are the huge geological deposits which contain hydrocarbons, though in smaller proportions than in coal. Foremost among these are the "tar sands" or "heavy oil sands" of the Prairie Provinces of Canada which are estimated to contain about 300×10^9 barrels of oil (Hubbert, 1969). They have the virtue of containing hydrocarbons which are chemically related to crude oil and, consequently, can be processed in existing oil refineries without these having to undergo major modifications. Mainly because of this, fairly large-scale exploitation has now begun, but it is important to emphasize its limited significance in the world picture as a whole. First, the on-site technical unit cost of producing a barrel of oil from tar sand in Saskatchewan is about five times as great as producing it at the wellhead in Nigeria or Venezuela; it is between 15 and 20 times as great as producing it around the Persian Gulf (Lovins, 1975). Second, this kind of deposit is a geological rarity. It is apparent, therefore, that although oil from tar sands may well feature in North American markets, as an expensive commodity, it is unlikely that it will be available to keep the wheels turning elsewhere.

Another kind of deposit which is often linked with the tar sands is "oil shale", but this material has very different physical and chemical properties. Apart from being a solid rather than a viscous fluid, it also contains a number of chemical substances which pose considerable problems in refining. A wholesale reconstruction of plant and redeployment of capital would be necessary in order to obtain a major proportion of world oil supplies from it. Furthermore, although vast quantities of oil shale are known to exist, containing more than 2×10^{15} barrels of oil (Duncan and Swanson, 1965) and well distributed over the continents, between 80 and 90 per cent of them contain less than 10 gallons of oil per ton. This is far below the limit of economic exploitability at the present time. In 1965 only 190×10^9 barrels of oil were held to be recoverable from oil shales, almost entirely from those containing between 25 and 100 gallons per ton. Even from the highest grade oil shales in the most advantageous situations, the technical unit cost of a barrel of oil in 1973 was between 20 and 30 times as great as at wellhead around the Persian Gulf. Indeed, for a variety of reasons, "there is no general agreement that oil shale will ever become an important energy source, though minor production seems possible in a few regions." (Lovins, 1975).

A rapid increase in the conversion of coal to liquid and gaseous fuels seems to offer much more promise if only because its energy yield per ton is about four times as large as the most productive oil shale. In the case of coal there is far less waste material to transport and dispose of, and useful biproducts accrue whose value can be set against the costs of production. The fact remains, however, that in 1973 the cost of production of liquids and liquified gases obtained by distillation from coal was about 30 times as great as that of crude oil at wellhead around the Persian Gulf.

A study of the relative costs of production thus makes abundantly clear why the production of petroleum from mineral solids is not already in full swing. Although for obvious reasons it was very unpopular among the large oil consumers, the great increase in price of Asian and African oil imposed by the producing countries in the early 1970s could be of considerable long-term benefit if it caused an increase in the exploitation of other sources of hydrocarbon fluids with a consequent slackening in the rate of exploitation of crude oil. (It is important not to be misunderstood on this point. Massive exploitation of tar sand and oil shale would cause great environmental damage and loss of land, and it would be best if it did not take place. The greatest blessing would be if the rise in oil prices caused a progressive diminution in consumption — but, at the present time, perhaps this is not the aim of the oil-producing countries.) Any increase in technological elbow-room that this might give beyond the year 2000 can be regarded as valuable.

On the other hand, expressing approval of unconventional sources of petroleum has great dangers. It suggests that a continued growth in the production of liquid fuels for traction and other purposes is of itself, a desirable thing, and this cannot be conceded. In a situation where energy for all purposes was increasingly in short supply, profligate use of it for the extraction and manufacture of fuel for automobiles would be a very dubious activity. If energy for fertilizer manufacture, food processing and domestic heating were threatened, it seems doubtful if even an unrealistic urbanized society would persist in devoting almost 100 joules of energy to the production of automobile fuel with an energy equivalent of 100 joules. And if this energy ratio were to tilt even further, one cannot imagine that the production of petrol for *any* purpose would be tolerated, quite regardless of pre-existing arbitrary price differentials between different forms of energy. It is in the light of this kind of consideration that one should view all technological discussions about the extraction of petroleum from materials such as low-grade oil shale.

COAL

If oil and natural gas are shortly to become unavailable for all but very special purposes, it is vital to consider what sources of energy might take their place on the industrial and domestic fronts. Coal, the staple fodder of the Industrial Revolution, is an obvious alternative: proved and inferred reserves seem to exist in sufficient quantity to fuel a vast world industrial complex for a protracted period. One assessment of total mineable resources of coal and lignite down to a depth of 1,800 m (6,000 feet) puts them at $7{\cdot}64 \times 10^{12}$ mt (Averitt, 1969) and there seems some agreement that this figure is of the right order of magnitude, though perhaps erring a little on the generous side (Hubbert, 1969). If the reserves were to be consumed at a rate approximating to coal consumption in the early 1970s — about 3×10^9 mt/year, they would last for about 3,000 years, but this is probably not a very relevant point. Over the 30 years since the second world war the mean annual rate of increase in consumption has been about 3·6 per cent, and this has been a period in which oil, for a great variety of purposes, has persistently ousted coal as a basic source of energy. If one envisages rapid world industrialization over the coming century, in the absence of a plentiful supply of oil, it is not unreasonable to postulate that the annual rate of increase in the extraction of coal might well be similar to that which occurred in the USA between 1850 and 1907, i.e. 6·6 per cent (Hubbert, 1969). Even if one takes a conservative view of this kind of development, and postulates an average annual rate of increase of only 5 per cent over the decades ahead, all mineable world reserves would have been used up somewhere between 2065 and 2070 AD.

Table 6.5 Estimates of world resources of minable coal and lignite (from Averitt, 1969)

Country or region	Initial resources (10^9 mt)
USSR and Eastern Europe	4310
USA	1486
Canada	601
Asia (outside USSR)	681
Western Europe	377
Africa	109
Oceania (including Australia)	59
Latin America	14
TOTAL	7637

In the case of such a bulky commodity as coal, however, particularly in a period in which energy generally was increasingly in short supply, it is not very realistic to imagine that there would be equal availability to all nations. If anything, coal is even less equitably distributed over the earth than oil (table 6.5), with over 55 per cent of the reserves in the USSR alone, and almost 93 per cent in four countries — the USSR, the USA, China and Canada. South and Central America have less than 0.2 per cent, and all the countries of the southern hemisphere along with southern Asia, North Africa, Central America and Mexico have only about 2·5 per cent between them. If oil fails, the underprivileged peoples of the world have little to expect from fossil fuels.

CONTEMPORARY SOLAR ENERGY

For some time past those of a conservationist turn of mind have insisted that, in the long term, industrial society cannot survive if it persists in trying to utilize any substantial amount of energy other than that which is currently being provided by the sun. Even the advent of nuclear technology (see below, p.96), because of its inherent perils, is not seen to undermine this basic precept. Thoughtful people, including some technologists, have even held to the view that if ours were a truly rational society it would be striving, as quickly as possible, to reach a situation in which precious and irreplaceable substances such as coal and oil would be cherished and conserved as industrial raw materials for the millennia to come, and not just destroyed in combustion. One cannot deny the force of these arguments; indeed, in a world without population pressures, one suspects that administrations would already be following such conservationist pathways. However, the nature and availability of energy from contemporary solar input poses problems, some of which may not be solvable in a crowded world.

DIRECT COLLECTION

The direct collection of solar energy is obviously a most desirable procedure and its many possibilities, at various levels of scale, have been discussed for some decades (Daniels, 1964). Many problems would evaporate and the world would rapidly become a cleaner place if each house, shop and factory could be supplied with a solar collector capable of supplying all the light, heat and motive energy it required. However, the mass production of electricity from such a source may not be practicable. Solar power at the surface of the earth, averaged over the whole twenty-four hours of the day, is only about 240 watts/m^2 (less in cloudy high latitudes, more in the tropics). Given that an appropriate energy-collecting surface is only about 10 per cent efficient, a large solar-electric power station of 1,000 Mw capacity would thus need to cover, on average, a continuous area of 42 km^2 (Hubbert, 1969). In intensively settled countries already suffering from land use conflicts, this is not feasible; indeed, even in those which have extensive areas of sunny semi-desert, the availability of materials and capital would pose enormous problems. Consequently, although there probably exists an adequate technology, and even though in the long term such large-scale installations might theoretically be an economic proposition, the chance of their materializing in time to make an impact on the problems of the early twenty-first century seems remote.

The same cannot be said about direct solar collection on a smaller scale. It has been maintained that the barriers to the widespread use of single-dwelling solar collectors are entirely institutional (Lovins, 1975). The technology is now available to provide domestic premises with wall and roof-top collectors entirely adequate to the task of providing hot water, air conditioning and lighting everywhere except in really high latitudes. There would be vast savings in fossil fuels before the end of the twentieth century if such an innovation gained widespread popularity in the near future.

INDIRECT COLLECTION: THE WIND

Indirect collection of contemporary solar energy seems to hold out even greater promise, mainly owing to the fact that the lateral movement of air and the vertical movement of water, taken together, are of universal distribution over the earth, in some ways being even more effective in high latitudes than in low. But even in the tropics where wind-strength generally is less than in higher latitudes, sea breezes and mountain winds are very important locally, often in those places where settlement is conveniently concentrated.

The use of windmills as energy converters has not received the attention it merits, probably because it does not lend itself to large-scale or centralized production. There can be no doubt about its applicability to a great range of small-scale usages, ranging from the heating of water in insulated reservoirs for background domestic warmth, to the provision of lighting, the charging of accumulators, and the supplying of mechanical energy at the domestic and small workshop level. The efficiency of windmills has been greatly improved in recent times and, with the great increases in price of fuel and energy that are now taking place, it would be unfortunate if the reinstatement of the windmill as a common feature in the landscape were to be hindered by large-scale vested interests.

There is a rather sad little tale about a miller who lived on a hilltop not far from Nottingham. His father before him had also been a miller — a good man who never sought a greedy margin of profit and whose services were so much in demand that he was persistently forced to turn away trade. To the end of his days he remained a small man, contented with his lot, the only land he owned being the acre of hilltop on which his mill was built. Upon succeeding to his father's business, the son embarked upon expansion: without delay he built another windmill on the croft in anticipation of doubling his income. From that day forth his fortunes faltered; ultimately the business crumbled and fell into decay. There was just not enough wind in one field for two windmills!

Until quite recently the sight of those two hulks silhouetted against the sky often provoked this story, and with a sophisticated twentieth century audience it was guaranteed a good reception. But during subsequent minutes the perceptive story-teller could detect a pregnant thoughtfulness. In the mind of most of us there lurks a misty shadow of something about the conservation of energy so that, very often (though not without embarrassed hesitation), the question would force itself to the surface: "How many windmills can one put in an acre field?"

In fact the story is doubly allegorical. In a world in which almost every facet of life has come to rely on the destruction of irreplaceable mineral material, it is a pity that no really satisfactory answer can be given to such all-important questions in applied meteorology. The wind is still free, but unfortunately it suffers from the limitation of being a little less reliable than one might wish. Has the time not come, however, when those who plan economies (see chapter 11) should be asking themselves whether it is not better for a man to be standing underemployed for a third of his time rather than to be drawing unemployment pay for the whole of it? The fact that a little capital equipment might stand idle with him until the wind began to blow again is perhaps of small account if the energy he used were free and non-polluting. Indeed, they should perhaps go further and enquire whether the level of concealed unemployment at the present time is not even less economic than the activities of the miller on those days when the wind failed him. We have surely now developed sufficient scepticism about "economies of scale" to realize that thoughts such as this are not mere unprofitable romanticism.

INDIRECT COLLECTION: HYDRO-ELECTRIC POWER

The main advantage of hydro-electric power over wind power, from the point of view of modern technology, is that the former can be much more concentrated. If condensed water were to return to sea level entirely in a highly dispersed form, it would be much less useful than wind, but since a large percentage of it runs off into channels or is returned to the surface via springs, it is eventually concentrated in large bodies of flowing water which can be used as medium- or large-scale sources of energy.

Hydro-electricity has frequently been presented as the great redeemer of the world energy situation. It was an essential element in the core-concept of the Tennessee Valley Authority (Lilienthal, 1944) and in the general philosophy of those conservationists who sought for a rebirth in the Great Plains and the other dry lands of the USA after the Dust Bowl catastrophe of the 1930s. As an energy-converting device based on a renewable resource, the hydro-electric installation is the best that we have and is likely to remain so for some time. Its main virtue is that it is capable of sustaining large-scale industry. Moreover, a world inventory reveals that the total potential water-power capacity of the earth is of the order of $2{\cdot}8 \times 10^6$ Mw, which is approximately equal to the world's total rate of energy consumption at the present time. Of this potential only about 7·5 per cent was exploited in the late 1960s (Hubbert, 1969).

Although of great potential importance, the future development of hydro-electricity is subject to serious limitations. Over 60 per cent of the potential capacity is located in South America, Southeast Asia and Africa south of the Sahara, far away from the present world centres of industrial production, but theoretically available to those countries which possess very little fossil fuel. Once installed, the running costs of hydro-electric dams are relatively low; the obvious deterrent to development is the enormous initial capital outlay and the repayments of capital and interest. These are the short-term reasons why development has not been far more rapid over the past half century.

There are long-term and much more fundamental problems associated with the wholesale development of the world's hydro-electric potential — problems which only time and a further doubling of world population could make obvious. It is already clear why great dams cannot be built across river valleys in the lowlands of Britain, Japan, Belgium and Java: to do so would drown irreplaceable land and huge numbers of homes and businesses. The intrinsic losses and the levels of compensation rule out such developments. It is only in countries

[3]The Kariba Dam inundated about 5,180 km^2 (2,000 ml^2) of slope and bottom land along 280 km (175 miles) of the Zambesi Valley.

where pressure on land is relatively slight, such as the USA in the 1930s or Rhodesia[3] and the USSR in the 1950s, that the submergence of vast areas can be contemplated. In order to develop most of the world's potential it would be necessary to flood bottom lands and lower slopes in nearly all those areas in the tropics which are inherently the healthiest and most invigorating — the upland and highland regions where the rivers have their headwaters. Huge lakes would also have to be made on plateau and lowland regions. Vast areas of forest and potential agricultural land would be submerged, thus reducing the total NPP of the earth even more rapidly than would otherwise happen. Furthermore, the nature and magnitude of all the ecological and economic side effects are incalculable.

One problem which would inevitably arise is that all reservoirs ultimately silt up, some more rapidly than others. If intense cultivation were displaced uphill and had to take place up-slope from the reservoirs, silting would be far more rapid than if the slopes were conserved beneath a stable forest cover. The vision of mankind living in perpetuity along the shores of artificial lakes, continuously supplied by hydro-electricity and irrigation water and untrammelled by problems of maintenance is illusory. Although persistent dredging might be capable of maintaining an equilibrium situation in some circumstances, the cost of doing so would ensure that, in the long run, hydro-electricity would not be cheap energy.

GEOTHERMAL AND TIDAL ENERGY

Energy derived from hot rocks in the earth's crust may well prove to be a substantial adjunct to that from more conventional sources. It already makes an important contribution in some restricted localities: a geothermal electric power station has operated at Larderello in Italy since 1904, and a number of others in California, New Zealand, Mexico, Japan and Kamchatka in the USSR have come into production since 1958 (Hubbert, 1969). A great deal of Reykjavik's urban heating system and horticultural production depends upon naturally heated water from a similar source. Up to the present time, however, success such as this has only been achieved in volcanic areas, usually where hot water actually emerged naturally at the surface in springs or geysers. Such naturally sustained systems can be expected to function indefinitely provided natural earth movements or the intensity of human interference do not disrupt them.

Rather more ambitious and novel schemes are now being discussed. It is known that rocks of unusually high temperature occur at relatively shallow depths in a number of non-volcanic areas: localities in southwestern England and County Durham have been mentioned particularly. It is suggested that if boreholes were drilled into these rocks and water pumped into them, it would be possible to draw off hot water continuously. Although there is no fundamental difference between projects such as this and those already operating in volcanic areas, the difference in degree could well be critical. Even in the latter, overexploitation over a period of time would make a project uneconomic or even non-functional. The geothermal electricity generating stations in operation at the present time are dependent upon deep-seated hot water which rises to the surface under pressure if it is tapped by boreholes but, in order for power from such sources to be sustained, a number of conditions must be fulfilled. First, sufficient water must be available in depth to be drawn off continuously as steam, and this must be supplied either naturally from some kind of groundwater source, or artificially from above. Second, the rocks at critical depth must be sufficiently permeable to permit this water to circulate freely through a large volume so as to raise it to a sufficiently high temperature at the extraction points. Third, the rate of heat conduction through the rocks of the area must be capable of maintaining the temperature of the aquifer even though heat is being extracted much more rapidly than would occur naturally. If, under exploitation, any one of these variables in the system is inadequate to maintain a state of equilibrium, then it will begin to run down. This applies equally to the use of natural steam for electricity generation and to artificial circulation of water in systems at a lower temperature except that, in the latter case, less energy is available to begin with.

It has been estimated (White, 1965) that if one per cent of the geothermal energy present in the top ten km of the earth's crust is in localities where it can be utilized, this is sufficient to supply about 60,000 Mw for fifty years. Since only about 1,000 Mw had been developed by 1970 (between 60 and 70 per cent of which is in Italy and New Zealand) then clearly there is scope for expansion. The fact that the time scale of "50 years" is mentioned is ominous. Obviously the process of extraction is not regarded as being automatically sustainable: one infers that there is some doubt as to whether the natural energy-producing capacity of the earth can sustain any substantial rate of extraction. Furthermore, although a 60,000 Mw capacity is very considerable, it is equivalent to less than 20 per cent of the earth's present consumption of hydro-electricity.

Possibilities for the development of tidal power have been summarized briefly but in a masterly fashion by King Hubbert (1969, p.209). He concludes that, in a limited number of coastal localities, conditions are very favourable for the large-scale generation of electricity; indeed pioneer projects are already in operation on La Rance estuary in France and in the Kislaya Inlet on the Barents Sea 80 km northwest of Murmansk. Again, this is an efficient and non-polluting way in which energy can be made available for large-scale industry; also it has the added advantage of being inexhaustible. Yet it can never be anything but very local: not only is it confined to coastlands but the number of coastal sites where it could be used profitably is very restricted. Its potential as a power producer cannot be more than about one per cent that of hydro-electricity.

NUCLEAR ENERGY

The foregoing review seems to indicate than an expanding world population, striving to prolong economic growth, would encounter insuperable energy problems before the end of the century. There is a further aspect of technological development which demands consideration, and this makes extrapolation and prediction much more complicated. A substantial body of conventional technological opinion would now maintain that the development of nuclear reactors makes discussions about the limitations of fossil fuels and solar power of only limited relevance. In the 1960s, the habit developed of anticipating a future not too far ahead where the mass production of nuclear power would ensure that energy would be almost free: it would therefore be possible to manufacture anything, and fresh water would be available from the oceans in virtually unlimited quantities. A large number of science popularizers in the 1970s still seem to think along these lines. It would probably be far more difficult to find serious thinkers quite so uninhibited, but great differences of opinion persist about the future availability of energy and these differences arise mainly because of nuclear problems.

The nuclear debate revolves essentially around two aspects of basic resources — first, their availability and second, safety problems arising out of their utilization. The second aspect will be considered later (chapter 11); the first requires careful analysis before one can appreciate fully the course of events that has led to the present situation.

Two kinds of nuclear reaction have been used to liberate the energy locked up inside atomic nuclei. The first was employed in the early atomic bombs such as those dropped on Hiroshima and Nagasaki: it depends upon the energy released when atoms of uranium are split and is consequently referred to as "nuclear fission". The second was used in the later and more devastating hydrogen bombs and depends upon the energy released when hydrogen atoms fuse to form helium. This "fusion" reaction has the great advantage of depending on raw materials which, for practical purposes, can be regarded as unlimited; indeed, for a variety of reasons, it is generally regarded as the most desirable base upon which to build a nuclear technology. As yet it is by no means certain that it will ever be possible to use it for the controlled production of energy, but the fact that cautious physicists feel that substantial and sustained progress is taking place does suggest that a prototype could be available by 2000 AD (Lovins, 1975).

It is clear, therefore, that nuclear fusion power stations will not be available to do anything for the vast majority of mankind in the critical decades at the beginning of the twenty-first century. It would be unreasonable to expect that the development, even of a prototype, could be achieved without the expenditure of sums of the order of ten billion dollars, and this would merely be a first step along the road to development. The economics of such a development are entirely conjectural, but one cannot imagine how even countries of modest means could afford such a technology, let alone the impoverished majority of mankind.

The reasons for persistence in the development of nuclear fission are therefore obvious: there can be little doubt that it would already have been displaced if fusion were simple and available at similar cost. The problems of fission development are more perplexing than is generally realized, however, and are bound up basically with resource availability. The conventional or "burner" reactor is one that actually consumes a naturally occurring isotope, uranium-235, one g of uranium producing the energy equivalent of 2·7 mt of coal. Accordingly, a 1,000 Mw nuclear power plant with a thermal efficiency of 0·33, would consume uranium–235 at a rate of about 3 kg/day (Hubbert, 1969). A nuclear technology based on burner reactors thus uses up U–235 at an uncomfortably rapid rate.

U–235 is a relatively rare substance, the uranium from most naturally occurring ores containing only one atom of U–235 to about 140 atoms of U–238. During the 1950s and early 1960s it thus became apparent that unless vast new deposits of uranium ore could be discovered, or unless a new nuclear technology could be developed which did not use up U–235 so quickly, the whole programme would rapidly grind to a halt. In 1965 one authority felt justified in concluding that, after 1976, it would not be possible to meet demand from deposits then know, and that production increases in the late 1970s would have to come from deposits not discovered in 1965 (Roscoe, 1965). A veil of secrecy shrouds a good deal of the information about uranium reserves, but the evidence available seems to confirm a serious resources problem. Peter Flawn (1966) put the world static reserve index (outside the Sino-Soviet Bloc) at no more than 24 years, the bulk of the known reserves of relatively high grade being in Canada and South Africa. It is clear, therefore, why the nuclear industry should have felt itself under great pressure to produce an alternative technology as quickly as possible.

The answer to the problem seemed to lie in another type of reactor, usually referred to as the "breeder" or "high-ratio converter" reactor. In 1968 the director of the Division of Reactor Development and Technology in the USA said: "It becomes evident each day how dependent we are going to become on the successful introduction of breeders" (Milton Shaw, 1968). An important point about the breeder reactor is that it uses the much more commonly occurring U–238, converting it into plutonium–239 which is a highly fertile fissionable material. But the most significant point of all is that breeder reactors are extremely unstable and, as such, have been regarded as "unsafe". The main aim during the development phases has been to produce a "safe" breeder reactor, a goal which proved to be far more difficult than originally imagined; by the mid–1970s, qualified nuclear scientists still regard breeder reactors as "dangerous beasts". This is mainly because of their instability, but one cannot ignore the fact that, when fully operational, they also contain tons of highly radioactive plutonium–239, one of the most dangerous substances known. The combination of these two features is viewed with disquiet by everyone concerned; to those who regard the co-existence of plutonium and many human traits and institutions as a long-term impossibility, this latest technological development is alarming in the extreme. The nuclear industry seems to be in a situation where fusion reactors are possibilities of the more remote future, where "burners" are in danger of running out of fuel, and where the only alternative seems to be the "breeder" — a contrivance whose existence would probably not be countenanced if a safer, sustainable option were available.

THE QUANTITATIVE PROBLEM

Viewed as an essential part of the human drama which will be enacted over the next few decades, the struggle to maintain a massive rate of energy conversion is all the sadder because, at the very best, it appears to be capable of only partial success. One is bound to ask the question whether, in such matters as fission energy development, partial success may not be far worse than making no attempt at all. Two quotations from Amory Lovins (1975, pp.21 and 73) seem to sum up the problem most succinctly:

> To place in perspective the supply problems of fossil fuels, we must stress a basic insight more common amongst engineers than amongst politicians: the truly formidable rate and magnitude problems of *any* major innovation. The aggregate amounts of energy now being converted are so prodigious that voluntary rapid change in supply problems is *physically impossible*. For example, suppose that our present world conversion rate of 8×10^{12} w — 97 per cent of it from fossil fuels — continues to grow (as most authorities predict and urge) at about 5 per cent/year for the rest of this century, yielding a $3{\cdot}7 \times$ increase to about 3×10^{13} w. If we could somehow build one huge (1 Gw = 1,000 Mw(e) = 10^9 w(e)) nuclear power station per *day* for the rest of this century, starting today, then when we had finished, *more than half* of our primary energy would still come from fossil fuels, which would be consumed about *twice* as fast as now.
>
> Some people still think that nuclear capacity in, say, the USA will increase $50 \times$ by 2000 (AD) and that the equivalent of total present US electrical capacity will then be built every 29 months. There is no accounting for what some people think.

7

National Mineral Wealth

If an index of the ultimate viability of individual nations is to be obtained, it is necessary to devise some kind of common denominator for organic and inorganic assets so that they can be assessed together. Only when we have a statement embodying both kinds of natural resource can a notion of population carrying-capacity be formulated. Quantifying national organic productivity is complicated enough as already demonstrated (chapter 5); putting a value on mineral production is also problematical; but devising some kind of expression which conflates the total resource of a nation is most difficult of all.

Much of what follows in this chapter, about the benefit that nations might derive from their mineral deposits, is exploratory and speculative. Detailed investigations along the lines envisaged do no seem to have been carried out, indeed it would be misleading to pretend that the methodology for what might be termed "potential mineral income analysis" has been fully thought through. Nevertheless, in a world of rapidly declining resources, the type of quantification at which pioneering attempts are made here seems essential and should be given far more attention with the minimum of delay.

ASSESSING THE VALUE OF MINERAL PRODUCTION

At first sight, it seems a relatively simple matter to put a value on a nation's mineral output. Accurate and detailed statistics of ore and raw mineral production on a national basis are readily accessible and an assessment of the actual metallic or refined content of the raw material is usually available. It is only when one attempts to evaluate the benefits a nation might derive from the production of unit quantity of a particular metal that both practical and methodological difficulties become apparent.

First, there is the basic problem that a ton of, say, one per cent copper ore, extracted from the ground in one part of the world, has a different price from a similar ton raised elsewhere. This is caused by a variety of factors — technical, locational, social and so on — which are mainly well understood. Until recently economists seem to have had some confidence that this could be rationalized adequately according to the principles of supply and demand: the low-cost producer could offer the product on the world market at a relatively low price so that the high-cost ones, for the time being, were forced out of production. Since the 1973 oil crisis, however, the world is rather a different place: dearth seems to be a great leveller, almost invariably in an upward direction, and who can say what will determine relative prices during forthcoming decades! It seems a reasonable assumption that if there is so little to go round that the expanding industries of the established industrial countries are unable to secure sufficient oil and metals to keep the wheels turning, then very "inefficient" producers will be in a position to determine the price level. Even without the formation of cartels it seems unlikely that the most efficient producers will try very hard to sell at a price well below that of the high-cost ones. The deeper implications of this will be discussed in the next chapter; one need only emphasize that, in the coming decades, it seems likely that there is going to be a continuing rise (though with inevitable fluctuations) in the world price of mineral raw materials as compared to that of manufactured goods, this rise only being equalled (possibly even surpassed) by that in the price of food. This basic point will be substantiated later, but it underlies a great deal of what follows.

The second basic difficulty when assessing national mineral output is that unit weight of a particular metal may have very different values to the countries which produce it because of the various states in which it is exported. In some cases it is still contained in the ore in which it was mined, in others it is in a semi-refined state, in a third category it is sold as ingots or bars of pure metal, while in a fourth it has been incorporated into a wide range of manufactured articles and its value to the exporting country must be assessed as a relatively small component of the total value of these goods. This diversity, of course, is a clear illustration of Adam Smith's precepts regarding the relationship between "wealth" and "the efficient use of labour": the value of unit weight of metal is enhanced at every stage where specialized labour works upon it. These different levels at which nations profit from their mineral production must be given close consideration if one is to assess the future role of minerals as national assets.

It is the great complexity that has grown out of the whole-hearted adoption of Adam Smith's philosophy which lies at the root of the practical difficulties experienced when attempting to evaluate national mineral wealth. Apart from the fact that the preparation of relevant and convenient statistics is a complicated exercise, there is the added difficulty that no really influential group seems to be particularly interested in having them. In the relative opulence of the technological world, people have not been accustomed to thinking in terms of using national mineral income as exchange for basic units of nutrition: industrial concerns involved in mining have used their income to pay higher wages (relative to the peasant's or farm worker's income in the country concerned), to make capital repayments, to meet running costs, and to pay dividends to shareholders who might well be resident in other countries. Even the politicians and administrators in the country of extraction, who might have been more concerned about the overall welfare of the inhabitants, have tended to regard the presence of extractive industry as a means of raising the general standard of living, rather than as a vital adjunct to the basic subsistence economy; they have allowed it to stimulate the inordinate growth of better-off, urban (but landless) social classes, rather than cherishing it as a life-line against the days ahead when population growth may make substantial food imports imperative.

THE CONCEPT OF A "NUTRITION-UNIT EQUIVALENT"

The problem envisaged here can be crystallized by enquiring how, on the world scale, one can assign a "food-equivalent value" to unit weight of metal produced for export. More specifically, for every ton of aluminium exported from a bauxite-producing country, how many kilocalories can be imported? It may be helpful to postulate a somewhat oversimplified hypothetical case as a first approach to the problem. In a country with a completely self-sufficient peasant economy[1] the average member of the community would produce and consume approximately 3,000 kcal per day in the form of food, at least 12 per cent of which would be protein (Borgstrom, 1973), along with a certain amount of plant, animal and mineral material for clothing, implements and shelter. The annual food consumption of such a nation, if it numbered a million, would thus be $3,000 \times 10^6 \times 365$ kcal.

If this same country were to begin to extract and export mineral material using exclusively local labour, this would involve the redeployment of a fraction of its peasants to non-food-producing work. With one per cent of the population (workers and dependents) affected in this way, the implication is that 10,000 people would then have to be fed from the proceeds of the exported minerals. This could be achieved either by importing food direct, or by buying fertilizers and agricultural technology in order to produce a home food surplus.[2] If the new mineral industry, in the short term, were neither an advantage nor a disadvantage to the country concerned, it would earn just enough per day to pay for food with a nutrition value of $3,000 \times 10^4$ kcal plus 10,000 units of clothing, utensils and housing material.

Pursuing this same hypothetical illustration, it is possible to explore some of the problems, already raised, which arise out of the possibility of exporting a particular metal in different forms. Let us say that the material being exploited was bauxite with an average alumina (Al_2O_3) content of 50 per cent, and an aluminium metal content of exactly 25 per cent. Thus, if four million tons of bauxite were extracted per annum, they would contain two million tons of Al_2O_3 and exactly one million tons of metal. Assuming that all the metal was exported, it is possible to envisage four distinct levels at which the country might profit from its mineral production:

[1] Such "pure" economies have almost ceased to exist in the modern world; they now have a precarious existence only very locally in places like Amazonia and New Guinea. National units of this nature have disappeared.

[2] It must not be inferred that these two methods of obtaining the 10,000 nutrition units are the only ones possible. Indeed one of the traditional hopes of administrations seems to have been that the remaining peasant population, stimulated by the acquistion of an industrial market, would work longer hours on an increased acreage, and produce the extra food without any further capital costs being incurred. The basic fallacy of this kind of expansionist philosophy is not fully explored here, but one should consider just how much of the soil degradation and derelict land over the earth is due to such extraction from the land without commensurate input.

Stage 1: The bauxite could be moved to the coast and exported as such at a price of $10 million for the four million tons. This amounts to $2·50 per ton of bauxite but, since the ore was only 25 per cent metal, it is $10 per ton for the actual aluminium content.

Stage 2: A concentrating plant could be built, employing additional labour, to extract pure alumina from the crude bauxite. This would involve a reduction in bulk to half the original. The alumina could then be exported at, say $20 per ton (i.e. $40 million for the two million tons), which amounts to $40 per ton for the aluminium content.

Stage 3: A hydro-electricity station and aluminium refinery could be built for the electrolytic extraction of aluminium metal from the alumina, reducing bulk to a quarter of that of the original bauxite. The metal could be exported at, say $400 per ton (i.e. $400 million for the million tons).

Stage 4: Finally, the industrial economy of the country could be "developed" and diversified, a large range of other metals and raw materials being imported to supply it. The aluminium could then be alloyed and fabricated into a great range of consumer and capital goods and exported.[3] The income from such a volume of goods would be enormous and the prospect of calculating what proportion of the total value was attributable to the aluminium component would surely satisfy the appetite of the most enthusiastic statistician. In the world at the present time it would certainly be well in excess of the $400 million value of the original aluminium ingots; what its relative value might be in future world situations is a field for speculation to which some further attention will be given later.

Leaving aside Stage 4 for the moment, one is able to take the postulated value of the mineral product for each of the first three stages and to assign it a "nutrition-unit equivalent". Indeed, in order to bring the exercise nearer to reality, one can use 1965 statistics because, in that year, the average world price of aluminium metal was not far removed from $400 per ton.[4] In 1965 the average export price of the three main cereals from the USA was:

unmilled wheat : $60·09/mt
unmilled barley : $54·96/mt
unmilled maize : $54·93/mt

As in most years, the prices of the three commodities were very similar, so it seems realistic to take their average — $56·66/mt — as a representative figure. Furthermore, since the USA has been one of the main providers of surplus cereals since the second world war, it seems reasonable to take its export prices as a broad indication of the cost of cereals on the world market over the past two or three decades.

[3] This is an artificial situation, of course. In the real world no country would industrialize to this level without absorbing some of its own manufactures.

[4] $486/mt in the USA (US Bureau of Mines, 1970b).

Taking 3,000 kcal as the standard daily nutrition requirement of an average human, it thus becomes possible to express money income from minerals in terms of annual nutrition units. Pure carbohydrates and proteins release about four kcal per g (Borgstrom, 1973), so one may take it that 1kg of unmilled cereal, at approximately 10 per cent cellulose and 15 per cent moisture content, on average, is equivalent to about 3,000 kcal. One metric ton (1,000 kg) of unmilled cereals is thus equivalent to the *daily* food requirement of 1,000 people or, very approximately, the *annual* food requirement of three people. In 1965, at US prices, this amount of food would have cost $56·66. For the hypothetical country of our illustration, therefore, it is possible to say how many people could have been supplied with food on the proceeds of mineral exports at each of the first three stages:

	$		mt cereals		nutrition units
Stage 1:	10×10^6	=	176,000	=	529,000
Stage 2:	40×10^6	=	706,000	=	2,118,000
Stage 3:	400×10^6	=	7,060,000	=	21,180,000

Although this is a hypothetical set of situations, the figures used are sufficiently realistic, in the light of recent market conditions, to serve as a basis for consideration of the real world. There are two salient points arising from the calculations — first, the outstanding difference in buying power between the proceeds from bauxite and those from the equivalent amount of aluminium metal; second, the very large number of nutrition units that a million tons of aluminium metal would purchase. On the face of it, a generally "underdeveloped" country with large reserves of bauxite (or any other important ore) is *potentially* in a strong position: if it were able to extract the metal within its own frontiers it could support a very large non-food-producing population (so long as the ore lasted and surplus food was available on the world market).

The general truth of the point that has just been made seems inescapable, but it is important to reflect a little on the details of the illustration that has been presented before contemplating the significance of 21 million nutrition units to an "underdeveloped" primary producer. In the first place, in 1970 only five countries in the world produced more than four million mt of bauxite, and only three of these, Jamaica, Surinam and Guyana, could be classed as "underdeveloped". Secondly, in 1970 only two countries, the USA and the USSR, produced more than a million mt of aluminium metal; indeed, all those who produced more than 100,000mt, with the exception of India (161,000 mt), were countries with a long-established industrial base (US Bureau of Mines, 1970b). Our hypothetical country, therefore, is an inordinately large producer; moreover, if it were to achieve Stage 3 and smelt all its bauxite, it would have achieved far, far more than any other "underdeveloped" country at the present time. Jamaica, the world's largest producer of bauxite (12 million mt in 1970), smelted none at all in 1969; it produced alumina from less than a quarter of it.

THE DANGERS OF "STAGE 4" DEVELOPMENT

The difference in value between aluminium in bauxite, in alumina and in pure metal is no revelation: it is exactly the kind of situation which Adam Smith envisaged. From his eighteenth-century standpoint, he would probably have had no reservations about the desirability of any and every country developing from a Stage 3 to a Stage 4 economy and of fabricating metal into a wide range of goods for internal consumption and for export. And there can be little doubt that the majority of economists at the present time would subscribe to the same view, if only they could think of ways in which the capital could be made available.

Seen simply in the context of the mid–1970s, it is by no means evident that there could be any grounds for dissenting from such a view: what is the point of producing aluminium if there is no intention of producing usable goods from it, and what better than that this should be done in the country of origin? Before committing oneself unreservedly, however, it is important to envisage sophisticated industrialization from the viewpoint of a world somewhat different from the present one — in which population has almost doubled but food production has not kept pace. This is the world which reasonable extrapolation indicates for the year 2000 AD — just twenty-five years hence. In such circumstances it seems likely that administrations in the great majority of underprivileged countries will be under continuous pressure. Maintaining an infrastructure with acceptable health, educational and transport services will be increasingly difficult and, in such circumstances, one cannot visualize the persistence of a moneyed class sufficiently large to maintain a substantial internal market for sophisticated manufactured goods. The point has already been made that the development of modern industry subsumes large imports of exotic raw materials and would have to be accompanied by an influx of expensive technology and expertise. Even the manufacture of basic capital goods such as railway waggons and simple machine tools must be viewed with reservation. It seems unreasonable to expect that most countries which, up to the present time, have barely begun to industrialize, will be able to develop in this way during the next two or three decades.

The best that can be expected from foreign capital is that it will be made available to assist up to Stage 3 — often not beyond Stage 2. On first consideration it seems only right and equitable to view the industrial aspirations of non-technological nations with pleasure and approval, but one should always bear in mind that the initiation and diversification of industry are the first steps to economic nationalism. The question has already been asked (chapter 5) as to what will happen to the older industrial nations (who must import food and industrial raw materials) if their manufactures are no longer required. The "moral right" of newer nations to industrialize cannot be denied, but unless they have a market, either internal or external, and *without economic growth,* such a development will not only have a disruptive effect on the established industrial countries, but will also be ineffective and even hurtful to their own economies.

All the evidence of the mid–1970s indicates that the imminent arrival on the world scene of new industrial nations, with few exceptions, must be regarded with scepticism. Apart from the internal market problems they would experience and the general poverty of other unindustrialized countries around them, the possibilities of large exports to established manufacturing nations would seem to be remote. Even with the relatively mild kind of recession that has already been experienced in the twentieth century, the way in which industrialized countries begin to seek refuge behind import restrictions on manufactured goods as soon as a slackening world market threatens, gives no basis for confidence.

It is for this reason that there must be serious doubts about any substantial development into what has been designated Stage 4 in the foregoing hypothetical discussion. One might add that this fundamental reservation lies at the root of the thinking of most of those who advise against industrialization along Western lines by the new nations of the world (Schumacher, 1973).

In the discussion which follows, therefore, there is the underlying assumption that the maximum benefit which an "underdeveloped" nation can expect to derive from its minerals is at what has been designated as Stage 3 of mineral exploitation. There is no suggestion, however, that all "underdeveloped" nations which possess mineral reserves can achieve this level of development; the assumption of Stage 3 merely provides a useful basis for comparison. For the same reason, the minerals extracted by nations which are already industrialized have also been assessed at this stage, though this is less realistic. Calculating the actual value of its mineral production (in nutrition units) to an industrialized nation would be extremely complicated, and appropriate data are certainly not available. This is a task which must await the attentions of economists.

THE MAJOR PRODUCERS OF IMPORTANT MINERAL COMMODITIES

Published statements of the total value of the minerals extracted by different nations are of very limited utility; indeed they can be very misleading for someone primarily interested in world trade. Thus, in 1968 West Germany and the United Kingdom are found to occupy sixth and seventh places respectively in the world list of producers, well ahead of countries like Saudi Arabia, South Africa and Australia (US Bureau of Mines, 1970a). The case of the United Kingdom is particularly interesting: although she was the leading world producer of copper, high grade iron ore, tin, lead and zinc at different times in the eighteenth and nineteenth centuries, these were virtually exhausted by the time of the first world war so that, by 1968, she had become almost entirely dependent upon imports. She occupies seventh positon among the mineral producers of that year by virtue of a huge production of road metal, limestone and cement for internal consumption, and of low grade iron ore, coal and North Sea gas for home industries and domestic use. The iron ore and fuels were important in the production of manufactures (some for export), but the excess of home-produced mineral material (either crude or refined) for export was very small.

Any realistic assessment of the exchange value of national mineral extraction must therefore adopt a selective approach and in the analysis which follows, only

Table 7.1 Potential value of 20 main minerals extracted in 1965 (in US $\$10^6$ at American prices)

Mineral	Total value	Major producers	Other producers
1 Oil (crude)	32787·2	30243·0 (92·2%)	2544·2 (7·8%)
2 Iron	20402·7	16736·1 (82·0%)	3666·6 (18·0%)
3 Copper	6554·9	5667·1 (86·5%)	887·8 (13·5%)
4 Chromium	5078·1	3971·7 (78·2%)	1106·4 (21·8%)
5 Aluminium	5028·8	4336·4 (86·2%)	692·4 (13·8%)
6 Manganese	2840·9	2313·6 (81·4%)	527·3 (18·6%)
7 Tungsten (WO_3)	2823·5	2610·9 (92·5%)	212·6 (7·5%)
8 Gold	1669·0	1445·1 (86·6%)	223·9 (13·4%)
9 Zinc	1342·8	1150·3 (85·6%)	192·5 (14·4%)
10 Potash (K_2O)	990·3	920·8 (93·0%)	69·5 (7·0%)
11 Lead	854·8	603·1 (70·6%)	251·7 (29·4%)
12 Tin	794·8	606·1 (76·2%)	188·7 (23·8%)
13 Nickel	745·9	695·3 (93·3%)	50·6 (6·7%)
14 Phosphate (P_2O_5)	623·6	582·4 (93·3%)	41·2 (6·7%)
15 Platinum group	464·5	455·6 (98·1%)	8·9 (1·9%)
16 Molybdenum	349·2	343·2 (98·3%)	6·0 (1·7%)
17 Uranium (U_3O_8)*	337·6	332·9 (98·5%)	4·7 (1·5%)
18 Silver	326·3	206·7 (63·5%)	119·6 (36·5%)
19 Mercury	167·1	158·0 (94·6%)	9·1 (5·4%)
20 Cobalt	59·1	56·0 (94·8%)	3·1 (5·2%)
	84241·1	73434·3 (87·2%)	10806·8 (12·8%)

*Non-communist countries only

20 commodities are considered (table 7·1). These are the 16 most important metals along with uranium, oil, phosphate and potash. It is realized that such a selection must be arbitrary in some degree, but careful reflection seems to indicate that no serious distortion or misrepresentation of the world picture results from confining one's attentions in this way. The 20 materials chosen are all of industrial and commercial importance and are in great demand on the world market. Others such as antimony, arsenic, asbestos and diamonds might have been included, but since no single country which is not already a major producer of one of the selected 20 commodities is a major producer of any one of these four, no serious misrepresentation seems likely to result from their omission. Obviously a case could also be made for the inclusion of coal, salt and gypsum, but relatively little of these bulky commodities enters international trade. Consequently, although all three are of very great importance to the countries possessing them as bases for internal industrial development, they cannot be regarded as important direct earners of foreign exchange: broadly speaking they

have been the means by which developed countries have been able to raise themselves to a Stage 4 economy, and by which they maintain themselves at that level.

Data for 1965 have been selected for the purpose of illustration. This is not because the pattern or volume of mineral production in that particular year is in any way peculiar, merely that comprehensive figures for mineral extraction, grade and price, as well as for cereal prices, are readily available. In the cases of all the commodities considered here, with the exception of oil, it is the weight of refinable material extracted from the ground that has been taken into account. With aluminium, chromium, cobalt, copper, iron, mercury, manganese, molybdenum, lead, nickel, platinum, tin, zinc, silver and gold, this is the actual metal; with tungsten and uranium it is the oxide (WO_3 and U_3O_8 respectively); phosphate is assessed on the basis of P_2O_5 content and potash on its K_2O equivalent,[5] while oil has been assessed as "crude oil".

Every country which produced 5 per cent or more of the world production of at least one of the 20 selected commodities in 1965 has been regarded as a "major producer"; indeed, for some of the more widely distributed materials, countries producing less than 5 per cent have also been included. The "major producers" as listed here accounted for 87·2 per cent of the world potential income from these materials (table 7·1) and one can feel confident that no significant producer has been overlooked.

On this basis 65 countries emerge as major producers of at least one commodity (appendix V), and the list reveals several striking features (table 7·2). The pre-eminence of the two superpowers overshadows all, with the USSR well ahead of the USA and with no other country producing even one third as much as either of them. The two taken together account for more than 43 per cent of the total world potential value and, if this is added to the value of the production of Canada, South Africa and Australia, one has 52·6 per cent of the world total.

Another significant point is that six of the first twelve countries in the list — Venezuela, Kuwait, Saudi Arabia, Iran, Iraq and Libya — occupy their positions solely because of oil production. Of the six, only Venezuela is a major producer of another mineral commodity. Between them they account for over 18·3 per cent of the total value. In 1965, therefore, eleven countries produced 70·9 per cent of the potential value of these 20 commodities.

[5] It is realized that these methods of assessment have distinct limitations. In particular the *total* metal content of each ore has been taken and a value assigned to it; but it should be understood that no smelting or refining process is completely efficient so that these values, to a greater or lesser extent, must be in excess of what could actually be realized. There is also a particular problem in the case of chromium: it has been assessed here as chromium metal and its actual trade value is much exaggerated as a consequence. This is because a large percentage of the chromite mined is used as refractory or chemical material: elemental chromium is not extracted from it so that the metal content does not achieve its full potential value. A further difficulty has been encountered with regard to aluminium and phosphate. The exact proportion of refined mineral content in the bauxite and the rock phosphate is not made explicit by the statistics available. The aluminium content of the former has thus been assessed at 25 per cent and the P_2O_5 content of the latter at 33 per cent, these being approximations to the world averages for these materials in the 1960s.

Table 7.2 The producing countries of 20 selected minerals in order of potential value of refined product

Country	Potential value of product ($10⁶)	Equivalent in nutrition units (10⁶)
1 USSR	17038·0	851·9
2 USA	14718·0	735·9
3 Venezuela	4498·9	224·9
4 Canada	3983·8	199·2
5 China	2410·2	120·5
6 South Africa	2407·9	120·4
7 Kuwait	2286·7	114·3
8 Saudi Arabia	2108·6	105·4
9 Iran	1991·2	99·6
10 France	1707·5	85·4
11 Iraq	1349·8	67·5
12 Libya	1234·5	61·7
13 Jamaica	1157·6	57·9
14 Sweden	1148·8	57·4
15 India	1135·1	56·7
16 Brazil	1062·2	53·1
17 Zambia	903·1	45·2
18 Chile	781·2	39·1
19 Liberia	682·1	34·1
20 Australia	660·1	33·0
21 Turkey	587·0	29·3
22 Surinam	583·5	29·2
23 Rhodesia	572·5	28·6
24 Mexico	563·7	28·2
25 Algeria	557·5	27·9
26 Indonesia	503·0	25·1
27 Zaire	439·3	22·0
28 Peru	407·3	20·4
29 Guyana	390·4	20·0
30 West Germany	372·5	18·6
31 Albania	353·7	17·7
32 Argentina	293·4	14·7
33 Yugoslavia	283·3	14·2
34 United Arab Emirates	283·0	14·1
35 Nigeria	283·0	14·1
36 UK	275.5	13.8
37 Malaysia	254.1	12.7
38 North Korea	252.2	12.6
39 Guinea	250.3	12.5
40 Qatar	232.7	11.6
41 Colombia	225.0	11.2
42 South Korea	220.8	11.0
43 Gabon	219.2	11.0
44 Japan	207.8	10.4
45 Hungary	197.2	9.9
46 Bolivia	184.6	9.2
47 Greece	168.7	8.4

Country	Potential value of product ($\$10^6$)	Equivalent in nutrition units (10^6)
48 Trinidad	146·7	7·3
49 East Germany	139·0	6·9
50 New Caledonia	90·7	4·5
51 Morocco	86·4	4·3
52 Portugal	81·0	4·0
53 Thailand	75·2	3·8
54 Italy	71·2	3·6
55 Austria	58·7	2·9
56 Spain	50·3	2·5
57 Poland	48·0	2·4
58 Bulgaria	31·6	1·6
59 Cuba	29·8	1·5
60 Ghana	26·4	1·3
61 Tunisia	24·8	1·2
62 Philippines	15·2	0·8
63 Nauru	11·9	0·6
64 Vietnam	8·4	0·4
65 Togo	7·7	0·4

A further observation which may surprise is that, were it not for these six large oil producers, Jamaica would occupy seventh place on the list. The position of the world's large bauxite producers is often overlooked, but an assessment of mineral potential value leaves one in no doubt about the significance of the production of countries like Jamaica, Surinam, Guyana and Guinea. They remain impoverished, but if they possessed energy resources (or the capital to develop hydro-electric power and other reserves), the establishment of refineries could transform their average income levels.

A number of countries in the list, which produce other minerals,[6] are in a similar position.

The nations of Africa (less South Africa), in 1965 accounted for 7·2 per cent of the total world value, those of Asia (less the USSR) for 18·9 per cent, and those of Latin America for 14·0 per cent — a total of 40·1 per cent. When one reflects that these commodities are all vital materials for industry, agriculture and commerce, and that Europe (less the USSR) accounted for one 6·7 per cent of their total world value in that year, the strategic plight of much of the industrialized world is seen in sharp relief.

Of course, a great variety of real situations lies behind this theoretical conspectus. At the head of the list the two superpowers not only converted *potential* value into *actual* value, but also fabricated and consumed the refined mineral materials in Stage 4 economies. In the USSR the emphasis was on the

[6] As already indicated chromium is an exception. The metal content of much of the chromite never achieves its full potential value so that Turkey, Rhodesia and Albania, who feature as main producers, are all overdignified in the list (table 7·2). Even South Africa would probably come below Kuwait, Saudi Arabia and Iran if a more realistic value were assigned to its large chromite production (309,297 mt).

production of capital goods for industrial growth; in the USA it was on consumer goods and on capital goods to produce more consumer goods. In other privileged nations such as Canada, Australia and (in part) South Africa, the picture was more diverse: a large percentage of the extracted commodities was brought to its Stage 3 potential, indeed some was fabricated; but a large excess was exported in a refined, partly refined and raw state. In Brazil, India and China similar levels of development were found, though in very different social milieus; in Zambia much of the material (mainly copper) achieved its Stage 3 potential before export, and the same can be said for Chile; but in Jamaica, Surinam and Guyana only a very small percentage of the aluminium taken from the ground was brought to Stage 2 (alumina) before export, and only a negligible amount was exported as metal. The position of large oil producers such as Kuwait, Saudi Arabia and Iran is a unique one as well as being highly advantageous: oil refining processes are comparatively inexpensive and involve only a small reduction in bulk, so that the crude material extracted from the ground commands a high price and the exporters of crude oil cannot reasonably be regarded as Stage 1 producers comparable to the exporters of metallic ores.

MINERAL INCOME IN NUTRITION UNITS PER CAPITA

In the hypothetical country considered earlier, $10 million, at 1965 USA prices, purchased 529,000 nutrition units in cereal form. In view of the approximations that have to be made, any claims to precision would be unrealistic, and it seems reasonable to assess a mineral income of $10 million as being equivalent to a round half million nutrition units. On this basis the potential nutrition exchange capacity of a considerable minority of the nations of the earth is found to be substantial (table 7·2). Given that the cereals were available and that the nations concerned had required them, 29 had the potential to import sufficient for 20 million people or more. A further 15 nations had the potential exchange for between 10 and 20 millions, and another 13 for between two and 10 millions. At the foot of the list Vietnam and Togo each had a potential sufficient to feed 400,000.

At the other end of the scale are the nations which do not appear in the list of major producers. As far as can be ascertained there are a few like Chad, Malawi, Somalia, El Salvador and Paraguay whose production of the 20 commodities in 1965 was nil, and a substantial number who produced negligible amounts. They fall into two distinct groups: on the one hand there are industrialized countries like Denmark, Belgium, the Netherlands and Switzerland with a high material standard of living; on the other there is quite a long list of countries, populated in the main by poor peasants and pastoralists — Mali, Niger, Upper Volta, Central African Republic, Mozambique, Yemen, Sri Lanka, Khmer Republic, Laos, Guatemala, Costa Rica and Panama. Clearly the implications of a lack of important mineral production are rather different for the two groups, but they share the fundamental disability: none of the nations in either group receives the annual bonus which inevitably benefits countries possessing mineral resources.

The most realistic way of viewing potential mineral income, however, is

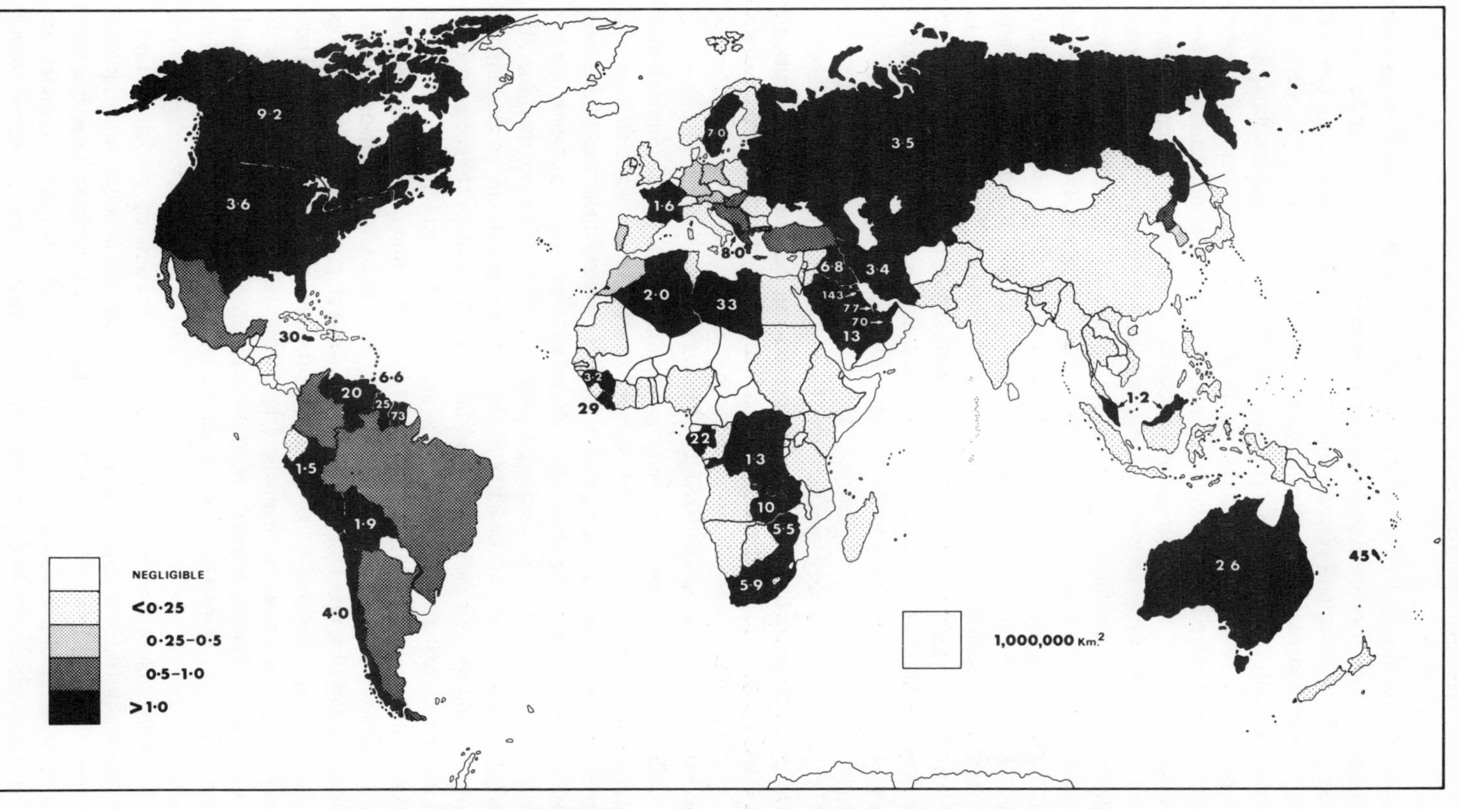

7·1 The potential value of national income from 20 mineral commodities in 1965 (in nutrition units per capita)

against the background of population. A country with a very large mineral income but a vast population may derive far less benefit per head than one with a much smaller income and very few people. Thus Gabon, Guinea and Trinidad, though well down the list of producers, nevertheless have large per capita incomes because of their small populations (figure 7·1), while China, India, Indonesia and Brazil, though high on the list, have much lower per capita income. Presenting the facts in this way also puts the enormous mineral production of the USSR and the USA in perspective: although 3·5 nutrition units per head is substantial as compared to the potential mineral income of most nations, it is far below the 9·2 per capita for Canada, the 30 for Jamaica and the 29 for Liberia. The case of Kuwait, with its tiny population, is outstanding: the 143 nutrition units per capita is far in advance of the figure for any other country. Another striking point which emerges is the way in which the potential per capita income of the large bauxite producers, Surinam, Jamaica, Guyana and Guinea (73, 30, 20 and 3·2 respectively) closely rivals that of big oil producers like Kuwait, Qatar, United Arab Emirates, Libya, Venezuela and Saudi Arabia (143, 77, 70, 33, 20 and 13 respectively). And what is true for the bauxite of Surinam is almost equally applicable to Liberian iron ore and the manganese ore of Gabon. It becomes very apparent why United Nations development schemes have laid such emphasis on mineral exploration and the provision of capital for the manufacture of mineral materials.

THE FUTURE OF NATIONAL MINERAL PRODUCTION

In the decade since 1965 no really important change in the production of important mineral commodities has occurred except that it has greatly increased. This should not surprise us, indeed it is the one thing that could have been forecast with a large measure of confidence. And unless a catastrophe of worldwide dimensions or an unprecedented social revolution occurs during the coming decade, there can be little doubt that this growth in production will continue. However, all the evidence indicates that the basic pattern of production will not change materially (chapter 6): by and large those nations which were the larger producers of important minerals in 1965 will continue to be so, and most of those whose production was small or negligible will continue in their deprived condition. Statistical probability suggests that some important discoveries will be made: between 1965 and 1975 oil beneath the North Sea and in Oman and a large copper deposit on Bougainville Island have been major additions to the world picture. But an average of three substantial acquisitions per decade between now and 2005 AD will not make a significant impact on the basic world pattern.

Obviously, nations which at the present time know of no large mineral deposits within their frontiers, would be very unwise to anticipate important discoveries. The dates at which established sources of supply will cease to yield material of acceptable grade is a matter far more worthy of careful consideration and of deep concern. In the immediate future, however, those countries which possess the known mineral reserves would seem to have distinct advantages — in some cases perhaps even commanding ones.

8

The Wealth of Nations

The basic aim in preceding chapters has been to provide some measure of the organic productivity of the nations along with an assessment of the potential food-earning capacity of their mineral production. A number of approximations have had to be made but there seem reasonable grounds for feeling that these data provide an adequate basis for a conflated statement for each nation, so that all the countries of the world can be assigned to broad resource categories.

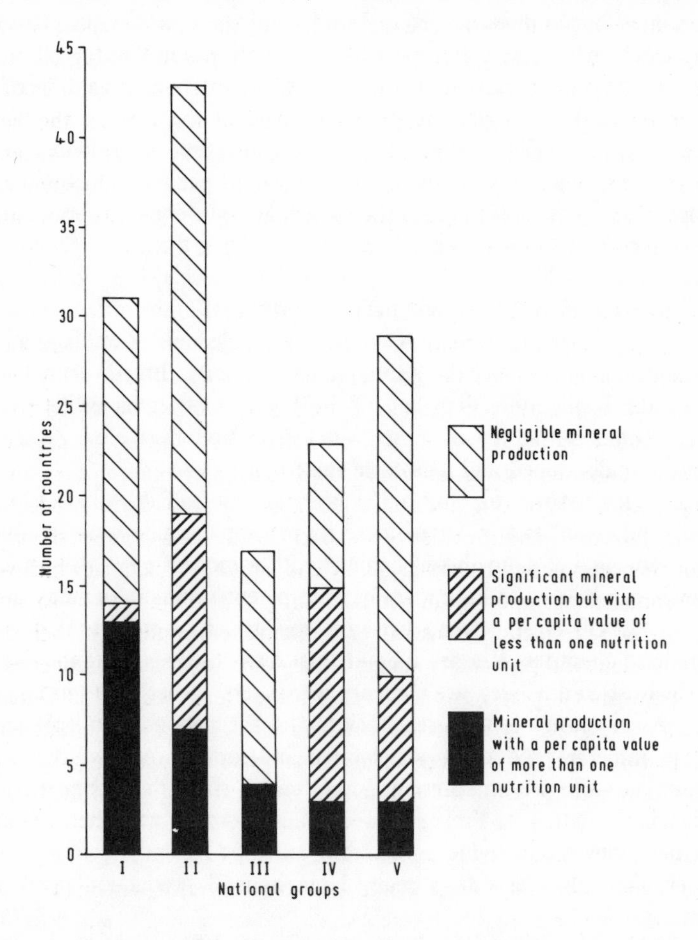

8·1 Potential national income from 20 mineral commodities (1965) in the countries of Groups I to V (in nutrition units per capita)

Whether or not such groupings are a true reflection of national well-being or "wealth", either now or in the future, will then require discussion.

A CLASSIFICATION OF NATIONS

In 1965 the land areas of the earth comprised 143 independent nations and major colonial territories. These can be differentiated into five groups (figure 8·1) on the basis of their potential per capita net primary productivity (PPCNPP). Group I contains those countries with over 100 mt per capita, Group II those with between 20 and 100, Group IV those with between 10 and 20, and Group V those with less than 10. The middle group, Group III, comprises all those countries which have a relatively high PPCNPP but whose general climatic and hydrological characteristics preclude the development of substantial agricultural production.

There are 31 countries in Group I and, with the exception of Canada and New Zealand, they all lie either partially or entirely within the tropics. It is also significant that almost half of them have very important mineral production (figure 8·2): in 13 of them the potential value of the 20 selected minerals (chapter 7) was equivalent to more than one nutrition unit per head in 1965, and in a fourteenth, Brazil, it was equivalent to 0·5 units per head. It would appear, therefore, that almost half the countries which are best endowed organically are also very fortunate in their mineral resources. Among them are technologically advanced countries like Canada, Australia and Venezuela, but the majority are industrially undeveloped: the potential per capita value of the mineral production of countries like Gabon, Surinam, Guyana, New Caledonia, Zambia and Liberia is enormous, and that of Bolivia, Zaire, Guinea, Peru and Brazil very substantial. On the other hand, more than half of these 31 countries have little potential mineral income and all 17 of these, with the exception of New Zealand, are industrially undeveloped and located in the tropics.

Of the 41 countries in Group II, again almost half (19) have significant mineral production, but in 12 of these its per capita value was less than one nutrition unit in 1965. In these countries with a moderate PPCNPP, therefore, only seven can be said to have a really large potential mineral income per head (figure 8·3). Of these seven, two are the superpowers, three more are industrialized countries (Rhodesia, South Africa and Sweden), and the remaining two (Malaysia and Chile) are primary producers rather than industrialized nations. As in Group I, the great majority of the nations with only small or negligible mineral production are located in tropical regions, but whereas European countries are unrepresented in Group I, six of them appear here: the Scandinavian countries of Finland, Sweden and Norway, with their remarkably similar per capita productivities, are accompanied by Ireland, Spain and Greece. However, the only one with a really large mineral production per capita is Sweden.

The countries in Group III, like those in Groups I and II, all have a PPCNPP of more than 20 mt but, for obvious reasons, they cannot be placed in the same

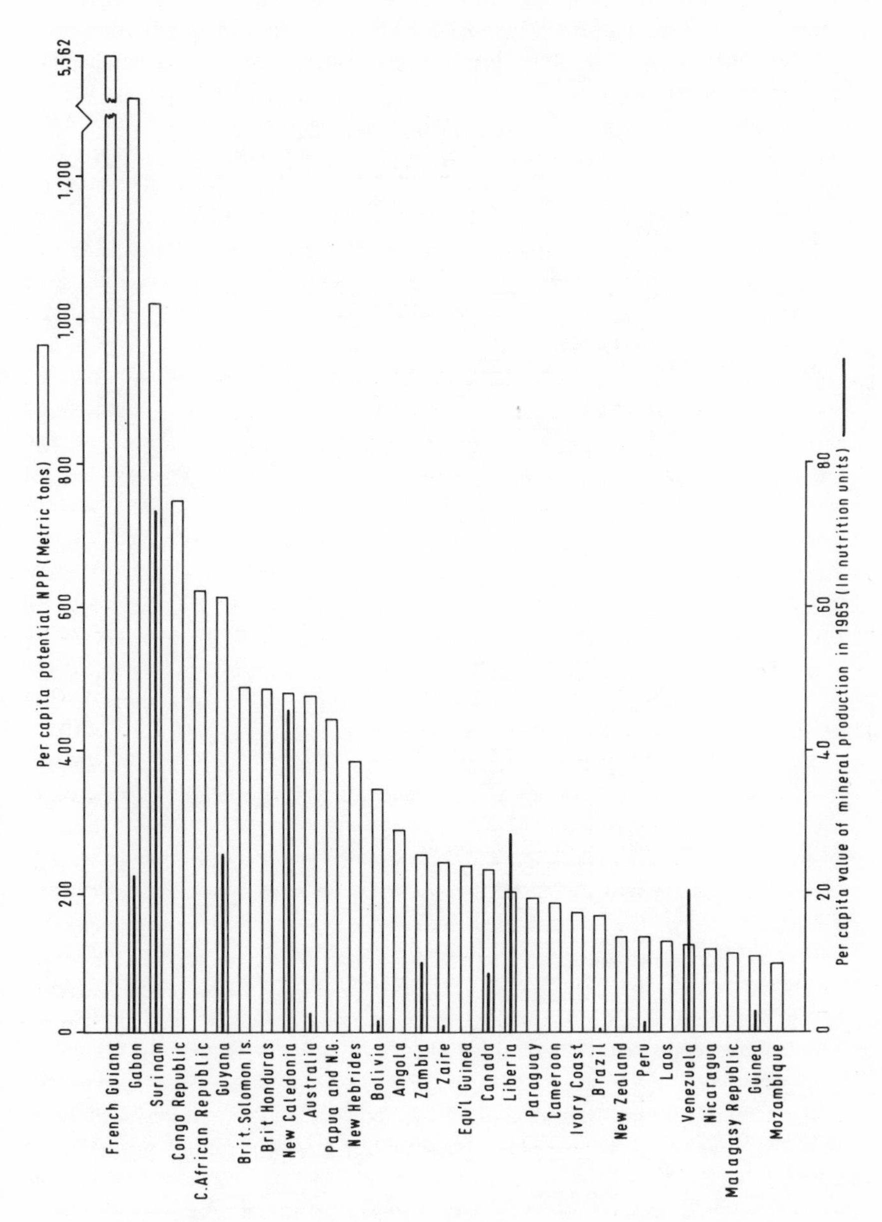

8·2 Potential organic and mineral production in the countries of Group I

categories as other countries of high organic potential. The nations in Group III occupy territories which are predominantly desert, semi-desert or seasonally dry scrub forest, with the exception of Iceland which is almost entirely treeless tundra. They have a high PPCNPP, not because their wild ecosystems are very productive, but because of small populations relative to area: their environments which, for one reason or another, are hostile to agriculture, have dictated this.

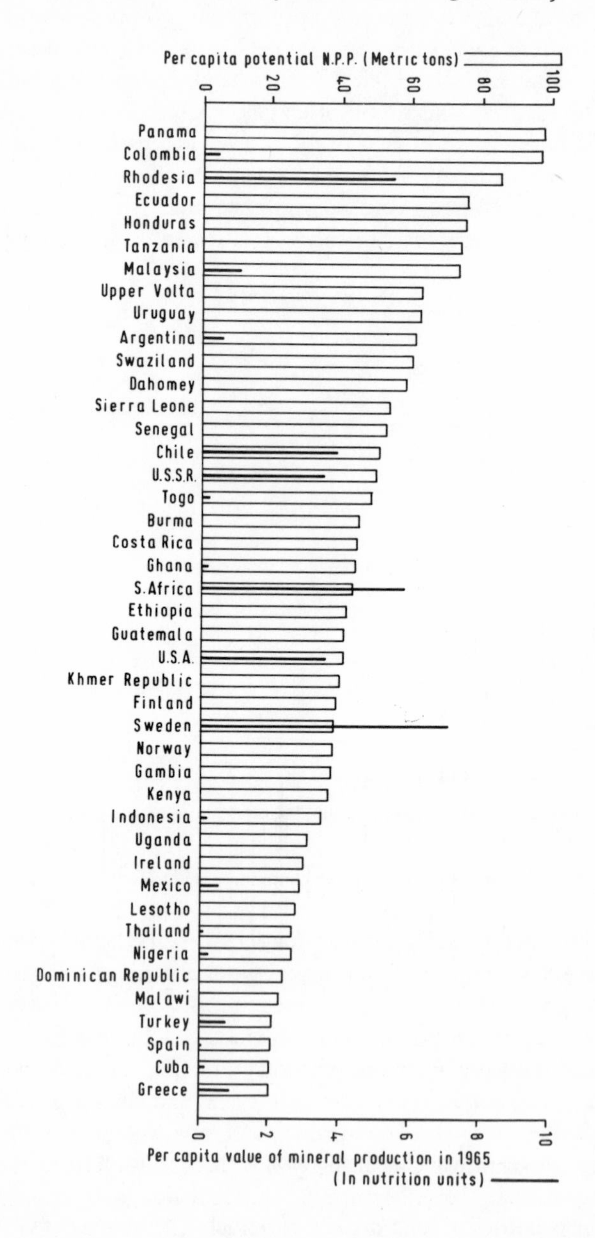

8·3 Potential organic and mineral production in the countries of Group II

The seventeen countries in this group (figure 8·4) have a variety of economies: ten are dry tropical countries with negligible mineral production and very little industrial development, while four were already major oil producers in 1965. Of the remaining three, Oman has become an important oil producer since 1965 and the former Spanish Sahara has begun to exploit its phosphate deposits since that date; the economy of Iceland, on the other hand, is dependent basically on the harvest of the sea. It is this group of countries which illustrates clearly the dangers of taking too simplistic a view of the concept of "national PPCNPP": on the face of it, they are all capable of producing large amounts of organic material per head but in reality, so large a percentage of their areas is either too dry or too cold for cropping, that permanent agricultural settlement is virtually precluded.

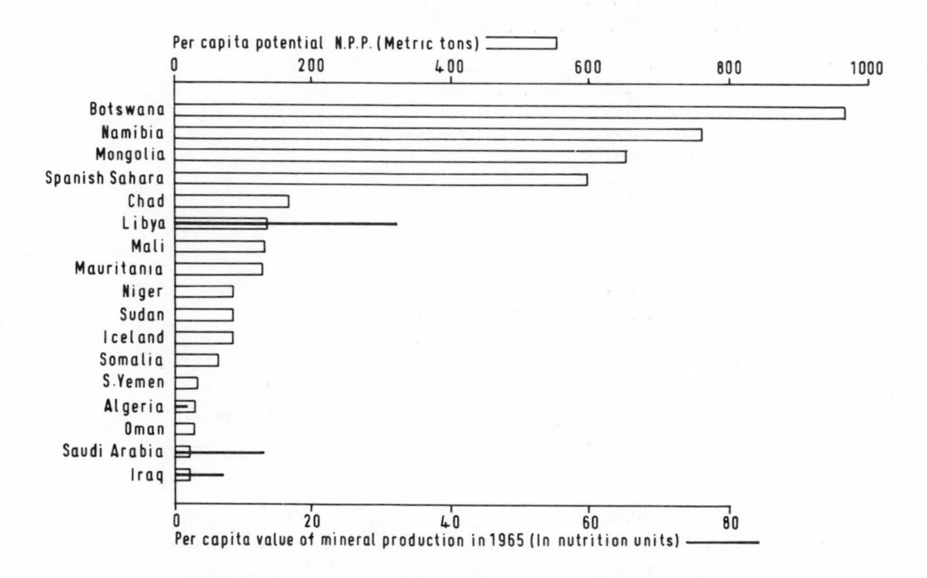

8·4 Potential organic and mineral production in the countries of Group III

Group IV comprises 23 countries with the fairly low PPCNPP of between 10 and 20 mt (figure 8·5). Fifteen of them have significant mineral production but only three — Albania, France and Iran — are really important producers. Of the 12 European nations in the group, only Albania and France had a mineral production valued at more than one nutrition unit per capita in 1965, but Hungary (0·96), Yugoslavia (0·68), Portugal (0·42) and Austria (0·39) all had substantial production. It is also noteworthy that China, with a PPCNPP of 10·8 mt, just manages to achieve inclusion here, but that the value of its very large mineral production, when shared among its vast population, only amount to 0·16 nutrition units per capita.

Finally, Group V comprises all those countries with a PPCNPP of less than 10 mt. The organic productivity of most of the 29 political units included here

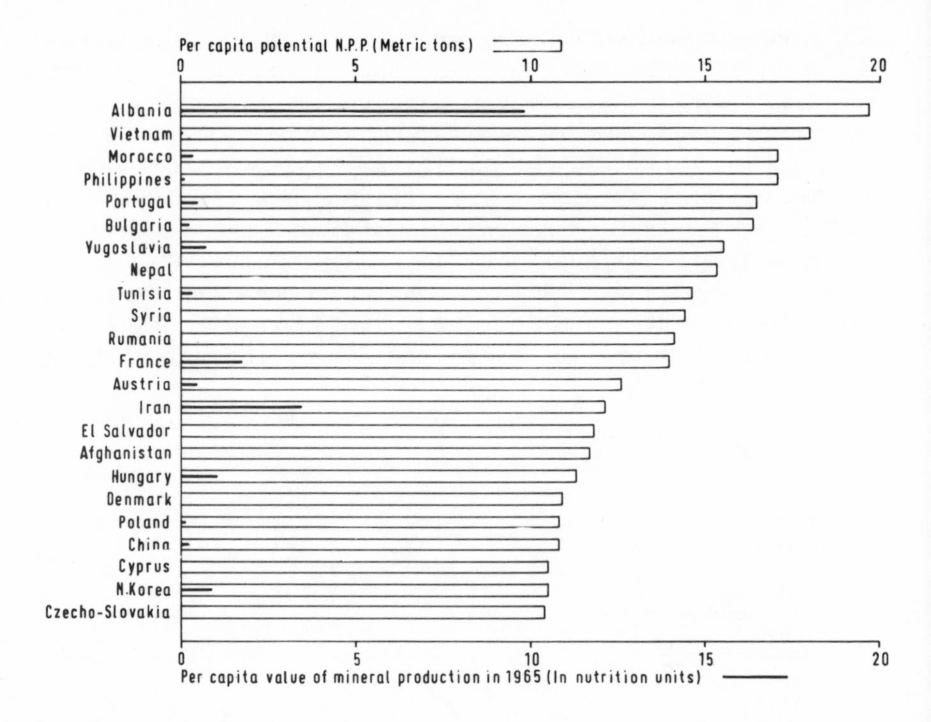

8·5 Potential organic and mineral production in the countries of Group IV

(figure 8·6) has already been analysed in chapter 5. It is also worth noting their small mineral income: only ten are significant producers of the 20 minerals and only three — Kuwait, Qatar and Jamaica — produced a potential mineral value of more than one nutrition unit per capita in 1965. Of the remainder only East Germany, West Germany, South Korea and the United Kingdom had substantial production. Seventeen of the 29 are heavily populated countries in Europe and Asia.

THE SIGNIFICANCE OF A RANKING OF NATIONS ON A RESOURCE BASIS

This ranking of nations may seem very unconvincing on first consideration. Is the suggestion really being made that, in the relatively near future, the material well-being of individual people will correspond to the relative position of their countries within the classification outlined? Such a view of the future may well appear unthinkable, if not outrageous, in the light of conventional criteria. We have become conditioned to a division of the nations of the earth into "developed" and "underdeveloped" — the former having a high gross national product (GNP) and the latter a low one; the former, generally speaking, being concentrated in Europe, North America and Australasia, and the latter in Africa, Asia and Latin America. And it cannot be denied that there is a great deal of evidence to justify this view of the world: even those "developed" countries

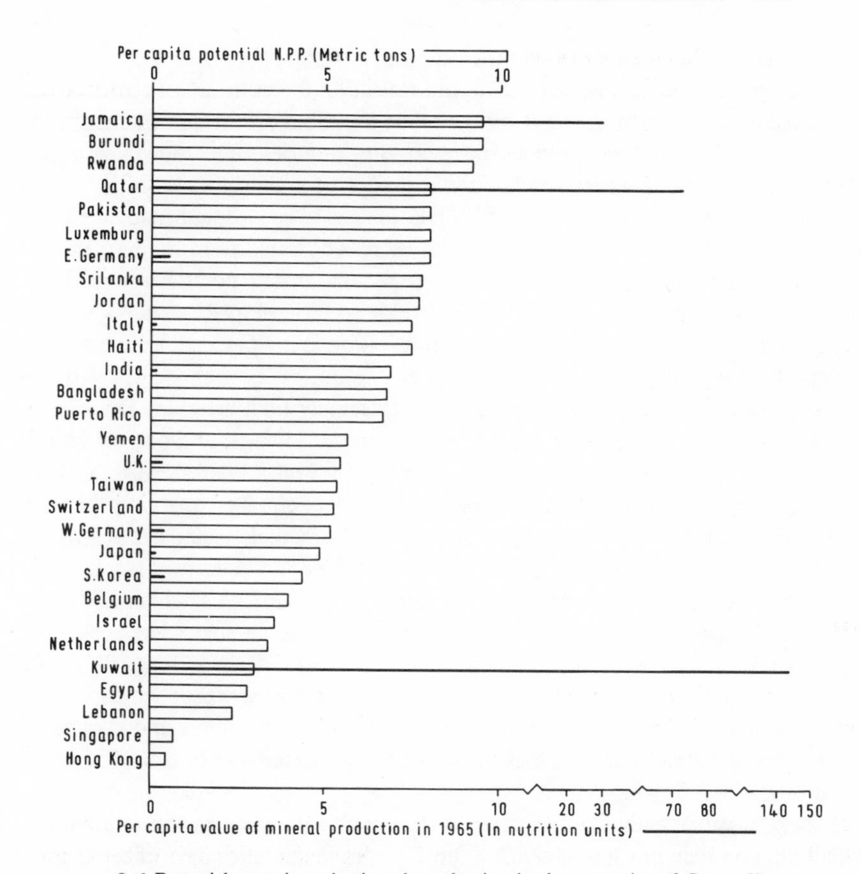

8·6 Potential organic and mineral production in the countries of Group V

which seem to have fallen on hard times in the 1970s still have enormous material emancipation comparatively speaking: their consumption of sophisticated manufactured goods is very large, and they export great quantities of manufactured goods, technical services, industrial capital and insurance to pay for their food imports. Can it be possible to take any classification of the nations seriously when it places Zambia, with its low GNP and one of the highest infant mortality rates in the world, in the top bracket, and countries like the Netherlands, the United Kingdom and Japan in the lowest one?

Incredulity is understandable, and certainly no suggestion is being made that the people of Zambia will shortly enjoy a material standard of living similar to that at present experienced in the United Kingdom. But before dismissing such a classification as unrealistic, if not grotesque, one should reflect upon a selection of items from the pages of history. The opinion of the Athenians about the peoples to the north and northwest of them in the year 450 BC cannot have been very high: they did not deal in concepts such as "GNP" but they certainly committed themselves to comments which reflected adversely on the intellectual and material achievements of the less "developed" people of their world — and with some justification. Similarly, one can reflect on the attitudes of settled West Europeans some two hundred years ago to the log cabin dwellers of Canada, and, with even more immediate relevance, on the attitudes of car-owning urban populations in the Western world only a quarter of a century ago to the camel drivers of the eastern Arabian Desert! The centres of wealth and influence have changed with the passing years, and with increasing rapidity in modern times.

There seem substantial grounds for suspecting that a point has now been reached where the high GNPs of badly endowed "developed" nations are no longer a true reflection of "wealth". An illustration at the personal level will help to clarify this point. Most people in Western countries, even those of relatively modest means, are capable of living at an extremely high standard for a short time. If we sell our house and furniture, cash all our savings, and borrow on the strength of any credit we may have had, we can go on a luxury cruise, eating, drinking and generally indulging ourselves at a level equal to anything that has ever been possible in the history of the world. Our actual "standard of living" over this period could not be excelled. But one does not refer to a person who does this kind of thing as "wealthy": "wealth" is something which is clearly sustainable. On this issue there seems no reason to doubt that what applies to personal circumstances also applies to national affairs. Regardless of investments, skills and employment structure, can a nation whose whole way of life is dependent upon mechanical energy, metals, plastics, fibres and chemicals be regarded as "wealthy" if it has to import almost all of these things and a great deal of its food as well?

There may be many still inclined to answer this question in the affirmative. After all, one only needs to go back a few decades to the latter days of the British Empire to encounter an economic philosophy which maintained unreservedly that the most admirable kind of terrestrial arrangement would be one in which large parts of the earth's surface, particularly in the tropics, would be devoted to cash crop production, because it could be done more cheaply there than elsewhere. The other part of the world (either because of natural advantages or existing circumstances) would concentrate on the production of manufactures. The two would then co-exist indefinitely, in a state of constantly increasing material welfare, inextricably interdependent and locked together in a massive trading system. This view of the future, of course, merely projected a trend which was already well established: it envisaged nothing which did not seem to have been proved feasible already.

An arrangement which can be made to work over a period of a few decades, however, does not necessarily provide the basis for an entire world economy in perpetuity. World trading such as this, on a massive scale, has now been given a fair trial for about a century and, in addition to the very weighty ecological objections to it, there are two very significant economic trends which should cause the most unecologically inclined to have grave doubts about its future. First, in recent years the world prices of food and industrial raw materials, both mineral and organic, have increased far more rapidly than those of manufactured goods (table 8·1). This seems to indicate fairly clearly that scarcity of the essentials for life and for manufacturing industry is beginning, inexorably, to make itself felt. Any argument that the trend is merely a short-term swing caused by inevitable fluctuations in the availability of a few basic commodities is without foundation: it is apparent across the whole range of primary production, and it is something which has not occurred previously in the modern world. Nor can it be said to arise out of artificial manipulations of the money market: the powerful nations engaging in world trade are on the whole the industrialized ones, and it is they who are in the best position to manipulate prices. Ever since the beginning of the Industrial Revolution they have tried to ensure that the relative pricing of industrial goods and primary commodities has not been disadvantageous to the former, and only in times of war and famine has local, temporary scarcity caused relatively high prices for food and raw materials. Even in times of depression, when the prices of industrial goods fell, those of primary commodities on the world market declined equally if not even more precipitously.

The second disturbing trend is that the amount of agricultural produce entering world trade, relative to the amount of other materials, is steadily declining. This has now been going on for at least two decades and is shown very clearly by world export figures for the period 1959–70 (table 8·2). This fall from 29·8 per cent to 19·9 per cent in the relative *value* of agricultural exports occurred during a period in which the price of agricultural commodities relative to all other materials remained fairly constant (table 8·1); consequently it cannot be said to exaggerate the fall in the relative *quantity* of agricultural produce which entered the world market. Although one must exercise caution when drawing inferences from these trade figures about the actual conditions in the exporting countries, it seems reasonable to assume that, taking the world as a whole, the production of cash crops for export is not keeping pace with the production of other exports, and that this may be due in great part to the fact that the growing populations in the countries concerned are consuming a larger percentage of the produce of their soil. There is certainly plenty of independent evidence to support this view.

THE WEALTHY AND THE POTENTIALLY WEALTHY

There is thus clear evidence that the primary-producer nations are occupying an increasingly strong position in the world, despite their low GNPs and the poor conditions of material welfare that are still to be found in so many of them. On the other hand, the inherent weaknesses of manufacturing countries with small PPCNPPs and negligible mineral reserves are equally obvious. However, between the extremes to be found in Groups I and V there is clearly a great diversity of resource basis.

The fundamental strength of countries such as Canada, Australia and Venezuela requires no emphasis: their organic basis is so sound that no matter how profligate they may be in its exploitation, their inherent capacity for primary

Table 8.1 World export price indexes (1963 = 100) (from UN, 1974)

	1958	1963	1965	1966	1967	1968	1969	1970	1971	1972	1973
All commodities	100	100	103	105	105	104	107	113	119	128	153
Food	103	100	103	105	104	101	104	111	117	132	194
Agricultural non-food	99	100	103	104	96	96	101	101	105	120	181
All minerals	108	100	104	104	103	102	104	111	127	141	180
Non-ferrous base metals	92	100	135	156	142	150	175	180	154	154	211

Table 8.2 The world value of agricultural exports in relation to that of total exports (in $\$10^9$ US) (from FAO, 1973)

	1959–61 (average)	1962–4 (average)	1967–9 (average)	1970
Agricultural exports	37·5	43·2	53·1	62·3
Total exports	125·7	155·8	242·0	312·7
Agricultural/total	29·8%	27·7%	21·9%	19·9%

production will support substantially larger populations than are carried at the present time. (Whether they will gain anything at all by attempting to do this is another matter.) Furthermore, they have far more mineral reserves than the great majority of nations and, if they so wish, this will provide them with the capability to import exotic materials from the rest of the world for another two or three decades. On an equally sound footing, though not profiting from the fact at the present time, are countries like Gabon, Surinam, Guyana, New Caledonia, Zambia, Liberia and Guinea. Given a minimum of internal development along with a world in which some international trading and large-scale manufacturing still took place, it is difficult to see how such well-endowed political units could not continue to be capable of supporting their present populations, and probably considerably increased ones. In spite of their apparent lack of significant mineral resources, it is also difficult to imagine that countries such as Congo Republic, Central African Republic, Cameroon and Ivory Coast could not be capable of supporting their present populations, and more, in the decades ahead.

Similar points can be made about many of the nations in Group II. The fundamentally strong resource base of the USSR, South Africa, the USA and Sweden is very obvious, but what is not always recognized by those who base their views on conventional criteria is that, potentially, countries such as Chile are in the same category. Moreover, among those which do not have significant mineral production but whose PPCNPP is quite large, are to be found not only Norway and Finland but also a substantial number of humid tropical countries who are usually regarded as "impoverished".

THE POOR AND THE POTENTIALLY POOR

It may seem a cruel quirk of fate that, whereas 14 of the 31 countries in Group I have a large supplementary income from minerals, only three of the 29 with low PPCNPP in Group V are similarly endowed. But this is not entirely fortuitous. In the first place a number of states like Hong Kong, Singapore and Lebanon are in Group V only because they are small and densely populated: the became discrete territories with a greater or lesser degree of autonomy because they were important trading centres with populations largely dependent on commerce. It would have been a very fortunate accident if such small territories had chanced to contain important mineral deposits. Secondly, about half of the countries in Group V only because they are small and densely populated: they became discrete long period so that their former mineral deposits have been depleted to insignificance. The small per capita production of the 20 selected minerals in the United Kingdom, West Germany and East Germany is not entirely due to unkind geological godfathers, or even to large populations at the present time: in great part it is because of many centuries of exploitation and depletion.

Whatever the reasons, the fact remains that about a quarter of the world's population lives in countries which not only require large imports of organic materials but also have little mineral production to supplement the products of their vegetation. Almost half these countries are among the most heavily industrialized in the world and thus require huge quantities of mineral material to maintain their economies. One might add that there are a further seven European countries in Group IV whose per capita production of minerals is very small or negligible.

In the light of this, again one asks whether these industrialized countries can be regarded as "wealthy". Without exception their allegedly productive agricultural systems are utterly dependent on imported feed grains, fish meal and fertilizer; their factories would grind to a halt but for imported minerals and fibres; and their entire commercial and social fabric would disintegrate were it not for complex transport systems dependent on imports of mineral oil. The classic response to this point has been that it is *because* they are so "wealthy" that they can function in this way and will continue to do so; indeed the entire burden of Adam Smith's thesis was that the wealthy nations are those which utilize their labour in an increasingly complex (i.e. "efficient") way. Later economists seem to have inferred from this that if these countries continue to use their ingenuity to produce manufactures that are much sought after by the nations who produce the raw materials, then the world commercial system will continue to operate to the benefit of both. Indeed, this view may seem to be supported by the point already made (chapter 7) that those industrially undeveloped countries which produce much of the mineral material and fibres may still find it more advantageous to import sophisticated manufactured goods in preference to attempting to produce their own.

Although this may well be true, it will not necessarily happen. Just because an industrially undeveloped country exports all its modest production of metal as such, and would like to import machine tools and manufactured consumer goods in exchange, does no automatically imply that it will be in a position to do so. One of the more regrettable aspects of the oil problems of the early 1970s has been that non-industrial countries have found it almost impossible to purchase sufficient liquid fuel to maintain their supply and communications networks; in some cases, even their meagre infrastructure of government and services has been threatened. If fuel shortages, accompanied in some cases by food shortages, are to be the common experience of these countries during future decades, it is hard to imagine how they will be able to find sufficient foreign exchange for expensive imports of manufactured goods. Indeed, leaders such as Julius Nyerere of Tanzania have already had the wisdom to disclaim any intention of following the "Western" road along which they would be compelled either to import manufactured goods on a massive scale, or to construct an industrial base with which to produce such goods. Even those technologically undeveloped countries with substantial mineral production may have severe food problems because of their rapidly expanding populations, and may feel impelled to trade their products in directions where the most profitable food bargains are to be made. It is not difficult to visualize a world in which scarcity of primary products caused a great increase in bilateral agreements between those who have vital commodities to offer.

THE SQUANDERING OF RESOURCE ADVANTAGES

On the other hand, it would be misleading to suggest that the position of big mineral producers is one of unqualified advantage. In the short term the benefits may be substantial but the short term may be very short indeed. One can appreciate that the temptations of a brief bonanza could lead a nation into a predicament far more unhappy than anything experienced by one suffering permanently from dearth, with its economy and aspirations attuned accordingly. The oil producers of the Middle East and North Africa probably provide the extreme manifestation of subjection to bonanza temptations. With enormous annual income from petroleum there is every incentive to use up royalties in the construction of vast urban appendages to the oil wells in these arid and semi-arid environments. Already in the early 1970s the annual rates of population growth in Kuwait, Iraq and Libya were 8·2 per cent, 3·4 per cent and 3·1 per cent respectively. When income seems almost limitless, the task of importing almost every scrap of food, every drop of water and all the other necessities for a large and growing urban community in the middle of a desert may appear to be quite normal and rational. But when that income is derived almost entirely from a wasting asset, which within a generation will dry up almost completely if exploited at the maximum rate, those most closely concerned can surely be expected to reflect on the dangers of unbridled economic growth. Consequently, if a nation in this kind of situation proposes to slow down exploitation, this should earn approbation rather than vilification and threat of reprisal.

To a greater or lesser degree all relatively undeveloped countries whose economies lean heavily on one or two types of mineral are faced with the same basic choice as the Arab oil producers; the latter are regarded as extreme cases only because their organic basis is so very slender.

Nor should the best endowed among the nations delude themselves that, by virtue of their natural resources, they are automatically immune to serious resource problems. The possession of such an advantage may be helpful in the decades ahead, but no resource base, no matter how bountiful, can shield a nation from the consequences of economic and political blindness. Unfortunately, the most blatant kinds of folly have often gone unrecognized, and still do so at the present time. One of the most striking examples is the overdependence on petroleum and natural gas which has developed since the second world war. In countries with a very weak resource base this could prove to be sheer suicide, but the signs are growing that even in well endowed ones it could turn out to be disastrous. Sweden provides a particularly good illustration. With a relatively small population, sound organic base, and huge reserves of high grade iron ore, she almost certainly has the soundest resource foundations of any country in Europe outside the Soviet Union. But Sweden has negligible deposits of fossil fuel and so, in order to keep in the mainstream of twentieth-century technological development and to achieve a standard of material welfare equalled in few other places, she has become dependent on petroleum imports to a degree which some illustrious critics find frightening (Lovins, 1975, pp.x–xi; foreword by Hannes Alfven, Nobel Laureate in physics).

The case of the USA, though it has developed differently, is now similar in a number of ways to that of Sweden. Despite being the first country to commercialize oil extraction, and initially possessing some of the most productive oil and gas fields in the world, the USA is now on the brink of an energy crisis of startling dimensions. In the face of demand which she seems politically incapable of controlling, and an exploitation rate which is now racing ahead of the rate of discovery of new reserves, imports from Venezuela and the Middle East are rocketing. And yet, in 1975, the price of petrol to the consumer was still less than half that in Western Europe. Overdependence on a resource which is rapidly running down, or which one has never possessed, is a kind of national madness which future generations, in retrospect, may view with incredulity as well as resentment.

The second and most widespread development which future generations may regard as unmitigated folly is that of massive urbanization. All relatively well endowed nations, and many others, have indulged in this at an ever-increasing rate during the course of the Industrial Revolution. And all those legislators, administrators and planners who continue to countenance swelling cities within their frontiers can take refuge behind the fact that conventional social science has viewed urbanization with approval as the main means by which a nation's standard of living could be raised. Even in the 1970s, in the midst of the seething problems which embroil almost all large urban areas, it is doubtful if one who regards the wholesale urbanization of society as fundamentally unsound would be regarded as anything but a heretic. And yet the basic objections to urbanization seem obvious enough: they rest on economic and social considerations and not just abstruse psychological ones. No matter how sound the organic foundations of a nation, if a large segment of its population becomes divorced from the land, after less than a generation or so it cannot quickly return to it. Even if ample land is available for the production of food and other organic necessities, urban masses cannot suddenly be settled upon it in times of dearth and stress. Quite apart from the fact that the necessary skills and attitudes have been lost, the cost of such an operation is intimidating. Borgstrom (1973) has calculated that even with a people who are predisposed to agriculture, "the cost of transferring one single family and establishing it on newly settled land amounts to at least $5,000." He goes on to point out that the total annual budget of Indonesia would scarcely be sufficient to transfer Java's annual *increase* of population to the more thinly peopled outer islands. How much more costly and hazardous would it be to transfer huge urban populations back to a rural way of life if the basis of their urban subsistence were suddenly removed!

Well endowed countries with some mineral resources are the ones most liable to suffer rapid urban accretion. The establishment of refineries, communications centres and ports is quickly followed by growth of service industries and, in a remarkably short period, hundreds of thousands may flood to them from the surrounding peasant communities. It must be admitted that in many circumstances this is difficult to prevent, but the fact remains that such vast agglomerations of people are very vulnerable. A variety of subsequent developments can cause chaos: depletion of the original resource, failure of a vital import, poor harvest in the hinterland, or merely some chance occurrence in a remote part of the world, can deprive this urban population of its main subsistence base even though the country as a whole has a relatively large PPCNPP.

Humanity now seems to be moving into a stage where resource exploitation of a sporadic and unplanned nature, though of a kind which was viable in the past, will no longer be so. Formerly, well endowed nations had sufficient elbow-room to evade the extreme punishments of resource mismanagement; the evidence indicates that the future will not be so kind.

NATIONAL OUTLOOKS

It is important, therefore, to avoid the simplistic view that the future prosperity of nations will be directly proportional to the per capita yield of their natural resources. It is certainly not a foregone conclusion which kind of nation will feel the blow most keenly if shortages of particular resources have world-wide repercussions. Indeed, the economic and social characteristics of nations are so complex that any kind of national forecasting is fraught with hazard. Nevertheless, the restrictions imposed on a nation by its resource limitations can be identified and quantified so much more rigorously than can many other aspects of its affairs that it seems useful to review the groups of countries that have been recognized above with a view to making some generalizations about their outlook and expectations.

Obviously, those industrially undeveloped countries with a negligible bonus from mineral assets, and with meagre organic resources already much depleted under relatively intense population pressure, cannot hope for anything but intensifying poverty, particularly if their populations continue to increase at the present rate. Nevertheless, the rank and file of peoples such as these have never known opulence or even a reasonably leisured and comfortable existence, nor have they any great expectations of the future. As population pressure increases and the chance of external aid decreases, one can anticipate that the general level of infant mortality will rise even higher — exactly as both Thomas Malthus and Adam Smith would have expected — and that the frequency of minor and major famines will increase. But whether or not this will spark off migrations or invasions across national frontiers is very much dependent upon the social organization and general character of the people concerned.

On the face of it one might expect that those industrially undeveloped countries who lack mineral resources, but who do possess a reasonably high PPCNPP, would be in a much stronger position. They too have never known easy living, nor do they have high expectations. Provided, therefore, that they have maintained a reasonable social flexibility, they will be in a position to absorb an increase in population without experiencing a real decline in material well-being or a feeling of deprivation.

But the outlook for the peoples of mineral-rich countries which have only just begun industrial development is far more unpredictable. They differ very much in their degree of dependence upon wasting assets. At one end of the scale there are the desert oil states who, at the present time, possess vast quantities of a substance which has come to be valued almost like gold, but who have hardly anything else. It is now customary to regard these peoples as having a rosy future, their only problem being that of finding the most profitable resting place for accumulating royalties. Indeed, personal owners of such royalties have every reason to look forward to a future which will be as leisured and emancipated as for any of the inhabitants of the earth. But the ultimate fate of the great majority of the people living in desert cities is far less assured. No one seems to have squarely faced the problem of the large community which has to import even the water it drinks, if its *raison d'être* dwindles to nothing over a mere three decades.

At the other end of the scale are countries like Brazil, Indonesia and Venezuela with vast and varied mineral reserves and organic resources on a scale which dwarfs those of the majority of nations. Clearly they have economic foundations which will support them through a variety of trials and vicissitudes; but if their mineral reserves are used up in profligate fashion and if, at the same time, urban agglomerations develop which are incapable of transplantation and resettlement in the event of a permanent world food shortage, one cannot feel confident that their resources are going to be adequate to avert catastrophe. Quite apart from the logistic problem, there would be the added one that most of their inhabitants would either have tasted some of the luxuries of Western industrial society or have been in such close contiguity with them as to have developed aspirations to a more emancipated way of life. Such people cannot be expected to suffer disappointment and deprivation without protest and violence.

Even more problematical is the fate of the peoples in those countries where mass industrialization and a "Western" way of life began to develop a long time ago. A number of ominous trends have already been noted; if these continue over the next two or three decades, the consequences for industrialized nations, heavily dependent upon imports of both food and minerals, seem inescapable. If the old colonial food suppliers continue to convert plantation land to food crops; if the traditional buyers of manufactured goods can no longer afford them, no matter how much they would like to; if essential imports of mineral fuel and metals become so costly that no manufacturer can produce competitive goods from them, even to export to the most wealthy nations; and if the most wealthy nations as a result become almost completely self-sufficient in manufactures as well as food — what then becomes of more than 50 million people in the United Kingdom and over 100 million in Japan? Is there not every reason to conclude that, even some time ago, they had reached a point where they were already over-industrialized?

Lastly, the outlook for the vast populations of the three great powers — the

USA, the USSR and China — is an interesting field for speculation. The dangerous dependence of industry and social structure on petroleum in the USA has already been mentioned. This is a hurdle of formidable dimensions, but there are others which are bound to be encountered in quite rapid succession. No other country in the history of the world has devoured inorganic resources so voraciously and developed an economy which seems so dependent on the continous enlargement of its own appetite. It is difficult to view the present trends and the continuing expectations of the large urban populations of this wealthy country with anything but alarm. In the other camp, the recurrent food deficits experienced by the USSR over the first half century of its existence seem to suggest that its problems are rather different. There is certainly no country in the world with more grounds for confidence about its mineral reserves; furthermore, some authorities suggest that even the food problems of the Soviet Union are organizational rather than fundamental (Goldman, 1972), and that with the abandonment of doctrinaire attitudes towards agriculture they would disappear. Up to a point these arguments are well supported; nevertheless, when one examines the marginal nature of so much of the agricultural and "potentially" agricultural land of the USSR with all its uncertainties of drought and frost, one cannot help but view with misgiving the rapid population rise which is taking place and the large percentage of the increase which is being accommodated in urban areas. Finally, there is the case of China — unique in so many respects. She possesses vast mineral reserves and her annual organic productivity, both potential and actual, is truly enormous. And yet, when viewed on a per capita basis, all this is made to appear very modest. There can be little doubt that if China has in some way managed to solve her population problem so that numbers will shortly stabilize and then decline, her resources are such that the future of this ancient civilization could be far more stable and assured than that of the majority of nations. But even her own leaders make no such claims about population stabilization: indeed they continue to assert that the population/resources crisis is no more than a capitalist invention devised in order to deny undeveloped nations their rightful aspirations. The public assertions of national leaders and their deeper motivations are not always entirely consistent, of course, but if those who hold the reins in China are able to envisage her 800 millions rapidly becoming 900 millions, 1,000 millions, and so on to a population of 1,600 millions by the year 2010, then they have a vision of the future which realists elsewhere find difficult to contemplate.

RESOURCE ANALYSIS AND PROPHECY

Sensible people in the secular sphere, pragmatists and idealists alike, do not pretend to be able to foretell the future; even in ecclesiastical circles it is probably far more difficult to find self-declared prophets now than formerly. On the other hand, the construction of scenarios is a less ambitious activity: the scenario writer restricts himself to a selection of criteria and assumptions, and projects current trends into the future in full knowledge that he is ignoring a myriad of other variables which operate in the real world. Because of this, if he is honest with himself, he knows full well that the chances of achieving an accurate and detailed forecast of future situations are very remote. If he is wise, his intention is merely to emphasize what the broad outcome is likely to be if certain current trends persist and are not offset or overridden by other influences that he has not taken into account.

It is because of these fundamental limitations that some of us choose not to indulge in scenarios. A disturbing scenario makes little or no impact on those involved in the day-to-day administration of national affairs for the reasons already given: it can justifiably be ignored as a forecast because so many parameters have not been taken into account. (The fact that the sober and reasoned forecasts of their trusted economic advisers suffer from similar limitations is sometimes overlooked.) The importance ascribed in this book to the simple quantitative assessment of population and resources arises from the fact that such an assessment has virtues which are denied to most scenarios. Although a close study of resources provides no more guidance than anything else as to what, among a vast range of possibilities, is actually going to happen, it does provide very clear pointers to the kinds of thing that almost certainly will not happen. Given that milk is milk and that a pint is a pint, it seems a fair statement of fact that, in the year 2000 AD, it will not be possible to put a quart of milk into a pint bottle. Much more to the point, neither will it be possible to make a pint of milk fill a quart bottle. It seems very likely that in the years ahead there will be those obscurantists who will seek to confuse the issue by speaking of litres and the superior quality of milk substitute; but for those who continue to think clearly the fact will remain that if, in a particular country, only 1,800 kcal/capita/day are available, then it will be impossible for the average person to consume 3,600. One can leave all the conjecture about the possible consequences of halving a nation's food supplies to the scenario writers.

THE HUMAN FACTOR

Unfortunately, there persists in many societies particularly in the Western world a frame of mind which, when faced with an apparently insuperable obstacle to national material advancement, maintains that literally nothing is impossible because of human ingenuity. This attitude has the support of the time-honoured precept that "people are the main resource", the implication being that a country populated by ingenious, hard-working people can find a satisfactory answer to any national problem which arises. Such a view obviously has great popular appeal and, if for no other reason, is difficult to undermine. It is not a rational view of human affairs, merely a declaration of faith, but because of its potentialities for obscurantism in national affairs it is important to consider its origins and examine its dangers.

In essence it can be regarded as a variation on Adam Smith's theme that "national wealth is dependent upon the efficient use of labour", though whether there is any evidence for direct antecedence is doubtful. There are, after all, several precepts of even greater antiquity which may well have nourished the roots of the idea. One recollects, for instance, that in the New Testament there is written: "ye shall say to this mountain, Remove hence to yonder place; and it shall remove; and nothing shall be impossible unto you." (Matthew, 17, 20). Is it possible that this statement of personal potentialities became elevated to the collective or national plane? Regardless of its ultimate origins, however, the economic flavour of "people are the main resource" makes it likely that Adam Smith must carry some responsibility.

Although it cannot be denied that national material well-being at the present time is correlated with a high level of technological development, this does not automatically imply that the nature of the "people" determines national wealth. Much already said indicates that the factor of human organization is secondary: it is dependent in very large measure on the possession and application of natural resources. Fundamentally, industrialized countries have done little more than substitute mechanical energy for muscular energy. This point is highlighted in a most incisive manner by Amory Lovins (1975) in his *exposé* of the staggering amount of "slave" labour at present at work in the world. His analysis revolves around the fact that man's global energy conversion from all sources (wood, fossil fuel, hydro-electric power, nuclear) at the present time is approximately 8×10^{12} watts. This is more than 20 times the energy content of the food necessary to feed the present world population at the FAO standard diet of 3,600 kcal/day. In other words each person on the earth, on average, possesses the equivalent of about 50 slaves, each working a 40-hour week (at 100 per cent efficiency). In terms of work force, therefore, the population of the earth is not four billion but about 200 billion, the important point being that about 98 per cent of them do not eat conventional food. The inequalities in the distribution of this "slave" labour between different countries is enormous, the average inhabitant of the USA, for example, having 250 times as many "slaves" as the average Nigerian. And this, substantially, is the reason for the difference in "efficiency" between the American and Nigerian economies: it is not due to differences in the average "efficiency" of the people themselves. There seems no way of discovering the relative average efficiencies of Americans and Nigerians: if Americans were shorn of 249 of every 250 "slaves" they possess, who can say how "efficient" they would prove themselves to be!

It might be argued that, on the evidence of history, there are firm grounds for supposing that the population of those countries which initiated and developed the Industrial Revolution must be innately more efficient than those which merely copied them later or have as yet scarcely begun to industrialize. Brief reflection indicates that this is by no means certain. Which of us in the industrialized countries can with honesty stand up and say: "I have not merely stood upon the shoulders of George Stevenson, Alexander Bell and Albert Einstein: with no prompting whatsoever I have had truly original thoughts which have initiated fundamental contributions to the development of science and technology"? If we subject ourselves to close scrutiny of this kind, individual by individual, it is doubtful if we can come to any conclusion other than that, as a population, we are no more innovative or fundamentally "efficient" than the populations of other areas. The tiny percentage of innovators in the countries which produced and nourished the Industrial Revolution made their discoveries in a responsive environment; the tiny percentage who innovated elsewhere (or who had the ability to do so) thought their thoughts in an unresponsive one.

Unfortunately it is not possible to test views on these matters in some kind of historical laboratory. It would be interesting indeed if one could experiment with the fundamentals of Adam Smith's hypothesis and rerun a couple of centuries of history with adequate controls. We could, for instance, take the five or six million people who inhabited the British landscape in the mid-eighteenth century, leaving them all the cultural endowments inherited from the Roman Empire, the Renaissance and the age of discovery, but neatly divesting the land of all coal, high-grade iron ore, tin, lead, zinc and copper. We could then invite them to set to work and make an Industrial Revolution. On the other hand we could select an area of similar size, inhabited by people of an entirely different race and culture, ensuring that it carried just the same minerals as Britain in 1750 in equally accessible places, and request them to do the same thing.

Such flights of fancy serve little purpose except perhaps to lead one to a strong suspicion that the possession of natural resources, conveniently arranged, has contributed far more to national success and opulence than history books usually suggest.

THE WEALTH EQUATION

On its face value Adam Smith's basic precept seems unassailable: there can be no "wealth" without the application of human effort, and the more "efficiently" this is used, the greater will be the return per unit of input. Whether or not one has reservations seems to depend mainly on the construction placed on the concept of "efficiency". If this is taken to imply merely the application of muscular effort and thought in appropriate quantities and in the right places, then it would be difficult to disagree; but if it implies the mass substitution of mechanical for muscular energy, using non-renewable energy resources (as is usually the case at the present time), then it is doubtful if real "efficiency" is under discussion. It is surely not "efficient" to burn up vast quantities of material in an astonishingly short time, when these might have been left for much more carefully considered utilization by the generations to come. It seems as though manufacturing industry at the present time is doing something exactly analogous to the fishing industry which, according to Paul Ehrlich (Ehrlich and Ehrlich, 1972), has an attitude to the sea suggesting that "if they were to go into the chicken farming business they would plan to eat up all the feed, all the eggs, all the chicks, and all the chickens simultaneously, while burning down the hen houses to keep themselves warm." If Adam Smith was envisaging this kind of development when he spoke of the "efficient" use of labour, then he was surely wrong: sustainable wealth is clearly not possible on such a basis.

Another aspect of this thesis also requires examination. Both nineteenth-century American capitalists and twentieth-century Russian communists have tended to turn it around and to speak of the land and its contents as being "valueless" until worked upon by labour. Legal theory and economic practice have been based upon this premise and indeed, in the USSR, economic philosophy and national book-keeping seem to have been founded on the assumption that both land and mineral resources are "free" (Goldman, 1972). It is fair to assume, therefore, that Adam Smith was ultimately responsible for both the capitalist and the communist views of labour as the sole determinant of wealth. And if all countries possessed infinite quantities of cultivable land and all the economic minerals, one could not dissent from this. Unfortunately the majority of nations now suffer from deficiencies in these commodities, and even the more fortunate ones are in danger of running out. The stage has almost been reached, which seemed so remote to Adam Smith that he gave it only a passing mention, where "the competition for employment [is] so great as to reduce the wages of labour to what [are] barely sufficient to keep up the number of labourers and, the country being already fully peopled, that number [can] never be augmented." (Adam Smith, p.88).

This being the case, the view that labour alone is the creator of a nation's wealth cannot be tenable. Indeed, it had probably ceased to be so before the end of the nineteenth century. Wherever there is the danger of dearth or exhaustion of a useful commodity, "wealth" should surely be regarded as the product of the interaction between labour and resources, and the quantities of both, in any country, should be the subject of careful and continuous assessment. After more than a century of intensive exploitation of resources in nearly all the countries of the world, it seems extraordinary that this basic equation has not become the basis of economic theory. One can only conclude that personal and national acquisitiveness, encouraged by the respectable rationale of Adam Smith's analysis, have perpetuated the acceptance of an outworn philosophy and effectively blocked the emergence of a new one.

Those who doubt this point might find it helpful to ponder one of the glaring facts of life as humanity embarks upon the last quarter of the twentieth century. Although it is now difficult to conceive of a single situation in which resources could be too plentiful, it is all to painfully obvious that, on the other side of the equation, labour is embarrassingly abundant. If Adam Smith could be with us today we might put an interesting question to him:

> If five million workers, along with their five million dependents, were, suddenly and painlessly, to disappear from the landscape of Britain, would the country be more wealthy or less wealthy?

It is, of course, a very emotive question, and if an audience of trades unionists, progressive politicians and committed social thinkers had been invited along to meet the guest, it would be imperative to elaborate with the minimum of hiatus. It would be necessary to emphasize that the five million ought to contain a fair proportion of prosperous people from the commercial and administrative sectors of society along with a very strong admixture from the stockbroker belt, as well as butchers, bakers, candlestick makers, university dons and some of those who happened not be gainfully employed at the time. It might also be sensible to add that if the hand of fate were to pass rather lightly and selectively over agricultural and coal mining areas this might also be advantageous.

The Great Man's answer would surely be awaited with intense interest. If he were in full possession of the facts of our present situation it is by no means a foregone conclusion that one of such keen insight and wisdom would favour the retention of the five million, despite the fact that every one of them would have been the recipient of at least eleven years full-time schooling and would be the end product of more than four generations of compulsory education. It is quite conceivable that he would feel that the saving of 10 million generous nutrition units, 10 million calls upon the accumulated national pension fund, 10 million units of housing accommodation and road space, along with vast quantities of other resources, would more than compensate for the loss of five million units of efficient labour.

9

The National Unit

Human affairs are managed within the framework of national units, each having a high degree of autonomy. Provided the activities of a nation are not seen to have adverse effects on the affairs of its neighbours, international law permits it to do much as it pleases within its own frontiers. True, there are now codes of behaviour outlined by the United Nations and its agencies regarding the way in which individual nations should treat their own peoples, and men of goodwill all over the world have banded together in various ways with a view to bringing the pressure of world opinion to bear on nations who flout internationally accepted precepts about the various "freedoms"; but in the main even the most internationally minded countries guard their rights to independent action with considerable jealousy. In the foregoing chapters it has been assumed that this kind of arrangement will continue during the coming decades — that the nations of the earth, as we now know them, will continue as economic and political entities, flourishing or declining according to the degree of success with which they manage their own affairs.

However, there may be those who regard this view as fallacious because they feel that, in the very near future, nations are going to amalgamate into coherent economic and political structures in which the resources and social advantages of the components will be blended to mutual advantage. In their support they can cite a number of recent developments which might reasonably be regarded as the first stage in such a trend. In particular the formation of organizations such as the European Economic Community (EEC), the Latin American Free Trade Association (LAFTA), the Central American Common Market (ODECA), the Arab Common Market and the West African Common Market, may be seen as particularly significant.

There can be little doubt that if a number of these plans and visions do materialize, then much of what has been said here about the long-term viability of existing nations is of limited significance: if countries with complementary resources and types of economy combine, then the political well-being of some of their populations will be much improved. It is necessary, therefore, to look carefully at current trends in nationalism and internationalism before one can decide whether or not extrapolations which assume present political frontiers can be regarded as useful.

THE TREND TOWARDS NATIONALISM

No realistic internationalist can find much encouragement in the general trend identifiable in world history over the past three quarters of a century. In the year 1900, ignoring the remaining small areas of "uncontrolled' tribal territory, there were 48 states on the earth which, on the basis of any acceptable criteria, could be said to have an independent foreign policy. They include small countries such as Liechtenstein, San Marino and Vatican City. Between 1900 and 1975 this number exactly trebled, from 48 to 144 (figure 9·1). There are now three times as many governments on the earth, each entitled by international law to take independent action which might have repercussions in the affairs of others.

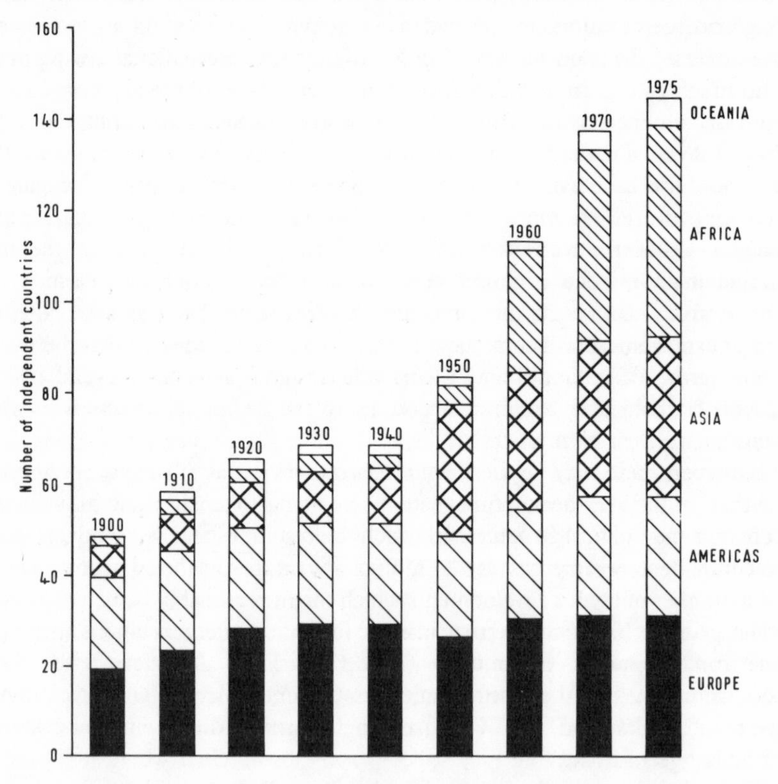

9·1 Increase in the number of independent political units, 1900–1975

The main reason for this development is obvious, but it is often presented in an oversimplified way. It is not sufficient to say that the Turkish, Austro-Hungarian, British, French, Belgian, Dutch and Portugese colonial empires have disintegrated and that their constituent peoples have "resumed" their independence. In fact many of the large tracts of territory which were managed as discrete colonies by the European occupiers were populated by a great variety of tribal peoples or, indeed, by quite distinct nations. When independence came, because such a diverse population had been organized for so long as a unit, both politically and economically, it seemed reasonable that the newly independent country should be coincident with the former colony. Indeed if the operation were to be completed as speedily as was so often demanded, no other arrangement seemed possible. But, in many cases, it was grossly over-optimistic to expect such a diverse unit to provide the basis for a stable and permanent political entity. The nationalism and the social resentments that had smouldered under the colonial regime were rarely allayed completely, and when the more recent sources of friction were removed, the bases of older antipathies and grievances often became more apparent. In few places were there sufficient statesmanship and forbearance (or sheer accident of mutual interest) to permit an amalgamation of separate colonies under unified leadership such as was achieved in the case of Tanganyika and Zanzibar. In many cases almost the opposite occurred: peoples with different aspirations from those of the dominant group were granted what seemed to them to be a spurious independence, so that the fires of nationalism were in no way quenched by the exercise of decolonization. To pretend that the former colonial powers prepared their dependent peoples for stable self-government, and then stepped down at an appropriate moment, is to indulge in delusion: in a number of cases subsequent unrest has already resulted in fragmentation, and who would be so rash as to forecast that the trend is about to be reversed? The roots of nationalism run deep and can derive nourishment from unexpected sources with remarkable alacrity; one cannot foresee when an ancient plant, so long pruned to apparent insignificance above ground, will suddenly burgeon and overshadow all around it. The case of Bangladesh comes readily to mind, and it would be invidious (if not positively inflammatory) to particularize on possible future parallels should the hand of central government be weakened. However, an Englishman can perhaps be excused the aside that whereas, a few years ago, a remark about a frontier along the Cheviots could never have been regarded as anything more than a good-natured hogmanay jest, in the 1970s it might well be taken rather more seriously.

The evidence for a continuing trend towards separatism is thus undeniable, while frontier revisions of the opposite kind have been almost negligible. Since 1900, the merging of Montenegro and Serbia into Yugoslavia, the reabsorption of Latvia, Lithuania and Estonia into the Soviet Union, and the rejoining of North and South Vietnam are the only cases which can be cited where independent political entities have been effectively amalgamated. On the other hand, several voluntary mergers have been mooted and even attempted, but without success. The union of Egypt with Syria in the United Arab Republic lived for only three and a half years, the life of the West Indies Federation lasted a few months longer, and in spite of clearly expressed enthusiasm by the Libyan government, no union of that country with Egypt has been effected.

INTERNATIONAL ORGANIZATIONS

Nevertheless, one must acknowledge the importance of recent attempts at international union. It would be foolish to deny that the progress made by the European Economic Community is more far-reaching than any other voluntary association of independent states that has occurred in modern times. The breaking down of political barriers has often been imposed by expanding empires, and resulted in a freer flow of economic activity. But, even so short a time ago as the 1930s, any suggestion that France and Germany, before the end of the twentieth century, would come together voluntarily in an economic union, and even begin to discuss the establishment of a political merger under a unified government, would have been regarded as political fantasy.

Nevertheless, no matter how close we seem to a final dissolution of frontiers in a United States of Europe, it would be premature in the extreme to conclude that this is already a virtual certainty. One of the most conspicuous aspects of the history of the EEC up to the present time has been the way in which strain and dissention have become apparent immediately a regional or a world economic problem has arisen in which some of the member states have felt they had divergent interests. This has happened on a number of occasions with regard to the relative prices of agricultural and industrial products, and it certainly occurred at the height of the oil crisis in early 1974. This suggests that each country is in the EEC because of the relatively short-term advantages it hopes to obtain from its membership, and not because of any long-term view or any fundamental attitude about the close identity of the peoples in the group of states involved.

It might be objected that this is only to be expected at such an early stage, and one cannot but agree; but just as in the past war has been regarded as a normal instrument of political policy to achieve national advantage, so now in the minds of many the lowering of economic barriers is seen in a similar light. The fact that the latter is inestimably more desirable from the point of view of ordinary people has little bearing on the point at issue: even among those people who have shown a preference for entering the "Common Market", the vast majority appear to have done so because they believe that their particular nation will be more prosperous inside than outside it. Should circumstances arise in which the people in the EEC countries find their absolute standard of living beginning to decline, the evidence suggests that separatism, protectionism, "patriotism" and sheer jingoism would rapidly displace any feelings of nascent internationalism that had begun to develop.

This may seem to be an almost perversely pessimistic view of what is usually regarded as one of the more constructive recent developments in the international field, but those Europeans who feel that a merging of the nations is about to provide the answer to their more difficult problems should reflect on two points — first, that nearly all national action arises out of national self-interest, and secondly, that one sad aspect of mass psychology is the apparent need for "alien" or "foreign" scapegoats when material welfare is threatened. If the world economic barometer were set fair for tomorrow and for the further outlook period, one might anticipate a United States of Europe with greater confidence.

Detailed examination of the relative effectiveness of international cooperation in other regional settings is not within my competence, but there seems to be some evidence that groupings such as the Latin American Free Trade Association (Argentina, Brazil, Chile, Mexico, Paraguay, Peru, Uruguay, Colombia, Ecuador and Venezuela) and the Central American Common Market (El Salvador, Guatemala, Honduras, Nicaragua and Costa Rica), though making valuable achievements in the field of common policy on production, tariffs and trade, and even planning to set up councils for the discussion of political, educational and defence policies, do not appear to have envisaged political integration at the level visualized in the EEC. Similarly the Arab League (Egypt, Iraq, Saudi Arabia, Syria, Lebanon, Jordan, Yemen, Libya, Sudan, Tunisia, Morocco, Kuwait and Algeria), in spite of the efforts made to form a unitary state or a political federation at the Alexandria Conference in 1944, have had to be content with a loose association of sovereign states. The subsequent institution of the Arab Common Market in 1965, providing for a progressive reduction in tariffs, did not really concern itself with any reduction in national sovereignty. Indeed, at the outset, if comprised only Iraq, Jordan, Syria and Egypt; the oil-rich states of Saudi Arabia, Oman, Kuwait, Libya and Algeria were not involved. Similarly, the West African Common Market (Dahomey, Ghana, Ivory Coast, Liberia, Mali, Mauritania, Niger, Nigeria, Senegal, Sierra Leone, Togo and Upper Volta), set up in 1967, aims to eliminate customs and trade barriers but sets out no provisions for the discussion of political unification.

THE OUTLOOK FOR NATIONAL AMALGAMATION

It might still be argued that, as population/resources difficulties increase, so nations will be compelled, in some way, to pool their resources. On first consideration this may seem a reasonable proposition, but closer examination reveals its weaknesses. It is an argument based on national self-interest and again the case of the EEC comes to mind. Here a group of relatively prosperous nations has collaborated economically in a milieu where, at the outset, welfare gradients were relatively slight. The name usually applied to the EEC in Britain, "the Common Market", is symptomatic of underlying attitudes: it was presented to the electorate as an organization in which there would be a wider area over which British goods could be sold more easily, and not as one which contained less privileged regions which would receive aid from a greater pool of wealth. It has certainly been necessary to take into account the existence of areas like Scotland and southern Italy, but the package was not presented as the "European Common Wealth", and certainly not as the "European Common Welfare Area". This being so, it is interesting to speculate on what the attitude of "the Six" would have been in 1970 if, tucked away in a corner of Western Europe, there had been a country with some tens of millions of peasant people with no known mineral deposits, very little purchasing power, and a standard of living far below that of the countries around it. If such a country had made urgent application for membership, would it have been accepted? One suspects that the measure of success already achieved in the EEC arises mainly from the fact that the standard of living of a large percentage of the population in all the component states is very similar.

This is not without relevance in any discussion of the likelihood of future national mergers on the world scale. With increased pressure on resources and decreased employment opportunities, it is quite conceivable that the governments of the poorest nations will become increasingly aware of the benefits to be gained from union with better endowed neighbours. Whether propositions of this nature would be acceptable to the other party is a very different matter: in the future the more prosperous countries may well have become much more conscious of the value of their assets and the number of mouths dependent upon them. An examination of the resources of the badly endowed nations, particularly those with large populations, leaves one with little doubt that they will have little to offer apart from hungry mouths and idle hands. If there is reason to suspect that even now the more fortunate nations would reject many of the proposals of marriage that might be made to them on the grounds that the suitors have inadequate prospects, how much more will this be true in the future!

There appear to be sound, logical reasons why industrially advanced countries which have used up many of their resources should amalgamate politically in order to enhance their bargaining power with primary producers; but there seem to be even greater reasons for doubting their determination to proceed with the plans which they have for doing so. There is also a good case for unindustrialized countries with few resources attempting to form beneficial political unions with more fortunate ones, but one suspects that their approaches would be unacceptable. There are strong arguments in favour of the very richest countries going into political union with the poorest countries; but even if the latter were reduced to a point of destitution where they were prone to accept such an offer from a powerful people of different race or cultural heritage, it seems unlikely that such an offer would ever be made. Taking a pragmatic view of the world scene, the kind of merger with the best chances of success would be one between a fairly prosperous industrialized country and an industrially undeveloped one with large resources: in such an arrangement, both would have something to gain. However, apart from the fact that ruling groups in nearly all young, ex-colonial countries have an understandable reluctance to relinquish one jot of their new-found independence, they are increasingly aware of their strong bargaining position. They may well adopt the reasonable attitude that, even economically, they have far more to gain from remaining strictly independent.

Of course, there always remains the unpleasant spectre of an attempted reimposition of enforced, exploitive imperialism of one kind or another. There were faint but unmistakable reminders of this during the height of the oil crisis in early 1974: political philosophies which, for more than a decade, had lived an almost entirely troglodyte existence did briefly thrust their heads above ground to suggest that if the very life-blood of industrial nations were seriously threatened, they had the "moral right" to safeguard their supplies. Such overt threats are now probably empty ones: they almost certainly cannot be implemented if the world is to retain even vestiges of an ordered existence. The evidence seems to indicate, therefore, that the better endowed among the newer nations will opt to remain independent and, provided Armageddon does not supervene, will succeed in doing so. The poorly endowed, on the other hand, will not even receive invitations.

Whether, in the long run, a merging of the nations into larger entities would be desirable (or even viable) is not at issue here (see chapter 11). The intention has merely been to demonstrate that, in the critical decades ahead, existing national frontiers seem likely to persist, and that even further fragmentation of sovereignty may well occur.

10

Human Problems, Education, and a New Regional Geography

As the intellectual blizzard of the late twentieth century gathers in intensity, bombarded by a welter of -isms and -ologies which obviously have some bearing on the problems of famine, pollution, unemployment, social disunity and general unhappiness, young people of goodwill are increasingly asking where they should go in order to study the really fundamental social problems which confront mankind. Though often arising out of rather naive assumptions about the relative simplicity of the real world this is, nevertheless, a good question, and probably deserves a better answer than can be given. Two hundred years ago, an honest succinct answer would have been: "Go to Glasgow and attend Adam Smith's lectures on political economy;" or a few years later, a recommendation to attend Professor Thomas Malthus's lectures on history and political economy at the College of the East India Company. Subsequently, no specific answer could have been given without reasonable expectation of contradiction: what constituted an authoritative statement in the field of human affairs became increasingly a matter of opinion. In the mid-nineteenth century there were a number of places where one might have gone to learn about political economy, but the flavour would have been very different from one to another. And certainly since the publication of the marxist interpretation of history and social development, opinions and academic courses have diverged at an ever increasing rate.

The problem has been exacerbated not only by the emergence of diverse political viewpoints but also by a rapid increase in specialization: the former field of "political economy" has been parcelled up into economics, economic history, social anthropology, sociology, social administration and politics, and though practitioners in each would modestly disclaim any prerogative to speak for the whole of social science, nevertheless each one may, on occasion, put forward his partial view with an assurance which betrays a deep faith in its relative importance. An economist might with some justification affirm that John Maynard Keynes in the 1930s was propounding a philosophy of far greater social and political significance than anyone else in his day. A sociologist could well refer to the great boom in the popularity of sociology in the 1950s and 1960s, though he might find it rather more difficult to suggest any dominant world figures, or any significant advance in social philosophy associated with it.

However, none of these practitioners, when speaking in a professional capacity, would attempt to review the whole human situation; indeed the separate specialisms arose specifically because of a conviction that intellectual respectability could only be achieved by someone who restricted his scope. But this fragmentation of study has now developed to a point where students search in vain for a holistic view, and where practitioners themselves are becoming concerned. An increasing number of thoughtful economists, in particular, are worried about their academic studies becoming less and less relevant to the more important world problems. As Professor Robert Solow of the Massachusetts Institute of Technology put it: the problem facing them is "whether to have more and more to say about less and less, or whether to have less and less to say about more and more." It is depressing that, having perceived the alternatives, he came down in favour of the former because he felt it would be better for economists to aspire to be competent technicians — like plumbers (Silk, 1976). Fortunately all economists would not make the same choice. Professor J.K. Galbraith, for radical reasons, comes down on the other side of the fence: he has made the point that economists "can, if they are determined, be unimportant; they can, if they prefer a comfortable home life and regular hours, continue to make a living out of the infinitely interesting gadgetry of disguise." But the alternative, he says, is for economists to enlarge their system, in the hope that it might provoke a reaction from those whose power would be revealed and examined as well as from those who find comfort in the fact that economists teach and discuss the wrong problems (Silk, 1976).

On their own admission, therefore, most economists do not regard their particular province as a place where, at the present time, concerned students can obtain a grounding in the nature of the basic problems facing humanity. And even if in the future economists do embrace the precepts of Professor Galbraith, it is very doubtful if they could achieve the scope and breadth of Adam Smith. In a single sweep of the intellect he could comment with some profundity on the contrasts in cattle farming in New England and Latin America, on the nature of rice growing in the Indies, on classical systems of agriculture, on the operation of the Poor Law, on the effect of weather fluctuations on crop productivity, as well as on the prices of almost every conceivable world commodity. The most broad-minded of modern economists would probably quail at the very thought of the corporate intellect of a large school of economics having to do this, much less that of a single academic. Even those with the breadth of vision of a Galbraith would probably never suggest that they should: the world obviously requires well trained econometricians, and all that the more liberal are urging is that they should seek their problems in the real world — that they should concern themselves with the messy, conflicting problems that clutter the affairs of men rather than with the pure, pristine and unsullied ones which have their origin (and perhaps even their market) in the world of the mathematician.

But if economists are not to take responsibility for reviewing human organization as a whole, who is? Or is there now mutual agreement that such a task is impracticable, and that all students who have a hankering after it should be made to appreciate their unrealism and diverted to responsible specialized study? Wholesale acceptance of such an educational philosophy would involve the renunciation of one of the most stimulating and rewarding fields of study that has developed in recent times — that of ecology. In its broadest sense ecology shows that it is impossible to understand any living organism unless one views it in the context of the environment in which it lives and in which it evolved — that it is not possible to appreciate fully the reasons for behaviour and physiological functions without an understanding of the nature of the surroundings in which they came into existence. This is true of every species of plant and animal and it must be true of *Homo sapiens*, the most complex and pervasive of all the animals, even though he has erected a complicated cultural apparatus between himself and the rigours of nature. Far from being of lesser importance now than in the time of Adam Smith, it is surely more important than ever that the whole field of investigation and learning should contain an aspect of study which concentrates on the nature of the interaction between human activity and the natural realities of the environment.

The division of labour, so categorically advocated by Adam Smith, seems to have led to a specialization in education which results in a breadth of vision far inferior to that which he possessed. Up to a point this has been recognized, C.P. Snow's "two cultures" being one important aspect of it. But the apparent lack of full comprehension between different kinds of scientist has certainly not been fully appreciated. When physical scientists and techologists indulge in little flights of unjustified optimism about the possibilities of future technological innovation, they often seem to assume a background of understanding in their audience which is quite unjustified. Many of the reservations — the "ifs" and "buts" — tend to be omitted. What they seem not to realize is that many of those in the social sciences and humanities, who obviously have interests in technological developments, will take the technologist more seriously than he takes himself. Technology can easily take the place of God — something beyond full comprehension but in which we can put our trust! On the other hand, when demographers and economists emphasize the complexity and unpredictability of the phenomena with which they concern themselves, the mind of the technologist may well seize upon this as an indication that a great range of social developments can occur, and that the courses open to mankind are almost a matter of free choice. A nexus of mutual trust thus develops in which each imagines all kinds of unrealistic things about the other.

Nowhere is this reciprocal trust more dangerously interposed than with regard to nuclear power development (chapter 11): on the one hand physical scientists are producing materials of almost incredible nastiness, with little thought or knowledge about the political and social systems which will be their custodians; one the other, many social scientists seem to be under the impression that little is being done which should concern them.

Apart from this most disturbing example, however, there are almost countless fallacies which gain attention and some credence in modern society, often in a blaze of publicity from national media; there is a no well established academic discipline primarily concerned with putting human and technological developments into their full ecological setting and viewing them holistically, and one is constantly assailed by commentators on "tomorrow's world" describing wonder-materials, wonder-machines and wonder-crops which will transform life-styles in the years to come. The fact that these objects of wonder would require vast and unavailable quantities of metal or energy or fertilizer is never even considered. If such *tours de force* were clearly labelled as science fiction then their full entertainment value could be savoured and no harm would be done: as presented, they serve as a constant bolstering of unrealistic hankerings for an unattainable future. Reference has already been made (chapter 6) to the publicity which was given, during the recent petrol crisis, to the distillation of methane from hen manure as though this could be the salvation of the whole of the British motoring public were petrol to disappear almost completely. This was without any reference to overall quantities, or to the overriding disirability of using hen manure in very different ways. Similarly, technological developments such as the expansion of hydro-electric power are frequently presented as though the land which would be appropriated is of no value for any other purpose. Possible conflicts in resource use are often disregarded completely.

The presentation of technological ideas *in vacuo* in this kind of way runs counter to the development of an informed public opinion. If academics are incapable of detecting the inconsistencies and deficiencies in the theses of their colleagues, how can those who are outside the charmed circle be expected to do so? There is an obvious need for an academic discipline whose main concern is a holistic view of man's utilization of resources; and the study should be incisively quantitative, concerned with actual amounts on both sides of the equation.

THE GEOGRAPHICAL CONTRIBUTION

In spite of the obvious recent trend towards specialization, it may still seem surprising that no academic discipline has arisen (or survived) which concentrates exclusively on the fundamental aspects of human ecology. The reasons are mainly historical, but they should be fully appreciated by anyone who crusades for the holistic viewpoint. During the nineteenth century the study of human communities in their natural setting was usually regarded as the province of geographers. This followed the publication of Alexander von Humboldt's *Kosmos* in 1842, acclaimed as the most mature digest of the products of scientific exploration and discovery over the earth during the previous few centuries: it not only presented a comprehensive picture of the natural environments of the earth, but also described the nature of many of the human societies and economies which seemed to be adapted to them. The study of geography was also becoming more widely recognized as a logical framework in which to present the facts of history. In the same year as the publication of *Kosmos,* Thomas Arnold, Regius Professor of Modern History at Oxford, felt it appropriate to deliver his Introductory Lectures pleading for a new outlook in geography. The real geography, he claimed, "embraces at once a knowledge of the earth and of the dwellings of man upon it; it stretches out on the one hand to history, and on the other to geology and physiology; it is just that part of the domain of knowledge where the students of physical and moral science meet together." (Baker, 1963). One finds a similar viewpoint in Mary Somerville's *Physical Geography* (1848). Although rather more optimistic about man's ultimate control of the environment than some of us today, she clearly had the same view of her role as a geographer when she wrote: "The influence of external circumstances on man is not greater than his influence on the material world. It is true, he cannot create power; but he dextrously avails himself of the powers of nature to subdue nature." G.P. Marsh, in his classical work *Man and Nature, or physical geography as modified by human action* also provided evidence about the nature of geography in the middle of the nineteenth century.

Nevertheless, it is clear that academic geography had only an uneasy existence at this time. Even where its practitioners had the desire to study the relationship between human economy and the environment they must often have been unsuccessful in carrying conviction. Indeed, in their presentation of environmental information in what was termed "physical geography", they seem to have failed to achieve a satisfactory synthesis. Because he was so critical of most of the introductory works on "physical geography", T.H. Huxley preferred to use the expression "physiography" in his lectures to students. He felt that geographers often began at the wrong end and finished with "an *omnium gatherum* of scraps of all sorts of undigested and unconnected information, thereby entirely destroying the educational value" (Huxley, 1877). Subsequently Mackinder himself made it quite clear that he regarded the theory and practice of geography in the 1870s as unsatisfactorily disparate (Mackinder, 1887). Foremost in his arguments for a "new geography" was the claim that geography must be unitary — that a division into "physical geography" and "political geography" was both unsound and unreal.

The fact that Sir Halford Mackinder has often been referred to as "the maker of modern geography in Britain" (Baker, 1963) is sufficient evidence that his views carried the day. The decades that followed certainly seem to have been the most regenerative in the history of the subject. In this period the product of more than a century of world scientific exploration and recording was assembled into what was conceived as the great final synthesis. Not only were the patterns of world climate presented with some air of finality by workers such as Wladimir Köppen (1931), and world vegetation regions by A.F.W. Schimper (1903) and others, but these were correlated and rationalized by geographers, and the concept of "the natural region" came into full flower. In the rapidly proliferating departments of geography, the main preoccupation for three or four decades was the description and elaboration of these natural regions and of the settlement patterns and economies associated with them. This attempt to view human cultures in the light of environmental contrasts and to put this interaction in a historical context gave rise to the most stimulating and important debate that the subject has ever had. It probably culminated in the works of Ellsworth Huntington (1907, 1915), highlighting the fundamental problems of determinism and human freedom of action which have exercised the minds of philosophers and theologians from classical times onwards, and in the debate of which many a heretic has been sent to the stake.

Basically the environmentalist-determinist approach sought to establish the nature of the causative links between the terrestrial environment and the human culture dependent on it. Vast quantities of new information from all the lands of the earth were now available and it was felt that some basic scientific laws about the natural history of society and economy were awaiting elucidation. Sadly for them, though predictably, no rigorous laws governing the relationship between man and nature were discovered. Massive compilations of material were made and voluminous regional accounts were written about almost every corner of every continent, but although many native cultures, understandably, were found to be superbly well adapted to their environments, the ultimate and unequivocal generalization could never be made: a particular type of climatic regime or environment-type had not automatically called into existence one specific sequence of human responses. Work such as Huntington's was stimulating because it indicated that in a particular set of circumstances a particular people have only a limited set of options open to them, if they are to survive. It was even successful in showing that, *in a limited number of cases,* cultures of very similar characteristics have arisen quite independently in climatically analagous environments. Studies like this were of the utmost importance because they emphasized the causal connection between man and the environment — something which the twentieth century would try to ignore completely.

Unfortunately there were large numbers of geographers who had no enthusiasm for establishing any level of environmental causation for any aspect of human behaviour. And so, for want of easy answers, and in face of a sea wall of crypto-religious prejudice, the invigorating waves of deterministic environmentalism were dissipated (Eyre and Jones, 1966, pp. 13–17). By this time, the earth had been largely discovered so that there was no recurrent stimulus to be derived from newly found environments and cultures. Even the numerous and diverse native cultures already discovered, often in such close ecological relationship with their natural environments, were rapidly being destroyed or transformed out of all recognition by the rising tide of Western industrialism and commercialism. To many geographers, therefore, investigation of peoples in intimate relationship with nature was made to seem increasingly irrelevant.

If, some time during the inter-war period, a geographer of stature and vision had emerged to take up the more realistic and profitable strands of Huntington's theses, in particular to emphasize the dependence of the swelling hordes of men on ever-decreasing resources, then Keynes might have had a worthy competitor and serious analysis of man's ecological plight would not have been delayed until the 1960s. But this is merely to wish that history had been other than it was, and to imagine a foresight and penetration not normally granted to mortal man. In fact, by the time of the second world war, academic geography seems to have been sinking back into an unmotivated descriptivism: the systematic aspects of regions had been established and the broad regional framework had been outlined; much that remained was the mere incorporation of more detailed information and a more sophisticated resolution of boundaries.

But the modern world does not permit academic disciplines to rest on their oars for long periods of time. They encounter difficulties in recruiting good minds if they fail to offer an intellectual stimulus which is seen to be at once relevant and challenging. Accordingly, in the immediate post-war period, geography passed through an uneasy decade or so in which still-dominant regional courses competed with individual systematic studies within the subject as a whole. This competition was not always obvious, nor was it widely advertised; indeed some of the more illustrious personages involved clearly experienced an ambivalence within themselves. Thus, for his presidential address to the Institute of British Geographers, S.W. Wooldridge (1950) took the title "Reflections on Regional Geography in Teaching and Research". Although a fully committed and eminent geomorphologist, he felt logically impelled to emphasize that regional geography remained the raison d'être of the subject. He recognized full well all the difficulties that beset the path of a self-declared polymath scientist, but he could not escape from the conclusion that regional synthesis must remain the distinctive contribution of the geographer.

Nevertheless Wooldridge's contributions to knowledge were largely (though by no means entirely) in geomorphology, and most of the subsequent contributions of his many students were in the same field. Indeed, during the late 1940s and early 1950s a large percentage of the post-graduate work in British geography was in geomorphology. It was only in the latter part of the 1950s that the volume of research in most of the other distinct systematic aspects of the subject achieved comparable proportions. Many senior geographers continued for some time to affirm their concurrence with the Woodridgian tenet that regional synthesis constitutes the ultimate pinnacle of study but, in most places, conviction was insufficiently strong to stem the tide of specialization. Had it not been for the direct allocation of government grants to encourage university study in the linguistic and cultural aspects of certain parts of the world (the USSR, parts of the Far East, and Latin America in particular), regional study in British geography might almost have withered away during the 1960s, except in just one or two places.

The trend was understandable. In spite of affirmations of faith it was never made entirely clear just how one was to achieve an intellectually satisfying regional synthesis; and if one fell short of intellectual respectability, the spectre of Huxley's "omnium gatherum" was always there to haunt the failure. Even Woodridge felt impelled to admit that: "In some moods it may seem indeed that the complex interrelated unity for which we seek is an aspiration of faith rather than a fact of observation, and this is certainly a view to which our critics, at least in this country, are notably prone." In any case there are obvious reasons, many of them very commendable, why directors of study should see fit to divert postgraduate students to clear-cut specialist topics rather than to permit them to pursue complex integrative studies, no matter how much more attractive the latter might seem.

But the wholesale departure into specialization is not without hazards. Although one can sympathize with the desire to achieve academic recognition through specialization, nevertheless exclusive concentration on one aspect of systematic study inevitably brings the geographer into more direct competition with other specialists and the possibility of duplication becomes apparent. During the twentieth century, with the rapid growth and diversification of knowledge, studies such as meteorology, pedology, ecology, economic history, sociology, politics and demography have all gained recognition as discrete bodies of knowledge and joined geology, history and economics as distinct university subjects. Although those geographers who have become specialists in "economic geography", "social geography", "political geography" and so on may justifiably claim that they are now more professional and academically qualified, there is another way of looking at the matter: in a sense they may well be more competitive but by the very course they have chosen they are therefore in competition with economists, sociologists and political scientists. The "economic geographer" might object that his field of study is very different from that of the economist, but is the difference so great as to merit such a degree of separateness? Is it reasonable to insist that although someone else is a specialist in econometrics, your own studies are quite distinct because you study the spatial aspects of econometrics?

Only posterity will be the final arbiter on issues such as this, but it is well to be fully aware of the pitfalls. Probably the greatest danger of having two fields of study with widely overlapping subject matter is that one of them, in its efforts to remain different, will elect to concentrate on aspects of that subject matter which are both irrelevant (from the standpoint of day-to-day affairs in the real world) and unimportant. It might also be interpolated her that, in the long run, a sophisticated statistical treatment can do nothing to redeem a field of study which is essentially trivial. An unsympathetic mathematician was once heard to remark that he could conceive of no more trivial event than when a new-found devotee of numeracy, leaning over a computer, was so utterly overcome by wonder and amazement at what he saw that he actually fell into it. No realistic geographer can feel anything but pleasure and gratification at the increase in numeracy and the desire for quantification that has permeated the subject in recent years, but the use to which the acquired skills have been put gives cause for some disquiet. It is increasingly clear that growing computerization is no indication whatsoever of a general tendency towards greater awareness of the need to view resources quantitatively. Indeed the evidence seems to suggest the opposite: in this age of almost pathological computermindedness, it is remarkable how the direct implications of simple arithmetic applied to amounts of people and amounts of resources can make so small an impact on the consciousness of those who spend their lives manipulating figures.

A NEW REGIONAL GEOGRAPHY

In spite of the manifest difficulties experienced by a geography comprised of rather disparate specialisms, anyone who feels the need for some kind of motivated culmination to geographical study hesitates before giving expression to his views. Any suggestion of returning to large-scale regional study may at best appear like putting new wine into old bottles; at worst it may seem to advocate a return to a cellar in which both the contents and the receptacles are of a vintage long since past its prime. The whole concept of "regional geography" may have an unhealthy ring, particularly to some of those from the more recent generations of practitioners.

But is it inevitable that a new approach to "regions" on the world scale would be stale and profitless? Those who have read the preceding chapters may well have developed a feeling that a vast field of study is lying virtually uncultivated, and that the best possible husbandmen might well be the cultural descendents of Humboldt, Mackinder and Wooldridge. The assessment of the organic resources of the United Kingdom presented here (chapter 5) is merely a brief, primitive and limited attempt to produce a motivated regional geography for a single country. Far more penetrating, detailed and comprehensive studies than this are urgently required for all the countries of the earth before their administrations can have sufficient information from which to devise long-term plans and to assess their national viabilities. A new regional geography which set out specifically to provide such studies would be very different indeed from most of the regional offerings of our youth.

It is often very easy to be unkind about the learning of the past, and to indulge in this gratuitously betrays a lack of historical perspective. Nevertheless, there is much point in recollecting that many books on "regional geography" were not written because the authors had some specific point to make: at best they were intended to indicate correlations in the distributions of various phenomena, at worst they had no more specific aim than to list and categorize the landscape features of an area in more or less orderly fashion. Probably the most interesting of them were those which presented each "region" in the context of its economic and social history, indicating the way in which the present landscape can be regarded as the final product of sequent occupance.

But the main limitation of most former regional geographies is that, in a number of ways, they were almost entirely academic. Although they often contained great quantities of information which could have been useful to planners and administrators, they themselves did not reach useful planning or administrative conclusions. For the most part they did not attempt to do so — the authors were concerned with producing "pure" not "applied" geography. Scholars of all kinds still subscribe to this kind of thinking: they hold that universities are places where knowledge is pursued for its own sake. There is ample justification for this, for enquiry into all aspects of knowledge must be pursued and where else if not in universities? But with a subject like geography, such a precept has its hazards and limitations. In departments of music and Latin a perfectly reasonable case can be made for just studying or creating, regardless of the affairs of the world; but in geography, as in economics, where all one deals with is so obviously part of the stuff of everyday life, it is probably very unwise not to devote a great deal of energy to presenting the results of study in a "relevant" framework. The puritanical among us might even go further: if one has expertise and knowledge which might be helpful in the clarification or resolution of vital world problems, is there not an element of immorality in devoting one's energies entirely to purely academic pursuits even though by chance, at some future time, someone else might use one's "academic" findings for practical purposes?

Others certainly had planning problems in mind but failed to produce work of lasting value because, even at the local planning level, they had little or nothing to say about the really basic issues of human ecology. Although they described resources and considered population, they did not even broach the subject of the fundamental and inexorable (though complex) formula which must link the two. They renounced completely that part of the cultural heritage which Malthus and Huntington had bequeathed them — the insistence on a cause-and-effect relationship between humanity and the realities of nature. Along with the rest of the world, they seem tacitly to have accepted a garbled version of Adam Smith's premise — that the population-carrying capacity of an area (parish, county, country) is unlimited, provided its labour force produces sufficient industrial goods.

The second main reason why most former regional geographies can be regarded as unacceptably academic is that, at the more extensive levels of integration, they concentrated on entities which did not relate to political reality. Many were purely formal regions — areas which, on the basis of a selection of criteria, possessed a measure of homogeneity. With a few notable exceptions, functional regionalism seems to have been practised only at the more local level — the areas within the "sphere of influence" of individual towns and industrial complexes. In other words, the "regions" with which geographers were concerned either transgressed national frontiers or else were contained entirely within one particular country as elements in a patchwork of small units. Between the large formal region and the small functional region there was a gap, both in size and conception, which was usually unbridged. Over the last half century there have been few who, like C.A. Fisher (1959), have continued to emphasize the fundamental geographical significance of the national unit.

And yet, in the minds of the vast majority of thinking people, the one areal entity which has reality and meaning is the "national unit" or "country". This is not without sound logical and observational foundations: a particular country may embrace fragments of a number of different "natural" or "cultural" regions, and may even transgress the boundaries of recognizable areas of a particular industrial or economic activity; but because of the actual or potential restrictions imposed by frontiers (chapters 8 – 9), that which is contained within them must be regarded as having an essential unity. On the other hand, that which lies beyond them, because it belongs to somebody else, must be regarded as very separate. Much of former regional geography had an other-worldly view of realities; indeed it sometimes indulged in exercises which aimed to demonstrate what a better world it would be if only national frontiers were drawn in different places. Although undoubtedly true in many instances, it was of little more use than a partisan historian's demonstration that the situation in the British Isles would be so much happier today if the Normans had conquered Ireland instead of England. (Some may feel this is an unfair comparison. Nevertheless, it must be insisted that, unless there is resort to war, it is fanciful to imagine that nations are going to relinquish portions of their territory, no matter how much this would benefit the recipient or the inhabitants of the area concerned. One would probably have to search a very long time to discover a case in which a beneficial transfer of territory could be effected by means of a mutually acceptable exchange.) Both these flights of fancy are invigorating exercises for the imagination, but they cannot be regarded as satisfactory endpoints for geography and history. Although a division of the world into formal regions on the basis of a wide range of significant criteria must be regarded as essential in teaching young people what the world is like, there are good reasons for concluding that some more profound kind of political regional geography provides a more satisfying culmination for geographical study.

To those who might still protest that present national units are so arbitrary and unsatisfactory that we must continue to devote all our energies to complete unification of the world political system, one can only re-emphasize the points that have already been made (chapter 9): we are saddled with existing realities and the tide of nationalism runs very strong. However, the protagonists of internationalization could well ponder the view that the best way to bring most nations to a full realization of the limitations of their separateness would be to present them with the stark truths which become apparent when realistic national stock-taking is carried out. (One might add that there is, perhaps, an equal chance that internationalizers themselves, having considered the results of stock-taking on the world basis, might change their views about the roads which lead to human salvation. What is the point of removing political and economic obstacles to trade if a scarcity of energy precludes the carting of vast and increasing amounts of material around the world and if, in any case, the goods are not available?) Many new countries which began a slow rise to a slightly increased emancipation when they were parts of empires, might husband their resources more carefully if presented with more clear-cut statements about their resource/population predicaments now that they are independent states. Similarly, Scots, Basques and Eritreans might well have second thoughts if presented with a clear inventory of their own per capita production in so many of the "essentials" of life. That some of these peoples have been exploited for the benefit of others is not in doubt, but the point remains that their present standard of living, inferior though it may be by comparison with that of others, only reached its present level because, as colonies or dependent provinces, they were part of a greater whole which linked them to a world trading system. This "greater whole" has now disappeared as a political reality, and there is every reason to suppose that the world trading system itself is beginning, perforce, to atrophy.

A coherent body of knowledge awaits compilation and evaluation which will demonstrate clearly to the nations (and would-be nations) what resources they possess, and what resources they cannot possibly have for their peoples, if outside sources should fail or be denied to them. This body of knowledge and enlightenment is what is being envisaged here as the new reinvigorated regional geography. Such a field of study would certainly possess the *raison d'être* which former regional geography lacked.

THE SKILLS OF GEOGRAPHERS

There is reason to feel confident that geography, as at present constituted, is adequately equipped to undertake national stock-taking authoritatively and responsibly. One of its great achievements over the past two decades — probably the really outstanding one — has been the gain in systematic skills arising out of the trend towards specialization. It now has properly qualified hydrologists, pedologists and ecologists, and in many of the seats of learning where geography is established, they possess properly equipped teaching and research facilities. Furthermore, many of them have profited from the so-called "quantitative revolution" and are at a level of numeracy and statistical dexterity far in advance of their counterparts of twenty years ago. In addition, there is now a more profound knowledge of economics, demography, land tenure and political science among those who are concerned primarily with social aspects of the subject.

Two important changes in emphasis may well be necessary, however, before the subject will be able to focus its assets with full effectiveness on the problem-oriented regional studies that are envisaged here. First, some of those geographers who are now quite justified in regarding themselves as adequate specialists in aspects of natural and social science will have to divest themselves of the assumption that their only claim to academic respectablility lies in the practising of their specialism. So long as this persists, the corporate development of the subject is deprived of the wholehearted participation of some of its most illustrious minds. This is not to say that they should cease to insist on their students receiving a sound scientific training, merely that they should realize that some present attitudes can lead to a situation where the different things being studied in departments of geography can appear to the student (and to any impartial observer) as unrelated as if they appeared in the schemes of study of entirely distinct university disciplines.[1] Such attitudes are not justified, and probably arise out of past inferiority complexes; insofar as they may result in direct competition with the research and teaching being carried out elsewhere,

[1] The view that geography, as a viable discipline, can deal with all conceivable phenomena in isolation from each other, provided the material is viewed spatially, has been dealt with elsewhere (Eyre and Jones, 1966, pp.3–7).

they could cause the subject to lose its distinctiveness. A focusing of systematic expertise within motivated regional studies could produce both distinctiveness and high academic morale.

Secondly, those who carry some responsibility for the direction of studies in the social aspects of the subject might well reflect on the amounts of energy and resources that have been devoted in recent years to the study of the internal structure and functions of urban areas. Justification for this, of course, depends entirely on one's view of the very nature of geography: those who would still hold that the subject is primarily concerned with the spatial analysis of features on the earth's surface would feel impelled to assert that urban patterns are at the very core of the subject. They would argue that, *because they are there*, towns have an equal right to have their spatial patterns analysed as any other set of features. Some might go further and declare that towns demand even more intensive study because, in many countries, more people live inside them than elsewhere.

If such a view of the subject prevails, then clearly there can be little chance of achieving a coherence in which both natural and social scientists focus their studies on the resources/population problems of the nations. Most of the purely internal functions of towns are only distantly connected with the fundamental ways in which man is dependent on the environment; the geographer's impact thus stands to be greatly diluted if urban studies predominate in geography. It is not that nothing in towns is worthy of study — merely that the detailed nature of the urban scene is much closer to the basic interests of psychologists, urban sociologists, physical planners, architects and engineers than it is to those primarily concerned with population and resource problems.

Geography seems likely to make its greatest impact if it concentrates on the results of urban expansion rather than on the details of urban structure. It is the submergence and neutralization of agricultural land, the amounts of people and waste they pour out into the surrounding countryside, and the amount of materials that have to be supplied to them that make towns of fundamental interest. The majority of people in Western society are now urban dwellers and it is not entirely palatable to them to have to concede that the large town is probably a very ephemeral feature — that huge cities are perhaps no more than a frothy pollutant which has invested the surface of the great river of human development in the present reach of its course. But there is surely strong evidence that the multi-million urban agglomeration is psychologically and materially incapable of maintaining itself in perpetuity. A discipline concerned primarily with the interactions between men and their environment would probably be well advised to concentrate on the fundamental rather than the ephemeral.

11

Planning — Superficial or Fundamental?

An analysis of human affairs which diagnoses a fundamental ailment is in danger of being regarded as pointless and irresponsible if not accompanied by some suggestions regarding the kind of treatment which might effect a cure. It is for this reason that a chapter on planning has been included here, and not because of any delusion that a complete blueprint for the way ahead can be embodied in a few pages. This is not to say that the writer has no convictions about some of the things which planners and administrators should be trying to achieve in the near future: only that it would be foolish to imagine that one person — even were he a contemporary reincarnation of Adam Smith — could be capable of producing a detailed and comprehensive map of the road to salvation.

THE FUNDAMENTAL NEED FOR PLANNING

That it is necessary to take thought for the morrow will have become obvious from the foregoing chapters. If civilization is to survive, problems of this magnitude and complexity will not solve themselves by some kind of "natural" course of events. Those of us who are impressed by the ingenuity and potential good sense of mankind the world over still retain the conviction that deliberate action can be taken in time to break and flatten the exponential curve of swarming and environmental destruction before it can destroy us in the same way that it would destroy a swarm of any other animal. But we must not delude ourselves that this will continue to be true, for even in another two decades it may well be too late. No world-wide trend can be reversed instantaneously no matter how determined and effective the policy that is directed against it. A delay of only two decades or so in the application of a programme of population limitation could entail a final equilibrium population almost twice the size that it might otherwise have been (Cabinet Office, 1976).

It we delay too long, the views of historical fatalists will probably be of no more comfort to distant posterity than to ourselves and our children. If civilization does collapse or suffer a severe setback because of our lack of foresight and responsibility, its chance of rising from the ashes will be enormously diminished: the struggle back to a technological society will be subject to far greater restrictions than was formerly the case. Nearly all accessible minerals will have been exhausted and the gene pool of the earth's ecosystems will be greatly reduced as compared to that which was available to man when he set out on his hunting and collecting forays in palaeolithic times.

THE NATURE AND FUNDAMENTAL AIMS OF PLANNING

Planning has its roots in the one basic characteristic which is usually regarded as the reason for man's rise to predominance over the other animals: human beings have the faculty for logical anticipation. This evolved from the purely animal ability to recall former experiences — to remember that certain types of occurrence are followed by particular types of event — but in humans it is developed a stage further: we are capable of identifying ways in which an imminent event is likely to be different from anything that has occurred before and of taking appropriate action to deflect or avoid it. Since history never repeats itself exactly, this is a mental ability which has furnished us with enormous advantages over animate and inanimate nature. Some individuals seem to have this faculty developed to a far higher degree than others and this cannot be said to be entirely due to differences in innate intelligence: a large range of environmental influences (not least of which may be an overspecialized education) may result in a failure to achieve maximum potential.

The average human being may perform a considerable number of these acts of logical anticipation every day; indeed, at quite frequent intervals, most of us have to make decisions on a course of action, using a number of items of information which, in combination, have never been used by anyone before. Thus, we plan our future. Large numbers of people are capable of doing this with a sufficient measure of success to ensure that the outcome of their planning is broadly in line with the outcome they originally envisaged. By and large, thoughtful and responsible people plan their family circumstances in this way: they have objectives and they devise plans of campaign to achieve them. Those who drift along without objectives, living beyond their means and working on the Micawberite assumption that something is bound to turn up, are looked upon as feckless and irresponsible.

If responsible people plan their private lives in this way, might we not expect that the affairs of nations should be managed with similar foresight? Planning on this larger scale must inevitably be more complex, but are we not justified in expecting statesmen and their advisers to look in a sober and balanced way at the logical feasibilities and to arrive at a plan of action which the evidence indicates will have a successful outcome? The more incautious politician might strenuously assert that this is exactly what is done, but all the evidence, particularly that of some public pronouncements, suggests that in certain important ways, basic political planning is not really planning at all. We frequently hear those in positions of influence and responsibility expressing their "faith" in technology, and it is clear that they are hoping that unspecified future technological innovations will solve problems for which there are no solutions at the present time — problems which often cry out for immediate action. We are surely entitled to ask whether those in positions of responsibility have a right to base national survival on something which is still a field for speculation rather than on systems and processes which are established, proved and sustainable. A householder who squandered the whole of his substance on the expectations of a substantial legacy from an almost unknown relative still in very good health, could surely be regarded as irresponsible, and his wife and children would have reasonable grounds for complaint.

Such strictures on government are merited up to a point, but it would be misleading to carry analogies between the family and the nation beyond a certain point. For one thing it is far easier for a family to arrive at a clear consensus, while politicians are always in the position of having responsibility for people with a wide range of desires and long-term aspirations. In spite of the fact that our political representatives are often so unwise as to speak about what "the nation" wishes, they know very well that a proportion of their constituents will disagree no matter what policy decisions are made.

However, there are far more profound philosophical problems in the field of long-term, large-scale planning. It seems reasonable that there should be some agreement between planners and planned regarding the level of living beneath which existence would not be tolerable. For instance, would society ever settle for a life in which each individual or family was provided with a box-like living space and just sufficient food, air, light, heat, plumbing and other services to maintain life over an average span of seventy years? If this were presented unambiguously as an option to humanity as a whole, probably the vast majority would be of the opinion that any amount of privation and self-denial would be preferable in order to prevent our ever being reduced to such a condition. In other words it is unthinkable that our way of life and our planning decisions in the immediate future should be such as to consign posterity to the fate of just "keeping alive".

If we reject mere "existence" as an acceptable option, however, the decision has still to be made regarding the guidelines to which our planners should refer. One might infer from the present ethos of Western society that nothing should deflect them from striving for the opposite extreme — that material standard of living must remain the foremost criterion. Amounts of physical comfort, mechanically produced amusement and relief from physical and mental labour seem to hold pride of place in the aspirations of the great majority of people. Apart from the fact that such a consumer-oriented society is bound to be short-lived, there are surely the strongest possible reasons for rejecting a high level of consumption as the basic prerequisite for a satisfying life. If all those who devote so much of their consciousness and their conversation to their possessions were compelled to reveal their innermost feelings, would not most of them admit that much of their concern for the material is merely a feverish enthusiasm for second best? There seems to be plenty of evidence that they would exchange most of it for the greater contentment of more secure family relationships and more genuinely sympathetic social contact within more meaningful communities. The near-desperate mental state of so many rejected parents, rejected children and rejected wives, and the quantity of hardened cynicism which survives when the near-desperation has passed, seem to demonstrate the truth of this. One of the most dreadful visions that can be conjured up is of a society in which each individual is so hedged around with costly gadgets and mechanical luxuries that no other human being is able to approach; and even if propinquity is possible, there are so many buttons to push during the course of the day that no opportunity arises for conversation, much less for a demonstration of regard or understanding. At first glance such a scenario may seem exaggerated and ridiculous, but is it not the one which salesmen and the advertizing world are striving to achieve? In the eyes of someone living only a century ago, would we not seem already to be half way there? Fortunately, such a goal, as well as being undesirable, is also unachievable for more than a tiny minority of mankind, and must be ruled out as a planning target.

Many of those who might reject material welfare as the first priority for the planner might well opt for the largest possible measure of individual freedom. Along with economic emancipation it is this which has been foremost in the minds of most reformers from the Reformation up to the signing of the Atlantic Charter. But one must seriously question whether the happier future society which many of us wish to envisage would be achieved by fashioning a material and social structure in which almost unbridled personal freedom of action had absolute priority. If one looks even cursorily at those most privileged sectors of Western society in which there are individuals who can do almost anything they please at almost any time, one is not impressed by a pervading happiness or contentment; indeed one often gets the feeling that, were it not for the fact that they are so economically secure, many would perish at an early age through sheer disorientation and isolation. Personal freedom is clearly a limited precept, and all those fervent advocates of "doing one's own thing" would do well to ask themselves whether a fairly even balance between unhampered mental and physical freedom on the one hand, and the self-discipline which arises from having to live together on the other, is not the only basic prescription for a rewarding life.

REALISTIC PLANNING

It is fortunate that thoughtful and conscientious planners are spared many of these agonizing decisions. They are not in a position to attempt detailed models of future situations because so many relevant parameters must remain unidentified, and even those that are known and understood often cannot be quantified. The best that the realistic planner can hope to achieve is the identification of the impossible (chapter 8): he can identify those lines of development which, through inescapable circumstances, are bound to be dead ends. If only our long-term planners can gain acceptance for a range of "impossibilities" — a set of goals which must be discounted because, in the foreseeable future, they are unattainable — then their tasks will become immeasurably more easy. They can then concentrate on creating a situation in which there is sufficient elbow-room to ensure that posterity has a good chance of retaining and improving those important things about which there would be little disagreement between thoughtful people of all creeds and persuasions. They can plan a world in which intense bodily pain, ignorance, human exploitation, and internecine strife arising from gross inequality of opportunity, are reduced to the lowest possible minimum. Such an achievement will be difficult enough under any circumstances; it will be utterly unattainable if obstructed by frenetic efforts to produce an infinite quantity of consumables so that an indefinite number of people can have an illusory happiness and material emancipation.

But where are the planners who are stretching their intellects to distinguish between the essentials and the dispensables? Should one imagine that people really have been appointed to rethink the basic priorities of mankind? Those with experience of planning and planners may find it difficult to reconcile the impressions they have formed with these more fundamental activities. In the minds of most people, "planning" is concerned with more immediate considerations: it arranges, facilitates, obstructs or modifies the familiar objects of our everyday existence rather than devises new frameworks for a different way of life which will be in equilibrium with the constraints of the future.

Nevertheless, during the past few years, many governments have felt impelled to set up committees whose terms of reference are specifically focused on more distant horizons. This seems to have been in response to publications such as *Blueprint for Survival* (*Ecologist,* 1972), *World Dynamics* (Forrester, 1971) and *Limits to Growth* (Meadows, 1972) which, in different ways, emphasized resource/population problems. The Stockholm Conference on the human environment also seems to have been successful in convincing reluctant national administrations that such problems must be taken seriously. In the United Kingdom, a government interdepartmental committee was set up to consider long-term world trends in phenomena such as population growth, resource depletion, environmental impacts and economic growth. Its first findings were published in *Nature* (Cottrell, 1973) and, subsequently, a discussion paper on world trends and their implications has been issued (Cabinet Office, 1976). The latter emerged from the presses with so muted a fanfare that one could readily be forgiven for overlooking its existence: its arrival was noted only inconspicuously in one or two of the national newspapers. And yet it contained statements which would have been unthinkable from any organ of the establishment only a few years earlier. Thus, in one of the summary sections (p.24) we read:

> Although it should be theoretically possible to feed the world's growing population until the turn of the century, the enormous political, social and economic problems involved make it unlikely that this will be achieved .... Unless there are resource transfers on a scale many times greater than at present, the effective check to world population will be the Malthusian trilogy of war, famine and disease.

And a little earlier (p.22) there is the statement that:

> In the long term, only the improvement and widespread use of contraceptive methods can prevent mass starvation and the resources currently devoted to these problems are inadequate.

These are remarkable statements for a government publication particularly since, being a discussion paper, it was not required to draw conclusions. The fact that it refers to the possibility of a Malthusian outcome is particularly arresting. But, despite its clear warnings, there is every indication in its economic sections of an astonishing complacency regarding the fundamental capability of the present economic system of the United Kingdom to cope with the almost unavoidable upheavals ahead. The committee's most radical suggestions for future economic policy seem to be "a shift in the balance of economic research in favour of applied economics" and the need for research "to identify ... market imperfections" (p.17). It seems as though the strictures of Professor Galbraith (chapter 10) may well have reached British economics, but that the spirit of Adam Smith still determines all its fundamental modes of thought.

THE ART OF THE POSSIBLE

It seems clear then that national government is now committed to a consideration of long-term planning issues. The fact that as yet there has been no radical statement about methods and objectives should come as no surprise. Except in times of war, governments have rarely indulged in specific statements about long-term intentions, and no administration, however enlightened, honest and unified, could be expected to be completely forthright regarding the necessity for rigorous policies demanding economic contraction and rapid social change. Any democratically elected government which committed itself in this way might expect to be out of office within a very short time, and even in a totalitarian situation survival would be precarious and probably short-lived. Neither can the official advisers of government express themselves with complete freedom. Any profound changes must be preceded by a period in which public opinion is prepared for them, if there is to be any real chance of acceptance. Essentially, this is what is implied when politics is referred to as "the art of the possible".

There can be little doubt that this is one of the reasons why the unpleasant facts of life, even when democratic processes demand their publication, are heralded so softly. It is probably why there has been no insistent demand from members of parliament for a substantial parliamentary debate. Such a debate would imply a recognition of the seriousness and urgency of the situation with a consequent demand from thoughtful people for realistic action, and it is feared that such action could not possibly be acceptable to the great majority of the electorate. Consequently, no one dares to reach out towards the nettle, let alone grasp it. Regrettably, there is also reason to suspect that even the organs of the media, usually so eager to embrace potential governmental embarrassments, are unwilling to probe deeply and persistently into these matters. The champions of the people wish to remain as such, and not to compete with government for unpopularity. Where a viable husbandry for the future requires the slaughtering of a sacred cow in nearly every backyard, and where the entrenched positions of so many politicians, business men and religionists will have to be abandoned, it is easy to see why editors, columnists and commentators hesitate to ventilate the issues involved. None of us enjoy contemplating the implications of mankind at the swarming stage, but a fundamental biological phenomenon will not go away just because we do not like it. The disinclination of non-politicians to look squarely at the facts and to begin to suggest planning mechanisms and planning objectives, is probably the most depressing aspect of the present scene. Government cannot be expected to do more than set up working committees unless urged to do so by the informed and the articulate.

RESISTANCE TO PLANNING

There are a variety of reasons why the governed might regard planning with suspicion, if not aversion, particularly large-scale, comprehensive planning which strikes at the roots of the social order. It is understandable, for instance, why many of those in positions of influence in the world of industry and business might be opposed to it. Not only do they feel impelled to try to repel encroachments upon their personal interests, they are also able to call upon Adam Smith as an expert witness. Nothing was more central to his thesis than the view that "it is the highest impertinence and presumption ... in kings and ministers, to pretend to watch over the economy of private people." He held that the free play of the market, in the long run, provides the greatest good for the greatest number, and that any interference with those who operate for profit in the market will decrease the sum total of wealth available to humanity. One can only comment that, as an absolute precept, this is a position which was long since abandoned by those who have had to assume responsibility for government. Although it is not difficult to find people who still advocate a return to untrammelled *laissez-faire* economics, it is hard to see how a complex community could function if all the multifarious adjuncts and services of its public sector had to show immediate profitability. Indeed, how can industrial marvels such as Concorde, the pinnacle of Western technological achievement, be justified if even remotely foreseeable profitability is the criterion?

The point at issue, however, is not the long-term validity of Adam Smith's precepts: if once it is conceded that the ultimate aim can no longer be to maximize material standards of living (see above p.158), the argument that the ultimate social good is dependent on the "free play of the market" falls to the ground. Moreover, there is no sense in pretending that the economic system is trying to create greater ease and more leisure in society when that society discovers that it is trying to create work for millions of people. Out-and-out self-interest may be taken as grounds for opposition to planning, but the material welfare of society as a whole long since ceased to be an acceptable excuse for opposition to a planned economy. Unbridled consumption of materials in a *laissez-faire* economy over the next twenty years would probably carry humanity beyond a point of no return, leaving a massive industrial society high and dry with insufficient resources to maintain itself, and with insufficient flexibility to retract.

During recent years there has been increasing use of the expression "social engineering", and this also has given rise to misgivings about planning which are both fundamental and understandable. Discerning and independent people shrink from the contemplation of a future in which the nature and location of their living space, the kind of food they eat, and almost every facet of their daily lives are rigorously circumscribed, mainly (it would appear) for administrative convenience and tidiness. They ask themselves who the planners are, whether they know best, whether or not they are benevolent, and whether they are likely to remain so. In the mind's eye they have the nightmarish scenario which Orwell painted for 1984. Many would say that if the end of planning is like this, they would prefer to have none of it, regardless of the consequences.

There is no easy or fully reassuring answer to such anxieties, but two points should certainly be considered by anyone who leans to the view that planning is dispensable. First, the restrictions on human freedom of action will have become far, far greater a generation hence if successful planning of population and resource usage has not taken place. The signs of overcrowing, over-urbanization and competition for materials are already apparent in the rush-hour, price escalation and recurrent water restrictions; indeed, these and many other constraints on everyday life are already irksome, uneconomic and mentally debilitating for many people, particularly in the "privileged" countries of the world. If a lack of planning permits the continued rapid increase in population and consumption, along with a decreased commitment to deal with environmental problems as they arise, then the only option will be between a rather nasty, circumscribed existence on the one hand, and turmoil and collapse on the other. Any possibility of a degree of mental emancipation for the great majority of mankind will have been forfeited.

The second point is that no effort must be spared to contain planning in an effective democratic framework. Indeed, one cannot imagine that unpalatable courses of action will ever gain acceptance if this is not done. Cynics may well deride the possibility of whole nations accepting a planned decline in consumption without resistance, but this need not be a foregone conclusion provided the reasons for the unacceptability of all conceivable alternatives are presented clearly and openly. In a democratic society those who are governed should be expected to ask for the reasons for any national course of action. The writer is only too conscious of the fact that he is advocating political and economic action for the immediate future which, at first sight, may seem unthinkably drastic. He would be unrealistic in the extreme if he imagined that there could be an unreasoning acceptance of the need for it; it would be an indication of pathetic conformity in society if ever this could happen. No planning action should ever be taken without an overwhelming case being made for it: its logic should be inescapable.

It is at this point, however, that one encounters what is probably the greatest potential obstruction to an orderly solution of unpleasant problems. Although the innate reasoning capability of *Homo sapiens* is beyond question, it cannot be assumed that, in any particular set of circumstances, he will use it. The overriding logic of a situation, particularly if it has unpalatable implications, may well be ignored. This is probably because man has evolved as a social animal and, over the millennia, has accumulated a cultural heritage on which he leans very heavily. Consequently, in a particular situation, especially if it is one of great complexity, a man may not use his own innate intelligence, or even the experience personally accumulated, but may fall back on a pattern of thought and behaviour which his ancestors have bequeathed to him. Throughout most of history this has doubtless been beneficial: it has ensured that a man could call upon more than purely personal experience when beset by unusual difficulties. In passing, one might also reflect on the fact that this is not a pattern of behaviour which is confined to the less intelligent: the most ingenious and fertile minds may fall back upon their cultural inheritance as a matter of habit or for peace of mind.

Unfortunately, it seems likely that these unreasoning patterns of thought may now be a great obstacle. One can appreciate the benefit they may have conferred when men lived in small agricultural communities, carrying out tasks essentially similar to those performed by their forebears for many generations: the circumstances in which they lived were very similar to those experienced by the ancestors who had created the folklore. But with the rapid growth of an urban way of life, the traditional modes of thought have at best become less relevant: just as dependence on a massive and intricate technology would become a millstone around the neck of civilization should raw materials fail, so traditional habits of mind could become a fatal stumbling-block in the coming decades. If famine or plague threatened a rural community in former times, there was often little or nothing that could be done to avert it. Consequently, a fatalistic acceptance supported by the sanction of religious quotation probably suited the requirements of society better than anything else, if an ordered way of life were to survive the catastrophe. It therefore put its trust in the Almighty and took comfort from the scriptural "God will provide".

In a world of vast urban populations there can be little hope of an orderly survival in the times ahead if, faced with the obvious necessity for positive measures such as birth control, resource conservation and redeployment, the logical inferences are rejected in favour of fatalistic escapism. Nor indeed will the outcome be any less unpleasant if the age-old reference to the Deity is translated into modern idiom, and society seeks refuge behind an unreasoned expectation that "technology will find a way".

One final obstruction to fundamental planning should be mentioned. The accumulating problems of humanity are already so numerous and difficult that no quick solution, with a rapid return to increasing material emancipation, can be envisaged. No material incentives can therefore be offered even for enjoyment by our children and grandchildren. Provided we do not attempt the impossible, we may anticipate only that a more secure and satisfying way of life can be planned with a possible return to ease and comfort for people later in the twenty-first century. Regrettably this may appear a threat rather than an incentive to many consumers in the present world.

The situation at the present time is not even analagous to the one faced by the British people in 1940 when, bereft of allies, and with no hopeful signs on the horizon, they accepted with determination and purpose a spartan diet, disruption of personal life and the nightly threat of destruction. The difference between the two predicaments is that, in 1940, the time-scale of the prospective ordeal was very different: even if the war was a long one it would, hopefully, be concluded within the lifetimes of many of those engaged in it. The war was about something which all could easily appreciate: it was a contest between "us" and "them" so that innate characteristics of competitiveness and aggressiveness could be mobilized to meet the opposition. There are no "us" and "them" in the present difficulties (though, sadly, there will usually be those who will try to demonstrate otherwise): the contest is between the self-conscious, reasoning mind of *Homo sapiens* on the one hand, and his biological limitations on the other. It will not be easy to mobilize human effort for such a contest.

Lacking short-term incentives like "peace", " possessions" and "freedom from interference", all that can be offered for the near future are what most people would regard as "lesser evils". Instead of failure of food supplies and industrial collapse, private individuals can be given such options as family limitation and lower incomes, and businesses those of lower profits, reduced resource consumption and more labour-intensive processes. Our present economic systems (capitalist and communist) are not oriented to be able to offer such options (see below, p. 170); but there can be little doubt that, if they could be presented in the appropriate political and social framework, they would be very effective. It is clear, however, that no such fundamental changes in system can be achieved until there is resignation to the fact that, in the future, social improvement is not going to be effected by "levelling up". Reformers in the past have often been intimidated into silence by the accusation that their egalitarianism would involve a quite unacceptable "levelling down". Since there is now no chance of an over-all "levelling up" over the next few generations, reformers need no longer look over their shoulders on this account.

The problems of overcoming resistance to fundamental planning thus revolve around the selection of a set of "lesser evils" and convincing people that it is pointless to expect better. However, the problems of fashioning an economic and social framework in which such options could be presented, and of inventing ways in which we can discard those features of our present systems which will not be viable for very much longer, require deeper consideration.

The Greater Evils

The planned acceptance of "lesser evils" implies that "greater evils" are to be avoided. Although the former will at first seem irksome and painful, particularly to all the privileged peoples, they are mild and eminently bearable as compared to the world-wide disasters which could constitute the latter — disasters which many would not survive. Is it really an imposition to ask two parents to limit themselves to one or two children and to eat not more than about 75 per cent of what they do at the present time, when both complain constantly about the cost of bringing up children and frequently have to engage in weight-watching in order to safeguard their health? Contrast their case with that of the woman refugee with a baby, homeless and destitute on the streets of Calcutta, who knows full well that her child will be dead by morning and that it will require a very unlikely change of circumstances if she is to survive it by more than a week or two. With a rapidly deteriorating world food situation and a faltering distribution network, cases such as this, already all too common, could multiply with alarming rapidity over much of the world. This is merely a glimpse at the choice of "evils".

POPULATION PRESSURE

At the present time most of us would prefer to postpone acceptance of the lesser infringements upon our freedom of action in the hope that the need for them will go away. What we fail to realize is that this very procrastination will accelerate the advance of impending disasters. It could well be that for every year in which we continue with our present policies, particular types of danger are brought two years nearer. It seems perfectly justifiable, for instance, to enquire whether people wish to arrive at a situation, somewhere in the lifetime of many of us, where reasonable people would be forced to agree that compulsory sterilization had become a necessity. Do we wish to go on using up raw materials in an uncontrolled way so that, not far into the future, vast numbers of factories have to close without making provision for their employees? Does Britain really wish to reach a situation where the available resources cannot possible support 55 million people, so that all the rents, rates and taxes that can be squeezed from the community are insufficient to prevent tower blocks from disintegrating, sewage works from choking up and the air from becoming re-polluted? With the present pressure on land in Britain, and the enormous pressures on the public purse, the small environmental successes of the past two decades could be dissipated almost overnight if our basic resource foundations were to crumble. The "greater evils" are only too apparent if one cares to project present trends; nevertheless a closer scrutiny of the roads which may lead to them is illuminating.

One popular view of population problems is that they will solve themselves — that without any conscious or corporate effort, numbers will cease to increase at the appropriate time and come to equilibrium with terrestrial realities. If one is willing to accept the assumptions of Thomas Malthus and Adam Smith there can be no argument about this: if starvation, pestilence and conflict intervene as food becomes scarce and peoples begin to jostle each other, these controls will be very effective. But this is not usually what has been envisaged when twentieth-century social scientists have discussed the matter: they have postulated a variety of possible ways in which fertility could be lowered without the intervention of the more drastic controls. "Urbanization", "increased standard of living", "decreased standard of living" and "overcrowding" have all been suggested as possible reasons why population growth might cease. And indeed, it must be admitted that, in the past, each one of these may have caused fluctuations in growth rates. The salient fact remains, however, that, in all circumstances where they have occurred over the past few centuries, neither opulence nor grinding poverty can be demonstrated to have stopped population growth. On the world scale, except where pandemics have intervened, population trends have been persistently upwards (chapter 3); it is unreasonable to expect that the chance interplay of social forces will come to our aid now. As demographers have so frequently emphasized, the reasons for birth rate fluctuations must be complex, and it is for this very reason that the future should no longer be left to take care of itself.

Over the past century, the views of society about population change have been clearly reflected in the attitudes of local authorities. Nearly always, when they have had anything which might be regarded as a positive policy, it has been one of enthusiasm for growth. Cities have looked forward to the next census with some excitement, wondering whether or not they will have managed to pass the half, three-quarter or one million mark. They have vied with each other for numbers, and as these have grown so their pride has swelled accordingly. In only a few cases, such as that of Greater London, have the attendent problems become so acute that planning measures have been adopted in an effort to stem the tide. In the great majority of cases, planning effort has been concentrated on details — whether to permit expansion into the countryside on a continous front, whether to stop this and promote ribbon development or satellite towns, and so on.

In the train of this growth the authorities concerned have ranged around the surrounding countryside, seeking the means to provide services and space. Water supplies have been transported for scores of miles to meet the escalating demand and one has constantly heard such statements as, "by the year 2000 AD water consumption in the region will have trebled." One wonders whether, in the backs of their minds, officials who make such predictions imagine that in the year 2000 their successors will be making just the same forecast for 2020 AD and, likewise, that the officials in all the other water authorities will be saying the same thing. Judging by the way in which in times of drought our rivers and streams are already reduced to the merest trickles, water engineers in many countries must envisage purchasing water from the neighbouring states of, say, Ruritania and Cloud-cuckoo Land.

In the light of such attitudes, our present world may go down to posterity as "the Age of Unrealism". The breakdown of ancestral restrictions on mobility in the Industrial Revolution has brought us to a point where it is believed that everyone should have a basic right to live anywhere. Previously, legal, economic and other social sanctions prevented this. If a tribesman wandered away to do his own thing, the odds were heavily weighted against his survival, and if a manorial peasant forsook the place of his birth to find a livelihood elsewhere, he was fortunate not to be apprehended as a vagrant and forcibly returned to his native heath. Only the privileged minority could move around as they wished, and usually they did not do so because their privileges only applied in the place where they belonged. We must not imagine then that complete freedom of individual mobility is part of an established, normal mode of existence, the viability of which has been proven since time immemorial. Furthermore, with increasing congestion, the inherent difficulties of free mass mobility might be expected to increase rather than the reverse.

THE EMPLOYMENT DILEMMA

Restrictions on living space and the atrophy and decay of services, though perhaps the most obvious, are far from being the most serious of the "greater evils". The crumbling of the whole economic system because of its inherent contradictions is far more fundamental, and the nature of these contradictions becomes apparent when one examines the concept of "gainful employment" in our present industrial society.

The promoters of the Industrial Revolution did not set out to create a world in which conditions would favour population increase: this occurred incidentally. The difficulties arising out of it were not immediately apparent, however, partly because of the vast quantities of fossil fuel and other minerals available, and partly because of the size of the market which an expanding transport system put within reach. Continuous expansion of the new factory system was thus possible, employing larger and larger numbers of the increasing population. Moreover, millions of people from the industrializing countries were decanted into other parts of the world which were either empty or actively depopulated of their former inhabitants. This relieved population pressure in Europe in another way. As a consequence of these developments, the illusion developed that population growth, linked to economic growth, would continue indefinitely into the future. The Industrial Revolution was thus imbued with immortality.

The basic limitation of the whole of this social process, and one that has never been squarely faced (except by the Luddites!), is that the Industrial Revolution, by definition, was a technological revolution which resulted ultimately in men being replaced by machines, because this reduced the cost per unit of production. It continues today and its aims are substantially unaltered. What is more, it has now developed to a point where we have the technological ability to automate almost every type of factory procedure so that a tiny staff of electronic and mechanical engineers can operate a factory with the need for unskilled, semi-skilled and even skilled labour reduced to the absolute minimum. So a situation exists in which population continues to increase but where human labour is increasingly dispensable.

As yet, this contradiction is barely acknowledged by society. In 1976 a television news programme carried three features: first, an important official of the British iron and steel industry commented on the necessity to cut its labour force by about 40 per cent in order to remain competitive; secondly, a politician spoke with regret of the way in which the "temporary recession" had caused the number of unemployed to rise above the million mark; and thirdly, a respected humanitarian gave his opinion that the whole concept of "over-population" was misguided. As far as could be ascertained, this juxtaposition passed entirely without comment.

It is understandable why discussions about "work" should give rise to more acrimony in society than almost anything else, but the lines along which these discussions develop are usually far from profitable. Two themes seem to predominate: first, there are the expressions of fear and regret that unemployment is unavoidable, and secondly there are confident beliefs, often loudly expressed, that other people do not work hard enough. Taken at their face value the two are obviously contradictory: if there is a lot of hard work to be done, why should there be millions of unemployed?

An objective examination of realities leads one to the view that, in terms of what constituted "hard work" only half a century ago, most of those "employed" today are no more than half employed. Relatively speaking, a great deal of "work" at the present time is very easy work. Whether one should regard this widespread "half employment" as "concealed unemployment" is obscured behind a semantic smoke-screen: in one sense of the expression a man is "fully employed" if he is paid a full wage for attendance at an official place of work; in the other sense he is "fully employed" only if he is hard at work for much of his waking hours. It is necessary to penetrate beyond this if one is to focus on the problem of employment in the context of resources and population pressure. Those who fulminate about the interminable coffee breaks or the almost continuous consumption of tea in both the public and private sectors of the economy, should ask themselves whether, if labour were twice as productive and more flexibly employed, half the labour force would not be made redundant and have to receive unemployment benefit. The choice would seem to be between employing half the population in "hard work" and paying much of the product of this to keep the other half in "idleness", or else paying the whole of the employable population a "living wage" for working half speed or half time. Without admitting to itself what it was doing, society in the privileged countries has already gone a long way to choosing the second alternative, but the question whether or not this "living wage" can in perpetuity be sufficient to support life is the fundamental issue.

There will be those who object that this argument is too simplistic — that if those employed in industry and commerce did work much harder for the same wages then far more would be produced, profits would be greater, and more would be available for investment so that more work would be created. This is the classical argument which leads straight into the logical *cul de sac* already explored. Such a course of action involves economic growth, and growth will not be possible for much longer: the energy, the raw materials and the markets will not be available. Rather than attempt to follow this disastrous course up to a situation where, not far hence, we pass the point of no return, we should reconcile ourselves to a set of lesser evils.

Unfortunately there is every indication that whatever plans exist are almost entirely designed to direct our feet along the wrong road. Economic growth is still regarded as inescapable; although half the world is already industrialized to a point where overinvestment in the production of expensive dispensables is a persistent threat (Watt, 1974), most of the other half is striving to achieve the same precarious state of affairs. Even if the materials for such a vast expansion of industrialization could be made available, markets for its produce would not materialize: with exploding populations in so many countries, purchasing power will be spread so thinly that the problem of securing adequate food will pre-empt all the energies of the vast majority. In the relatively opulent countries a large proportion of sales is already achieved by means of credit and hire purchase, so that any substantial lowering of real incomes threatens disaster: future income is mortgaged for years ahead in large sections of the community. As a consequence, consumers, trades unions and industrialists all concur: because the sale of goods must not be permitted to slacken substantially, income must be maintained even if it involves the employment of too much labour (though preferably in somebody else's establishment). The probable reason why the bubble has not already burst is because technologists have been so successful in lowering the *technical* costs of production, and factories have been able to carry on at a profit even though employing far more labour than they really need. But in the long run such a trend can only continue if growth is achieved. This is why growth has become far more than an index of commercial success: with the present system it is essential for survival.

THE FINAL CONVULSION: PLUTONIUM TECHNOLOGY

The issue just outlined lies at the root of the energy crisis, because economic growth cannot be maintained without making ever-increasing demands on energy supplies. Static reserves of fossil fuel are still substantial, but if the rate of depletion continues to increase exponentially then the date of virtual exhaustion advances at a frightening rate. The conclusion is inescapable: economic growth, imposed mainly because the system is overloaded with people, is pushing humanity towards the greatest of all impending evils — the development of a plutonium technology.

Ever since the first Pugwash Conference in 1957, the clearest and direst warnings have been issued about the dangers of nuclear fission. Consequently it is hard to believe that the plans at present in hand for its development would ever have been entertained if the world energy situation were not very serious indeed. Nothing demonstrates this more clearly than recent changes in emphasis in the pronouncements of some technological optimists. Whereas only a short time ago they were proclaiming that they saw no really serious problems in the world energy supply situation, since the petroleum crisis of 1973–4 they wear a more worried look and justify their continued support for the development of nuclear power by asserting that it *must* take place because the technological society cannot do without it.

And yet the implications of such a course of action are so horrific that good sense and all sound scientific and humanitarian considerations seem to demand that it be ruled out as an acceptable option. The only type of nuclear energy at present available involves the manufacture of the new element, plutonium, which does not occur in nature. It is so lethal to animal life that a few kilogrammes of it, appropriately distributed in the vicinity of the victims, would be sufficient to wipe out all humanity. A single fast breeder reactor of the size and type now being planned and constructed, would contain when fully operational between one and three tons of this element in its fuel inventory.[1]

Some very clear summaries of the nature and hazards of a plutonium technology are now available (see Lovins, 1975). It is only necessary here to emphasize those features which make it so dangerous and objectionable that almost any alternative discomforts and privations would be preferable.

First, plutonium has a half-life of 24,400 years so that, to all intents and purposes, once manufactured, all not consumed in energy conversion processes remains on the earth with man and his ecosystems into the indefinite future. There are no known methods (and none on even the more distant scientific horizons) of converting it into a non-radioactive, harmless material. Secondly, statements to the effect that increasing amounts of this radioactive substance (along with others which become radioactive by contact with it) can be accumulated without risk of serious accident or environmental contamination are worthless and should never be made. Such "assurances" seem to carry the implication that questions of safety in these matters are specifically confined to the province of the nuclear technologist — that he alone is qualified to provide the information on which final decisions can be made. This is far from the truth. When once the point has been made that these materials are noxious and long-lived, informed and thoughtful humanists are probably better qualified than anyone to reach balanced decisions. Essentially, the nature of the materials and the processes is no longer at issue: what matters is whether or not an earth with plutonium upon it can ever be safe, given that human beings and acts of God are as they are. In view of the behaviour of men throughout history, right up to the present day, it seems utterly unrealistic to have confidence that an ordered and stable way of life is going to prevail, unbroken, over all those parts of the earth where nuclear materials are being used and stored over the next 25,000 years and more. If the schemes of nuclear planners come to fruition we are asked to envisage, only a century hence, a world littered with thousands of nuclear generating stations, abandoned radioactive sites[2] and waste repositories, as well

[1]It has been pointed out that most of the plutonium in these reactors would not be in its most lethal elementary form, but combined in an oxide which one would not expect to be comminutable into respirable particles. However, in the case of technological failure, explosion or other possible disruptions, there is some doubt as to what state the liberated plutonium would be in (Lovins, 1975).

[2] The most optimistic prognoses allow an average life of no more that thirty-five years for a nuclear power plant.

as continuous streams of radioactive materials in process of transport over land and sea. A single terrorist bomb, or one intercontinental ballistic missile from an irresponsible government, exploding in just one of these, could project a cloud of deadly material into the atmosphere, capable of contaminating the earth's surface over a vast area with radioactive substances which would persist for an indefinite period. One serious earthquake, storm at sea, error of navigation or act of sabotage could cause the release of tons of the same kind of material into the ocean, rivers or groundwater, to diffuse out of control through the natural systems of the earth. And this is not to mention all the possible structural failures which some protagonists of a nuclear economy have assured us could not happen.

Such assurances seem particularly hollow in view of the resources dilemma of the nuclear industry. Because of the pending shortage of uranium-235 (chapter 6), the more stable burner reactors will have to be phased out as quickly as possible: the whole future of the industry thus depends upon the rapid development and proliferation of fast breeder reactors which, by their very nature, are far less stable and difficult to control. Indeed there are responsible nuclear physicists who now feel it to be unlikely that an *operationally* "safe" fast breeder reactor could be developed before the end of the century. The industry therefore finds itself under pressure to commit itself to even less safe procedures than it would probably have insisted on were uranium–235 a more commonly occurring isotope.

The Lesser Evils

The necessity for more rigorous planning of our daily lives is the main price we now have to pay for having journeyed so far with economic growth as our travelling companion. Furthermore, the nature and scale of the impositions upon us will have to change. Constraints upon the individual in recent years have predominantly taken the form of compulsory land purchase and the demolition of homes: it has been meso-scale planning rather than planning at the national and international level. But, as already implied, meso-scale planning will shortly reach the end of its tether if it is not supported by appropriate micro-scale planning, and unless there is fundamental macro-scale planning to ensure a viable social and economic framework for the operation of local government. Embracing the "lesser evils" implies an acceptance of greater restrictions on personal and national freedom of action.

PLANNING POPULATION REDUCTION

Population reduction is one of the more difficult issues which must be tackled simultaneously at micro- and macro-level. The main problem is that decisions made by the average individual and family must not be grossly incompatible with the economic constraints in which the community has to function. Clearly there is little chance of a concurrence of individual action and community requirements unless, first, people are told what these requirements are and, secondly, an adequate system of incentives and penalties is instituted to achieve them. It is undeniable that this is fundamental "social engineering", but it is the kind of thing which has been employed by society in most phases of history. Unless pressurized to desist, we are all prone to acts of self-gratification which may be quite contrary to what is required for survival. With regard to the promotion of population reduction at the present time, in most countries of the world no clear indications have been given regarding the most appropriate course of action. Social pressures are operating in a confused way, if indeed they are not entirely in the wrong direction. In spite of enormous efforts to promote birth control by national governments in a few countries like India (Johnson, 1970) and the Philippines (see *The Times,* 29 July 1976), in many of the poorer countries peasants still view children as economic assets (sources of labour) rather than liabilities. Moreover, in some more affluent countries such as the United Kingdom, where welfare services have become an important element in the economic system, the present scale of incentives and deterrents seems entirely contrary to the requirements of the situation: those who limit their families to one or two children receive negligible recognition for doing so, while rewards are piled upon those who produce far more, particularly if they are not capable of feeding and clothing them out of normal income.

It is realized that problems such as this bristle with social and political implications and that, in a just society, it is important to ensure that children do not suffer grossly because of the actions of their parents; but a system can surely be devised in which no one is in any doubt that if there are four children in a family, then the material standard of living of the parents will be only half what it would be if they had limited themselves to two. For a fair society which insists on personal responsibility and in which there is not gross inequality between the highest incomes and the basic minimum wage, this seems a not unreasonable proposition. (It is important to emphasize, however, that the most well-to-do people in society must not be left with the impression that they are morally entitled to have as many children as they like because they can "afford them". Every child which is born is a potential consumer of materials during its lifetime, regardless of its financial circumstances; indeed the opulent tend to consume a great deal more than the poor. A country which imports a large proportion of its requirements should be concerned about its total numbers: who is poor and who is rich is a purely internal matter.) It certainly seems preferable to continuing with our present system until a point is reached where sterilizing drugs have to be added to the municipal water supply. Any pretence at democracy will be hollow if ever this occurs.

However, population planning at the micro-level will probably be ineffective if it is not accompanied by equally determined activity on the international scene. In the first place it would be unrealistic to expect successful population limitation schemes to materialize in underprivileged countries without massive aid. But such countries should not object to a substantial percentage of aid and credit being earmarked for this purpose if there is clear evidence that measures for population reduction are also being undertaken by the privileged. Secondly, rigorous international action on immigration will have to be taken, since it would be unreasonable to expect people to limit their own families if the benefits of this were cancelled out by arrivals from elsewhere. This is a most difficult and emotive issue, not merely because it so often involves racial entanglements, but because the whole problem of inequalities between the nations also arises.

Any hope of obtaining international goodwill on immigration issues would seem dependent on two things. First, there must be practical demonstrations of real concern by the privileged. People in southern Asia and the West Indies cannot be blamed for wishing to migrate, either temporarily or permanently, to countries elsewhere in the world where average incomes are obviously higher. But their governments are only likely to embark on constructive discussions if genuine sympathy is shown for the social and economic problems which threaten to overwhelm them. Secondly, it is of the utmost importance that the privileged should view the whole world problem with impartiality. At the present time it is almost impossible to embark upon discussions about immigration without appearing to be inflammatory, and this is mainly because so many of those who have done so have been partisan and bigoted. If these protagonists of immigration limitation would make their points fairly and in full context, little exception could be taken to them: if they were to say that the time has gone when one nation can unload its population problems on to another, and that this applies to West Europeans just as much as to anyone else, then the wider problems could be discussed dispassionately. In the present climate, the man who declaims against recent arrivals in the United Kingdom and, in the next breath, announces his imminent departure to Canada or Rhodesia, seems to have no inhibitions about the inconsistency of his attitudes.

With regard to the main point at issue, national planners need have no doubts or reservations: short of a holocaust, there is no danger of there being too few people in the near future. Every effort (of a peaceable nature) can be devoted to the lowering of population by as much as possible and as quickly as possible. It is perhaps conceivable that, by the latter part of the twenty first century, some thought might have to be given to the threshold beneath which it would be inadvisable for world poplation to fall, but at the present time one can only contemplate the arrival of such times as a distant luxury. Nor should we worry about the problems of population age structure which a falling birth rate would bring. The point has often been made that, in such a situation, there would be a dangerous increase in the ratio of dependants to productive earners. What is so often overlooked is that an increase in the proportion of aged dependants would be more than offset by a decrease in that of young ones: with an average life-expectancy of 72 years and an average retirement age (men and women) of 62, the senior citizen group carries considerably less weight than that of the children, given a school-leaving age of 16. Society over the past few decades seems to have had no qualms about increasing the number of dependants: the school-leaving age has been progressively raised. In any case, considerations such as this are of a low order of magnitude as compared to the enormous threat of overpopulation. Increase must cease at some time, so all the lesser problems might just as well be faced now.

PLANNING THE ECONOMIC AND SOCIAL FRAMEWORK

Transforming our institutions to make them conformable with a falling population and rapidly decreasing consumption poses the most challenging problems of all. A new generation of radical Adam Smiths is needed to outline what most economists at the present time would regard as a contradiction in terms — a shrinking economy leading to a contented society in stable equilibrium. Essentially such a strategy must solve the very real problem as to how to maintain a sophisticated technology, producing the essentials for medicine, education and cultural pursuits, with no necessity for the mass production of our present consumer society. In other words it must reject the twentieth-century argument that culture can only be maintained by the spin-off from expensive research, vast machines and massive production, and devise an alternative system.

Concurrent with this, every conceivable effort must be made to encourage the acceptance of lower incomes. This can have little chance of success unless influential and respected people demonstrate by example that real pleasure is to be had from pastimes which are relatively inexpensive. It will be made easier if commercial advertising pressures are relaxed so that alternatives to the way of life epitomized in the glossy brochure can be given a fair chance of publicity. There is ample evidence to show that the tilling of one's own plot and the cultivation of local relationships can be satisfying far beyond most of the more expensive pursuits for people of a wide range of interests and aptitudes, but that these things have little chance to burgeon in a society where there is every inducement to spend each weekend travelling further and faster than on the previous one, and with an even more imposing load of expensive impedimenta.

Even then, such changes in attitude and aspiration are unlikely to be achieved unless the reduced economic circumstances which accompany them are seen to be fairly distributed. People are bound to resist if they are told that a lower material standard of living is inescapable only to observe that a minority, because of inordinately high income, are instrumental in keeping up prices and in diverting what few modest luxuries might be available into a limited number of channels. Indeed it is vital not only that great inequalities of current income are avoided, but that the ability to stimulate expansion of production by mortgaging future income, or using the accumulated wealth of others, should be made impossible. In the privileged countries, our present house of cards would really stand exposed if no man could furnish his house until he had earned the money to do so, or if an enterprise could not expand before it had accumulated the capital to finance it.

Pundits of modern business and economics may well deride any conception of the near-abolition of credit as simplistic, retrograde and utterly unthinkable. How, they may ask, would young people obtain their own houses if they could not borrow substantially to do so? Furthermore, would it not be iniquitous if companies had to leave large profits "lying idle" until sufficient had been accumulated to carry out expansion or replacement projects? With regard to the first question one might reply that with a falling population and no mortgages, the cost of houses would decline with remarkable promptitude, and houses for rent could well become amazingly plentiful. As for the second point, if the really "big spenders" in society had to wait a great deal longer before carrying out building projects or re-equipment schemes, many of these would never materialize and only essential ones would do so.

In fact we are perhaps far, far nearer than most people imagine to the kind of situation in which measures such as this will be inescapable. Escalation in the proportion of personal and corporate incomes which is being pruned away by rates and taxes, though partly arising from bureaucratic inefficiency and diseconomies of scale, results in very large measure from the enormous cost of renewing and enlarging vital services. The amounts that will shortly be left for voluntary investment will be very small; but the sums of money which will soon be required for food production, energy restructuring and basic public works of all kinds promise to be so astronomic that little will be left over for the continuing production of most of those consumables which we have erroneously come to regard as "essentials". It is difficult to see how society will be able to divert investment into the really essential channels without such credit restrictions through taxation, supplemented possibly by an almost prohibitive bank rate. Such restrictions are merely another set of "lesser evils" which will have to be accepted in order to avoid what could be a spectacular collapse of our water mains, sewers, tower blocks and other essential systems.

LAND USE PLANNING

In many countries of the world, land use planning is accepted as a necessary instrument of government; the machinery does not need to be created therefore, merely to be operated in a way which is consistent with a sane use of resources. An unrealistic view of the future has led so many nations to have profligate and destructive land use policies. It is perhaps understandable why countries with relatively large amounts of land per capita should continue to destroy timber and degrade their soil beneath extensive pastoral practices (chapter 4), but it is astonishing that one like the United Kingdom, in view of its resources predicament, should persist in slicing away hundreds of productive agricultural acres each year merely to accommodate road-widening schemes. As far as can be seen the questionable advantage of increasing the mean speed of car movement by five miles per hour is almost all that can possibly be achieved by such activities, and this is so slight a gain to set against the losses that one is again tempted to the conclusion that the only real reason is the creation of employment. Land use policies which permit and stimulate not only road-widening but a thousand and one other kinds of urban encroachment on the country's most precious resource are unrealistic beyond belief, but the institution of economic and social alternatives to them demands great ingenuity and persuasiveness.

RETHINKING OUR POLITICS

One is perhaps asking for the impossible, but a study of population/resource issues leads one to the view that there is an overwhelming case for the rejection of many of our salient political clichés. The author is only too well aware that many readers will be primarily motivated to discover whether the opinions expressed here subsume a "socialist" or a "free enterprise" economy. The answers inferred from the foregoing chapters will not greatly gratify either camp. The affairs of men have now entered a phase which is novel in so many ways that many standard political attitudes are no longer relevant. One forms the impression that throughout the capitalist world there are so many responsible people who would like to make radical proposals but who feel it would be pointless to do so within the economic framework in which they find themselves. On the other hand, they seem to have numerous counterparts in communist countries who dare not express themselves freely on matters concerned with population and resource problems lest they be branded as reactionaries. With mankind at the crossroads, one feels impelled to assert that it does not really matter who owns the gasworks, provided the gasworks are managed in a way which is most appropriate for the welfare of the community as a whole. All those of both persuasions who would hold that either "capitalism" or "communism" is the great agent by which "technological advancement" can be achieved, should be reminded that most kinds of "technological advancement" are now the last things that we should be striving for. Mental effort, flexibility of the intellect, and realism are the things which we should be requiring from legislators, not reaffirmations of belief in these two nineteenth-century doctrines which, indeed, both owe a great deal to Adam Smith.

PLANNING FOR NATIONAL AUTONOMY

At the present time, planning of resources on the macro-scale, generally speaking, is no more than sporadic and remedial. Apart from such developments as the lowering of tariffs in "common market" groupings (chapter 9), and water sharing schemes by countries which occupy different parts of the same river basin, progress has been made almost entirely through the Commissions of the United Nations. An outstanding exception was the setting up of the World Bank (International Bank for Reconstruction and Development) by the major powers at the Bretton Woods Conference in 1944, in an effort to stimulate world trade by arranging credit for the deprived nations. But international planning discussions on more problematical economic issues have been minimal. Indeed, international organizations might well not have survived had they attempted to interfere more in national economic affairs. It is only where a world resource, such as whales, has been in imminent jeopardy from over-exploitation that drastic measures have been considered, and often even then with little tangible result. It seems clear, however, that if the critical problems of world population, international trade, pollution, and conservation of scarce resources are to be resolved without violence and chaos, then careful and detailed planning, with mutual tolerance between all the nations of the world, is essential.

Fortunately this should not be taken to imply that the ultimate internationalization of all the countries of the world will have to be achieved in the near future. Even if possible this could well be a retrograde step. Given the clear indication that massive world trading is not going to be possible in the future, it would be undesirable to weaken national and regional autonomy: if the countries of the world have to achieve near self-sufficiency, the stronger their national organization the better.

This is a most complex and difficult subject which cannot be presented adequately here; it will certainly tax politicians and economists to the limits of ingenuity. The phasing of any planned, massive economic contraction will be critical, since established patterns of world trade could not possibly be terminated abruptly without causing collapse. Obviously, for a considerable time raw materials and semi-manufactured goods will have to continue to move in one direction, with a reciprocal flow of machine tools, plastics and other finished goods in the other. Nevertheless, a great overall reduction will probably have become inevitable by the beginning of next century, and one cannot visualize anything but strife and chaos unless the transfer of essential materials has been carefully planned.

The evidence seems to indicate that, for survival, there will be a time in the first part of the twenty-first century when most national governments will have to have achieved a situation in which the fundamental equation is balanced — where the population is supported by its own resources (at least so far as bulky commodities are concerned). Exactly what will constitute a viable national unit by that time is problematical. Whether the material standard of living of people in northwest Scotland, for instance, would be maximized if the area were part of an autonomous unit based in Inverness, or on Edinburgh, or on London, or on Strasbourg, can only be speculated upon. There can never be a final answer to such a problem because so much will depend on the volume and variety of resources which particular communities are able to exploit at any particular point of time. If in the distant future a happy balance can be re-attained between population and perceived resources, then the element of "choice" regarding the size of viable political units could again be restored.

Pursuing the example of northern Scotland, however, the fact remains that, in the foreseeable future whether as an independent state or an outlying province of a larger country, its population will have to be very small in order to permit a bearable standard of living unless it is subsidized from elsewhere: since one can discount considerations such as North Sea oil which will have been effectively exhausted by the end of the century, its long-term resource base is very slender.

But the denizens of the far north should not be unduly discouraged: inhospitable and peripheral areas are not the only ones with obvious problems when people and politics are viewed in the light of future resource availability. It is equally appropriate to reflect on the resource base of Greater London with its twelve million people and to delineate the area into which it would have to be incorporated to ensure survival in a situation demanding self-sufficiency!

Foretellers of Doom

Those whose observations have led them to the conclusion that our present consumer society is not sustainable have frequently been referred to as "doomsters". The full implication of the appellation is not entirely explicit, but if it may be taken almost literally as designating a group of people who take pleasure in contemplating the imminent misfortunes of humanity, then it is both inappropriate and unfair. Those who feel this kind of disquiet tend to be people particularly sensitive to human discomfort and unhappiness. In view of the fact that the vast majority of people like to contemplate a secure and settled future for themselves and their children and, consequently, are prone to consign unpleasant future possibilities to the backs of their minds, is it not likely that those who have reached uncomfortable conclusions are people of unusual objectivity, and that it is their detractors who are disposed to wishful thinking?

Nor is it entirely appropriate that those who have these serious reservations should be referred to as "pessimists". A man is not automatically a pessimist because he feels that our present socioeconomic institutions are unsustainable: indeed if he has convictions that humanity has the latent reserves of resourcefulness and flexibility to change these institutions in time to meet changing circumstances, he should surely be regarded as an optimist. In a sense, there is no more pessimistic frame of mind than the one which assumes that we have to continue with our present expansionist system because basic human and economic institutions cannot possibly be changed. "Pessimism" and "optimism" apart, one cannot but doubt the judgement of those who seem to have no doubts about the inevitable success of rapid, continuous technological innovation, but who assume that "human nature" and the economic system are immutable. Such a conclusion lacks either imagination or honesty.

To maintain that people will never, under any circumstances, accept long-term restriction and privation is both defeatist and contrary to historical evidence. A century ago many of our ancestors accepted an existence which was incredibly hard and restrictive as compared to that which the majority enjoy today in Western countries. What people will accept and tolerate is a reflection of their expectations, and there is ample evidence to show that the expectations of the majority can be profoundly influenced by an honest and forthright analysis of the difficulties which lie ahead. Commentators have been surprised by the way in which, in 1975 and 1976, the people of Britain accepted wage restraint. Indeed this is extremely heartening in view of the fact that they did so in the absence of any clear indication of the real, long-term seriousness of the national situation, and without any clear undertaking that future privations were to be fairly shared by all sections of the nation. If a clear indication of the real national predicament were to be provided, and if guarantees were given that when shortages and restrictions begin to bite they will be experienced by all, is it not reasonable to expect that people of good sense and goodwill will be even more likely to bow to the inevitable and make as rich a life as possible with what they have? The responsibility rests on those with knowledge and influence to create the framework in which such a transformation of outlook can take place.

12

A New Utopia

Confronted with a vista of tranquillity and plenty, one sometimes gets an idealistic flash of future human possibilities. I well remember on a showery day in June rounding the bend of a Lake District track and coming on a sweep of woodland, field and fell — gleaming greens and greys in the drifting sun and shadow. Embedded in it was a grey stone house with warmly painted doors, windows and gables, half-submerged in trees, beansticks and creeper. Alongside and behind, stables, barns and orchards were clustered in a happy blend of artistry and purpose. The fields and lower fells were quietly alive with sheep and lambs and cattle. The scene was almost unsurpassable for peace, abundance, and all those better things which men, through the millennia, have done to landscape. And I said to myself: if only all humanity could live like this!

Again, on the high plateau of Kenya we jolted for two hours over brown and blistered land where ragged tribesmen tended skinny herds, and the odd cluster of low, beehive huts baked and shimmered in the sun surrounded by patches of bare, red mineral stuff awaiting the next rains. And then, surmounting a low swell we came upon what seemed, by contrast, a kind of earthly paradise. It lay in a broad hollow between two outflung arms of the northern Aberdares — a low and rambling house with sheds and outbuildings, all set in a matrix of trees and flowering shrubs. The waters of a diverted stream, nourished by rainfall in the high Aberdares, wound its way through two acres of gardens where choicest flowers from five continents were blended, and where fruit and vegetables of almost every clime grew in profusion. Fields of well watered crops sloped down into the bottom lands and here and there half-tame crowned-cranes stalked between the rows. All around the hollow, flocks and herds were grazing on well managed pastures. Here was an enclave of plenty, peace and beauty, showing very clearly how Africa can burgeon. And again the thought arose — if only everyone could live like this!

And why not? Such emancipation and well-being are to be found in almost every corner of the world, so why not for all? Well, throughout the ages, it has been thought impossible: the argument has been that there must always be serried ranks of lower orders to do the unpleasant work and so bear up the pinnacle of the social pyramid, ensuring that leisured living and a cultured way of life survive from one generation to the next. The classical patricians in their marble halls were supported by their slaves and by the shepherd in his hut upon the mountain side. Behind the well-to-do Lake District farmer lies an urban proletariat and a factory way of life which produce his tractor and his car and all the modern gadgetry of home and farm which have replaced the former crowd of field workers and servants in the house. And the Kenyan proprietor has the best of old and new, with a little army of retainers as well as all the technical support of an industrialized world.

But is this still inevitable: at our present stage of technological advancement must there still be of necessity a vast substratum of less privileged? One might feel justified in thinking that it must now be possible to work towards a social system in which factory workers, truck drivers, and those who produce the goods and operate the economic machine, could have pleasant houses in peaceful surroundings with spacious schools and colleges for all their children. And might not the Kenyan farm be run without the enormous differentials of status and income between managers and managed?

There seems no technological reason why a measure of gracious living should not be made available for all. We already have the answers for all the technical, *qualitative* problems which would arise in the quest for such emancipation. But the fact remains that the *quantitative* problems would defeat us utterly. There can be no easy, cultured life for billions of people on planet earth: even if the present four billion were to increase but little, and an all-out, honest effort were made to raise them to the level of patricians, that effort would be vain. Before the exercise could be completed there would be little left to sustain what had been achieved, and the face of the earth would have become an unpleasant place where many a previous little paradise would have become a factory yard, a fetid swamp or dusty desert.

There are too many people. Even to begin the advance towards a new utopia we must reduce our ranks. That we require a new utopia can scarcely be in doubt: those to whom the task will fall to be custodians of culture and cohesion in the years ahead could well find life unbearable without one. But it must be a vision very far removed from the promised land of cultures of the past. It must not be like the one flowing with milk and honey which the Israelites went out to conquer, in which they were exhorted to be fruitful and to multiply. Nor must it be that white-porticoed golfhouse-in-the-sky with diamond-studded eighteenth green which has become the pinnacle of aspiration for so many opinion-formers in the West. Such ways of life could not be sustainable in the twenty-first century — certainly not for billions of people.

No, the vision must approach more nearly the one perceived by John Stuart Mill (1857). Of all the economists from Adam Smith till recent years, Mill alone prescribed a steady-state economy as the only sustainable one. The world in which he lived had little more than a quarter of our present population and yet he felt that the most populous countries of his day had already reached a stage where no more real advantage could be gained by further growth. He visualized a future in which cooperation and profitable social intercourse would depend upon restricting numbers — where culture and intellectual development could only be maintained with a system of no growth.

He did not elaborate on the ways in which men's attitudes would have to change in order to conform to such a system, and this is possibly because in his day a far greater proportion of the populace than today would be inclined to regard a stable community as normal: most people of the nineteenth century were still quite close to their agricultural origins. We of the late twentieth century will need re-education in the demands and recompenses of a sane, realistic world. It must be one in which peace of mind, deep-felt security and self-respect arising out of being someone in a real community, will be valued far more than conspicuous possessions, freedom from patient labouring, and exemption from having dirty hands. It will have to be labour-intensive rather than capital-intensive, small and intimate rather than pretentious and self-assertive. It does not follow that those of genius and independence of mind will lose identity and value in such a world, or that their qualities will go unrecognized — merely that their talents will find outlet in very different ways. Nor should we fear that a re-embracing of some of life's hard realities must entail return to a dark age: provided that we choose our way rather than have it thrust upon us, then surely we can salvage enough of the products of the Industrial Revolution to avoid returning to the pain, the horrors and the injustices of former times.

If the world of a century ago could have acted promptly on the advice of Mill, our present situation would of course be very different. It might well be that technology would not have advanced quite so rapidly, but this would have been more than compensated by the fact that it would not have reached the present impasse where a halt has to be called if civilization is ever to enjoy the new utopia. It will now have to follow a devious, circuitous route, practising rigorous self-discipline and economy to a degree which would not have been required if growth had been checked at an earlier stage.

The adoption of a utopia which makes modest demands on the resources of the earth will permit our little earthly paradises to survive and grow in number, though life within them will be different from now. Petrol, plastics, stripey toothpaste, snap, crackle and pop are not essentials for fulfilment, and there is no reason why, if science and an ordered way of life can be preserved, all those who then can live in quiet places should not be able to procure a little bit of metal and the tools with which to fashion most of their necessities.

Indeed it may well be, in some remote future time beyond the range of our utopia, that each small province of the earth will have its small reactor, safe and unpolluting, able to supply free energy for all and to disgorge wonderful materials as yet undreamt of. But the direct route to such a goal is blocked by a rising tide of humanity — there is no way to it by our present road. The coming generations must pick their way across a stony land, suiting their numbers to their means, and comforting each other as they go. And if they reach the new utopia they will number far fewer souls than those who populate our present world because, in the long run, the mess and heat and friction generated by vast multitudes will always be ruled out by the natural laws within which all things must function. Let the powers and potentates who have a hankering for bigger markets, more ratepayers, and ever-swelling numbers of the faithful, reflect on this and then hold their peace.

Appendix I

ABBREVIATIONS USED IN THE TEXT

BP	The British Petroleum Company Limited
cm	centimetres
cm^2	square centimetres
EEC	European Economic Community
FAO	Food and Agriculture Organization
g	grammes
gal	gallons
GNP	gross national product
Gw	gigawatts (10^9 watts)
ha	hectares
IBP	International Biological Programme
IUCN	International Union for the Conservation of Nature and Natural Resources
kcal	kilocalories (the "large Calories" of the dietarian)
km	kilometres
km^2	square kilometres
m	metres
m^2	square metres
m^3	cubic metres
ml	miles
mt	metric tons (tonnes)
mmt	million metric tons (million tonnes)
Mw	megawatts (10^6 watts)
NPP	net primary productivity
PPCNPP	potential per capita net primary productivity
UNEP	United Nations Environment Programme
UNESCO	United Nations Educational, Scientific and Cultural Organization
w	watts
WRME	wood raw material equivalent

Appendix II

THE METHODS, CRITERIA AND AUTHORITIES USED IN COMPUTING THE THEORETICAL NPP OF THE LAND AREAS OF THE EARTH BENEATH THEIR ORIGINAL WILD VEGETATION

The areas originally covered by the main world vegetation types have been calculated from the original manuscript maps (1:16,000,000) of my world vegetation map (Eyre, 1968), a simplified and reduced version of which has been presented here (figure 4.1). Measurements were made with a planimeter, the answer, in cm^2, being converted into km^2.

Although only 18 major world vegetation types have been listed in the text (table 4.1), it will be realized that a number of these are conflations of several sub-types. In all, 32 distinct vegetation categories have been recognized, and their areas measured.

An average NPP (in $mt/km^2/yr$) has been postulated for each of the categories. These average productivities have been based on a wide range of information from a large number of authorities. An element of subjectivity has been unavoidable here, since different workers have produced different productivity figures for the same vegetation type: in most cases this seems to have been merely an indication that productivity does vary even within the same kind of plant community because of environmental differences, so that it has seemed reasonable to take an arithmetic average of the different results. However, in a few cases, the findings of particular researchers have not been accorded the full weight they might have been. This is not necessarily because they were felt to be invalid in the context in which they were carried out, but because there was good reason to suspect that the vegetation concerned was far from being typical of its general type, or because the aims and precepts of the workers concerned were not in full accordance with those which have generally been followed in recent times.

The authorities whose figures have been taken into account in arriving at the average productivities for each main vegetation type are acknowledged in the following table. Full references will be found in the bibliography.

PRINCIPAL REFERENCES TO THE NPP OF THE MAIN VEGETATION TYPES OF THE EARTH

Tropical rain forest: Kira *et al.* (1967); Ogino *et al.* (1967); Lemon *et al.* (1970); Jordan (1971).
Tropical rain-green forest: Muller and Nielsen (1965); Misra (1972).
Broad-leaved and mixed evergreen forest: Kimura (1960); Tadaki and Hatiya (1968); Iwaki (1974).
Mid-latitude coniferous forest: Tadaki and Hatiya (1968); Forrest and Ovington (1970); Iwaki (1974).
Summer-green forest: Duvigneaud and Denaeyer-DeSmet (1970); Maruyama (1971); Lieth (1972).
Boreal forest: Tadaki and Hatiya (1968); Bazilevich and Rodin (1971); Iwaki (1974).
Savanna: Bourlière and Hadley (1970); Daubenmire (1972); Lamotte (1972).
Prairie and steppe: Kucera *et al.* (1967); Bazilevich and Rodin (1971); Sims and Singh (1971); Coupland (1973); Andrews *et al.* (1974).
Semi-desert: Chew and Chew (1965); Bazilevich and Rodin (1971); Lieth (1972).
Tundra: Warren Wilson (1957); Bliss (1970); Dennis and Johnson (1970); Bazilevich and Rodin (1971); Kjelvik (1973); Mue (1973); Svoboda (1973).
General: Cooper (1975); Bazilevich and Rodin (1971); Lieth (1973); Lieth and Whittaker (1975); Westlake (1963); McNaughton and Wolf (1973); Iwaki (1974).

Appendix III

WORLD POPULATION DATA

Country	Population estimates mid,1971 (millions)*	Births per annum (per thousand population)†	Infant mortality (deaths under 1 year old per 1000 live births)†	Population under 15 years old (%)‡	Annual rate of growth (%)	Number of years to double population at recent growth rates	Illiteracy over 14 years old (%)†
Northern Europe							
Denmark	5·0	14·6	14·8	24	0·5	140	0–1
Finland	4·7	14·5	13·9	27	0·4	175	0–1
Iceland	0·2	20·7	11·7	34	1·2	58	0–1
Ireland	3·0	21·5	20·6	31	0·7	100	0–1
Norway	3·9	17·6	13·7	25	0·9	78	0–1
Sweden	8·1	13·5	13·0	21	0·5	140	0–1
United Kingdom	56·3	16·6	18·6	23	0·5	140	0–1
Western Europe							
Austria	7·5	16·5	25·4	24	0·4	175	0–1
Belgium	9·7	14·6	21·8	24	0·4	175	0–3
France	51·5	16·7	16·4	25	0·7	100	0–3
Luxembourg	0·4	13·5	16·7	22	1·0	70	0–3
Netherlands	13·1	19·2	13·2	28	1·1	63	0–1
Switzerland	6·4	16·5	15·4	23	1·1	63	0–1
West Germany	58·9	15·0	23·3	23	0·4	175	0–1
Southern Europe							
Albania	2·2	35·6	86·8	—	2·7	26	20–30
Greece	9·0	17·4	31·9	25	0·8	88	15–20
Italy	54·1	17·6	30·3	24	0·8	88	5–10
Portugal	9·6	19·8	56·8	29	0·7	100	35–40
Spain	33·6	20·2	29·8	27	1·0	70	10–20
Yugoslavia	20·8	18·8	56·3	30	1·0	70	15–25

*Estimates from United Nations (1970b).
†See UN (1971).
‡See UN (1967) and (1969).

Country	Population estimates mid,971 (millions)*	Births per annum (per thousand population)†	Infant mortality (deaths under 1 year old per 1000 live births)†	Population under 15 years old (%)‡	Annual rate of growth (%)	Number of years to double population at recent growth rates	Illiteracy over 14 years old (%)†
Eastern Europe							
Bulgaria	8·6	17·0	30·5	24	0·7	100	10–15
Czechoslovakia	14·8	15·5	22·9	25	0·5	140	0–5
East Germany	16·2	14·0	20·1	22	0·1	700	0–1
Hungary	10·3	15·0	35·7	23	0·4	175	0–5
Poland	33·3	16·3	34·3	30	0·9	78	0–5
Romania	20·6	23·3	54·9	26	1·3	54	5–15
USSR	245·0	17·0	25·7	28	1·0	70	12
USA	207·1	18·2	19·8	30	1·1	63	0–3
China	772·9	33·0	—	—	1·8	39	40–50
Australia	12·8	20·0	17·7	29	1·9	37	0–1
Canada	21·8	17·6	20·8	33	1·7	41	0–3
New Zealand	2·9	22·5	16·9	33	1·7	41	0–1
Northern Africa							
Algeria	14·5	50	86	47	3·3	21	75–85
Morocco	16·3	50	149	46	3·3	21	80–90
Tunisia	5·3	45	74	44	3·1	23	75–85
Saharan Africa							
Chad	3·8	48	160	46	2·4	29	75–82
Egypt	34·9	44	118	43	2·8	25	75–80
Ethiopia	25·6	46	—	—	2·1	33	90–95
Libya	1·9	46	—	44	3·1	23	80–87
Mali	5·2	50	120	46	2·4	29	85–95
Mauritania	1·2	45	187	—	2·2	32	90–97
Niger	4·0	52	200	46	2·9	24	95–99
Somalia	2·9	46	—	—	2·4	29	90–95
Sudan	16·3	49	—	47	3·2	22	80–88
Western Africa							
Dahomey	2·8	51	110	46	2·6	27	90–95
Gambia	0·4	42	—	38	1·9	37	90–95
Ghana	9·3	48	156	45	3·0	24	70–75
Guinea	4·0	47	216	44	2·3	31	80–90
Ivory Coast	4·4	46	138	43	2·4	29	85–92

Country	Population estimates mid,971 (millions)*	Births per annum (per thousand population)†	Infant mortality (deaths under 1 year old per 1000 live births)†	Population under 15 years old (%)†	Annual rate of growth (%)	Number of years to double population at recent growth rates	Illiteracy over 14 years old (%)†
Liberia	1·2	41	188	37	1·9	37	90–95
Nigeria	56·5	50	—	43	2·6	27	80–88
Senegal	4·0	46	—	42	2·4	29	90–95
Sierra Leone	2·7	45	136	—	2·3	31	80–90
Togo	1·9	51	127	48	2·6	27	80–90
Upper Volta	5·5	49	182	42	2·1	33	85–92
Middle Africa							
Angola	5·8	50	—	42	2·1	33	90–97
Cameroon	5·9	43	137	39	2·2	32	80–90
Central African Republic	1·6	48	190	42	2·2	32	70–79
Congo Republic	1·0	44	180	—	2·3	31	50–55
Gabon	0·5	35	229	36	0·9	78	85–90
Zaire	17·8	44	104	42	2·3	31	80–85
Zambia	4·4	50	259	45	3·0	24	55–60
Eastern Africa							
Burundi	3·7	48	150	47	2·3	31	85–92
Kenya	11·2	50	—	46	3·1	23	70–75
Malagasy Republic	7·1	46	102	46	2·7	26	—
Rwanda	3·7	52	137	—	2·9	24	85–90
Tanzania	13·6	47	162	42	2·6	27	80–90
Uganda	8·8	43	160	41	2·6	27	65–75
Southern Africa							
Botswana	0·6	44	—	43	2·2	32	70–80
Lesotho	1·1	40	181	43	1·8	39	—
Malawi	4·6	49	148	45	2·5	28	85–90
Mozambique	7·9	43	—	—	2·1	33	90–95
Namibia	0·6	44	—	40	2·0	35	60–70
Rhodesia	5·2	48	122	47	3·4	21	70–75
South Africa	20·6	40	—	40	2·4	29	65–70
Swaziland	0·4	52	—	—	3·0	24	—
Southwest Asia							
Cyprus	0·6	23	27	35	0·9	78	20–25
Iran	29·2	48	—	46	3·0	24	75–85

Country	Population estimates mid,971 (millions)*	Births per annum (per thousand population)†	Infant mortality (deaths under 1 year old per 1000 live births)†	Population under 15 years old (%)‡	Annual rate of growth (%)	Number of years to double population at recent growth rates	Illiteracy over 14 years old (%)†
Iraq	10·0	49	—	45	3·4	21	75–85
Israel	3·0	26	23	33	2·4	29	10–15
Jordan	2·4	48	—	46	3·3	21	60–70
Kuwait	0·8	43	36	38	8·2	9	50–55
Lebanon	2·9	—	—	—	3·0	24	40–50
Oman	0·7	42	—	—	3·1	23	—
Saudi Arabia	8·0	50	—	—	2·8	25	85–95
South Yemen	1·3	—	—	—	2·8	25	—
Syria	6·4	47	—	46	3·3	21	65–70
Turkey	36·5	43	155	44	2·7	26	60–65
Yemen	5·9	50	—	—	2·8	25	90–95
Southern Asia							
Afghanistan	17·4	50	—	—	2·5	28	85–95
Bangladesh and Pakistan	141·6	50	142	45	3·3	21	75–85
Burma	28·4	40	—	40	2·3	31	30–40
India	569·5	42	139	41	2·6	27	70–75
Nepal	11·5	45	—	40	2·2	32	85–95
Srilanka	12·9	32	48	41	2·4	29	25–30
Southeast Asia							
Indonesia	124·9	47	125	42	2·9	24	55–60
Khmer Republic	7·3	45	127	44	3·0	24	60–70
Laos	3·1	42	—	—	2·5	28	70–80
Malaysia	11·1	37	—	44	2·8	25	70–80
Philippines	39·4	46	72	47	3·4	21	25–30
Thailand	37·4	42	—	43	3·3	21	30–35
Vietnam	39·9	—	—	—	2·1	33	—
Eastern Asia							
Japan	104·7	18	15	25	1·1	63	0–2
Mongolia	1·3	42	—	44	3·1	23	5
North Korea	14·3	39	—	—	2·8	25	—
South Korea	32·9	36	—	42	2·5	28	—
Taiwan	14·3	26	19	44	2·3	31	35–40

Country	Population estimates mid,971 (millions)*	Births per annum (per thousand population)†	Infant mortality (deaths under 1 year old per 1000 live births)†	Population under 15 years old (%)†	Annual rate of growth (%)	Number of years to double population at recent growth rates	Illiteracy over 14 years old (%)†
Central America							
Costa Rica	1·9	45	60	48	3·8	19	10–20
El Salvador	3·6	47	63	45	3·4	21	45–50
Guatemala	5·3	42	94	46	2·9	24	60–70
Honduras	2·8	49	—	51	3·4	21	50–60
Mexico	52·5	42	66	46	3·4	21	30–35
Nicaragua	2·1	46	—	48	3·0	24	45–50
Panama	1·5	41	41	43	3·3	21	20–30
Caribbean							
Cuba	8·6	27	40	37	1·9	37	15–25
Dominican Republic	4·4	48	64	47	3·4	21	40
Haiti	5·4	44	—	42	2·5	28	80–90
Jamaica	2·0	33	39	41	2·1	33	15–20
Puerto Rico	2·9	24	29	39	1·4	50	15–20
Trinidad and Tobago	1·1	30	37	43	1·8	39	15–25
South America							
Argentina	24·7	22	58	29	1·5	47	5–8
Bolivia	4·8	44	—	44	2·4	29	55–60
Brazil	95·7	38	170	43	2·8	25	30–35
Chile	10·0	34	92	40	2·3	31	13–16
Colombia	22·1	44	78	47	3·4	21	30–40
Ecuador	6·3	45	86	48	3·4	21	30–35
Guyana	0·8	37	40	46	2·9	24	15–25
Paraguay	2·5	45	52	45	3·4	21	20–25
Peru	14·0	43	62	45	3·1	23	35–40
Surinam	0·4	41	30	46	3·2	22	—
Uruguay	2·9	21	50	28	1·2	58	8–10
Venezuela	11·1	41	46	46	3·4	21	30–35

Appendix IV

NATIONAL NET PRIMARY PRODUCTIVITY

Country	Land area (in $10^3 km^2$)	Total potential NPP (in 10^6 mt/year)	Potential NPP per capita (in mt/year)
Northern Europe			
Denmark	42·4	54·6	10·9
Finland	305·4	181·3	38·6
Iceland	100·3	16·6	83·0
Ireland	68·9	89·7	29·9
Norway	308·4	146·9	37·7
Sweden	411·4	307·0	37·9
United Kingdom	241·5	308·6	5·5
Western Europe			
Austria	82·7	94·3	12·6
Belgium	30·5	39·0	4·0
France	540·0	713·6	13·9
Luxembourg	2·5	3·2	8·0
Netherlands	33·8	44·2	3·4
Switzerland	39·9	34·2	5·3
West Germany	242·6	305·5	5·2
Southern Europe			
Albania	28·0	43·3	19·7
Greece	129·3	181·0	20·1
Italy	293·0	402·9	7·5
Portugal	88·0	158·4	16·5
Spain	503·0	699·4	20·8
Yugoslavia	253·0	322·2	15·5
Eastern Europe			
Bulgaria	110·5	141·2	16·4
Czechoslovakia	125·7	153·4	10·4
East Germany	105·5	129·2	8·0

Country	Land area (in $10^3 km^2$)	Total potential NPP (in 10^6 mt/year)	Potential NPP per capita (in mt/year).
Hungary	91·0	116·6	11·3
Poland	303·8	361·0	10·8
Romania	235·0	291·4	14·1
USSR	21126·0	12237·2	49·9
USA	9191·0	8416·5	40·6
China	9499·0	8345·8	10·8
Australia	7679·0	6027·6	470·9
Canada	9220·0	4995·7	229·2
New Zealand	266·0	390·2	134·6
Oceania			
Papua and New Guinea	460·0	1090·0	436·0
British Solomon Islands	28·9	72·5	483·3
Fiji Islands	18·3	45·0	90·0
New Caledonia	19·0	47·5	475·0
New Hebrides	14·8	37·5	375·0
Northern Africa			
Algeria	2297·0	421·6	29·1
Morocco	434·0	279·0	17·1
Tunisia	155·9	77·6	14·6
Saharan Africa			
Chad	1269·0	626·2	164·8
Egypt	976·0	99·2	2·8
Ethiopia	1100·9	1062·3	41·5
Libya	1761·0	253·4	133·4
Mali	1241·0	674·4	129·7
Mauritania	1031·0	152·0	126·7
Niger	1187·0	337·2	84·3
Somalia	627·3	183·3	63·2
Spanish Sahara	266·0	38·7	595·4
Sudan	2376·0	1368·0	83·9
Western Africa			
Dahomey	110·0	163·0	58·2

Country	Land area (in $10^3 km^2$)	Total potential NPP (in 10^6 mt/year)	Potential NPP per capita (in mt/year)
Gambia	10·0	15·0	37·5
Ghana	230·0	407·0	43·8
Guinea	241·0	431·5	107·9
Ivory Coast	318·0	752·5	171·0
Liberia	96·3	240·0	200·0
Nigeria	916·0	1491·0	26·4
Senegal	179·0	210·0	52·5
Sierra Leone	71·7	144·0	53·3
Togo	55·0	91·5	48·2
Upper Volta	273·8	345·5	62·8
Middle Africa			
Angola	1226·0	1650·8	284·6
Cameroon	469·9	1083·5	183·6
Central African Republic	620·0	994·0	621·2
Congo Republic	340·0	748·0	748·0
Gabon	266·0	653·0	1306·0
Zaire	2306·0	4262·0	238·4
Zambia	736·0	1100·0	250·0
Eastern Africa			
Burundi	25·7	35·0	9·5
Kenya	568·0	412·3	36·8
Malagasy Republic	587·0	811·5	114·3
Rwanda	25·2	34·0	9·2
Tanzania	886·2	1009·5	74·2
Uganda	193·6	270·5	30·7
Southern Africa			
Botswana	544·4	581·0	968·3
Lesotho	30·0	30·0	27·3
Malawi	94·0	105·5	22·9
Mozambique	760·0	796·5	100·8
Namibia	820·0	455·9	759·8
Rhodesia	388·0	443·5	85·3
South Africa	1218·0	896·2	43·5
Swaziland	17·3	24·0	60·0
Southwest Asia			
Cyprus	9·2	6·3	10·5

Country	Land area (in $10^3 km^2$)	Total potential NPP (in 10^6 mt/year)	Potential NPP per capita (in mt/year)
Iran	1636·0	354·7	12·1
Iraq	434·0	212·6	21·3
Israel	20·2	10·7	3·6
Jordan	97·0	18·4	7·7
Kuwait	16·0	2·4	3·0
Lebanon	10·4	7·0	2·4
Oman	212·0	19·2	27·4
Saudi Arabia	2149·0	213·1	26·7
South Yemen	287·7	39·8	30·6
Syria	185·1	92·1	14·4
Turkey	770·8	761·6	20·9
Yemen	195·0	33·7	5·7
Southern Asia			
Afghanistan	646·0	203·9	11·7
Bangladesh	142·8	347·5	6·8
Burma	670·0	1276·5	44·9
India	3259·0	3949·6	6·9
Nepal	139·0	175·7	15·3
Pakistan	800·0	345·1	8·0
Srilanka	64·7	100·0	7·8
Southeast Asia			
Indonesia	1904·0	4315·5	34·6
Khmer Republic	176·6	288·0	39·5
Laos	236·0	399·0	128·7
Malaysia	332·0	819·0	73·8
Philippines	297·4	673·0	17·1
Thailand	511·7	986·0	26·4
Vietnam	330·0	716·5	18·0
Eastern Asia			
Japan	369·0	513·1	4·9
Mongolia	1560·0	845·6	650·5
North Korea	120·0	150·4	10·5
South Korea	98·0	143·9	4·4
Taiwan	35·4	77·0	5·4
Central America			
British Honduras	22·6	57·5	479·2
Costa Rica	50·0	84·0	44·2
El Salvador	20·3	42·5	11·8

Country	Land area (in $10^3 km^2$)	Total potential NPP (in 10^6 mt/year)	Potential NPP per capita (in mt/year)
Guatemala	108·9	215·5	40·7
Honduras	111·0	210·5	75·2
Mexico	1972·0	1488·8	28·4
Nicaragua	121·0	254·5	121·2
Panama	75·0	146·5	97·7
Caribbean			
Cuba	114·0	176·5	20·5
Dominican Republic	48·0	104·0	23·6
Haiti	27·0	40·5	7·5
Jamaica	11·0	19·0	9·5
Puerto Rico	8·9	19·5	6·7
South America			
Argentina	2723·0	1505·4	60·9
Bolivia	1079·0	1633·7	340·4
Brazil	8457·0	15811·9	165·2
Chile	752·0	506·1	50·6
Colombia	1096·0	2155·1	97·5
Ecuador	281·0	478·5	76·0
Falkland Islands	12·0	0·2	100·0
French Guiana	89·0	222·5	5562·5
Guyana	197·0	489·5	611·9
Paraguay	399·0	479·5	191·8
Peru	1281·0	1871·0	133·6
Surinam	163·0	407·5	1018·7
Uruguay	180·0	180·0	62·1
Venezuela	882·0	1415·5	127·5

Appendix V

MAIN PRODUCERS[1] OF 20 MINERAL COMMODITIES IN 1965

Countries[2]	Mineral commodity[3]	Quantity (mt)[4]	Value (USA $ × 10^6) at average US prices[5]
(1) USSR	Al	1190000	693·3
	Cr	534240	1590·3
	Co	1270	4·5
	Cu	753000	971·4
	Fe	87440000	5495·7
	Hg	1379	24·3
	Mn	7799000	1258·9
	Ni	86000	150·1
	Pb	372000	117·8

[1] Excluding uranium production in the communist countries.
[2] The 65 countries listed here are all major producers of at least one of the 20 mineral commodities listed under (3). The countries are presented in order according to the total value of the products.
[3] The mineral materials taken into account in this table are aluminium, chromium, cobalt, copper, iron, mercury, manganese, molybdenum, nickel, lead, the platinum group (taken together), tin, tungsten, zinc, silver, gold, phosphate, potash, uranium[1] and oil. With the exception of those noted below, it is the weight and value of the final refined product that is presented, though it is realized that, in the case of chromium, this is somewhat misleading: much of the chromite which is extracted from the ground is never converted into chromium metal but is used as refractory or chemical material. The actual chromium content of the ore thus never achieves its maximum possible value. The exceptions are as follows:

Tungsten: assessed as its impure oxide (60% WO_3)
Phosphate: the weight given is for rock phosphate, but the value has been assessed on the assumption of a P_2O_5 content of 33% (near the world average).
Potash: the weight and value are for K_2O content.
Uranium: assessed as its oxide U_3O_8.
Oil: assessed as crude oil.

[4] It must be emphasized that these are the amounts of metal present in the ores that are raised; they are not necessarily extracted from the ores in the country in question (if, indeed, they are extracted at all). Information derived from US Bureau of Mines (1966)
[5] This is the theoretical market value of all the metal content of the ore raised. Information from US Bureau of Mines (1966).

	Pt (group)	48	266·9
	Sn	21333	83·8
	W	11519	568·3
	Zn	413000	130·1
	Ag	765	35·1
	Au	173	213·5
	Phosphate	27755000	225·6
	Potash	2349000	169·9
	Oil	243000000	5093·3
			17038·8
(2) USA	Al	420000	224·4
	Cu	1225000	1582·4
	Fe	50630000	3182·4
	Hg	675	11·9
	Mo	35089	274·7
	Pb	273000	86·5
	W	7210	355·7
	Zn	554000	174·8
	Ag	1128	51·7
	Au	48	59·7
	Phosphate	26699000	216·8
	Potash	2848000	205·9
	U	9471	167·0
	Oil	387600000	8124·1
			14718·0
(3) Venezuela	Fe	10850000	682·1
	Oil	182100000	3816·8
			4498·9
(4) Canada	Co	1722	6·1
	Cu	469000	605·1
	Fe	19940000	1253·0
	Mo	4263	33·4
	Ni	244000	424·7
	Pb	275000	87·1
	Pt (group)	12·8	71·0
	W	2824	139·3
	Zn	826000	260·5
	Potash	1351000	97·7

	U	4030	71·1
	Oil	44600000	934·8
			3983·8
(5) China	Fe	19500000	1226·0
	Hg	896	15·8
	Mn	1000000	161·4
	Pb	100000	31·6
	Sn	25397	99·8
	W	16961	836·8
	Zn	100000	31·5
	Phosphate	907000	7·3
			2410·2
(6) South Africa	Cr	309297	920·7
	Mn	1567000	253·0
	Pt (group)	21·3	117·7
	Au	866	1069·4
	U	2669	47·1
			2407·9
(7) Kuwait	Oil	109100000	2286·7
(8) Saudi Arabia	Oil	100600000	2108·6
(9) Iran	Oil	95000000	1991·2
(10) France	Al	660000	356·4
	Fe	17860000	1122·3
	Potash	1878000	135·8
	U	1712	30·2
	Oil	3000000	62·8
			1707·5
(11) Iraq	Oil	64400000	1349·8
(12) Libya	Oil	58900000	1234·5
(13) Jamaica	Al	2160000	1157·6
(14) Sweden	Fe	18280000	1148·8

(15) India	Fe	14200000	892·3
	Mn	1504000	242·8
			1135·1
(16) Brazil	Fe	12340000	775·9
	Mn	1176000	189·9
	Oil	4600000	96·4
			1062·2
(17) Zambia	Co	8348	5·4
	Cu	696000	897·7
			903·1
(18) Chile	Cu	582000	751·4
	Mo	3810	29·8
			781·2
(19) Liberia	Fe	10850000	682·1
(20) Australia	Al	300000	157·8
	Cu	93000	119·4
	Pb	361000	114·4
	W	1993	98·3
	Zn	356000	111·9
	Ag	474	21·7
	Au	24·9	30·7
	U	336	5·9
			660·1
(21) Turkey	Cr	185941	553·5
	Oil	1600000	33·5
			587·0
(22) Surinam	Al	1090000	583·5
(23) Rhodesia	Cr	185941	553·5
	Au	15·4	19·0
			572·5

(24) Mexico	Hg	620	10·9
	Pb	170000	53·9
	Zn	233000	73·4
	Ag	1143	52·4
	Oil	17800000	373·1
			563·7
(25) Algeria	Oil	26600000	557·5
(26) Indonesia	Oil	24000000	503·0
(27) Zaire	Co	8348	29·5
	Cu	288000	372·2
	Zn	119000	37·6
			439·3
(28) Peru	Cu	178000	229·4
	Mo	673	5·3
	Pb	147000	46·6
	Zn	255000	80·2
	Ag	999	45·8
			407·3
(29) Guyana	Al	730000	390·4
(30) West Germany	Zn	109000	34·4
	Potash	2385000	172·5
	Oil	7900000	165·6
			372·5
(31) Albania	Cr	118821	353·7
(32) Argentina	Oil	14000000	293·4
(33) Yugoslavia	Al	390000	210·8
	Hg	566	10·0
	Pb	106000	33·6
	Zn	92000	28·9
			283·3
(34) U.A. Emirates	Oil	13500000	283·0
(35) Nigeria	Oil	13500000	283·0

(36) UK	Fe	4380000	275·5
(37) Malaysia	Sn	64681	254·1
(38) North Korea	W	4444	219·3
	Zn	104000	32·9
			252·2
(39) Guinea	Al	670000	250·3
(40) Qatar	Oil	11100000	232·7
(41) Colombia	Au	9·1	11·2
	Oil	10200000	213·8
			225·0
(42) South Korea	W	4476	220·8
(43) Gabon	Mn	1286000	207·6
	U	657	11·6
			219·2
(44) Japan	Cu	107000	138·1
	Zn	221000	69·7
			207·8
(45) Hungary	Al	370000	197·2
(46) Bolivia	Sn	23720	93·2
	W	1853	91·4
			184·6
(47) Greece	Al	320000	168·7
(48) Trinidad	Oil	7000000	146·7
(49) East Germany	Potash	1923000	139·0
(50) New Caledonia	Ni	52000	90·7
(51) Morocco	Co	1831	6·5
	Phosphate	9823000	79·9
			86·4

(52) Portugal	W	1643	81·0
(53) Thailand	Sn	19142	75·2
(54) Italy	Hg	1975	34·8
	Zn	115000	36·4
			71·2
(55) Austria	Oil	2800000	58·7
(56) Spain	Hg	2852	50·3
(57) Poland	Zn	152000	48·0
(58) Bulgaria	Pb	100000	31·6
(59) Cuba	Ni	52000	29·8
(60) Ghana	Au	21·4	26·4
(61) Tunisia	Phosphate	3039000	24·8
(62) Philippines	Au	12·3	15·2
(63) Nauru	Phosphate	1478000	11·9
(64) Vietnam	Phosphate	1043000	8·4
(65) Togo	Phosphate	961000	7·7

Bibliography

ALLABY, M., BLYTHE, C., HYNES, C. and WARDLE, C. 1975: *Losing ground* (London).

ANDREWS, R., COLEMAN, D.C., ELLIS, J.E. and SINGH, J.S. 1974: Energy flow relationships in a short grass prairie ecosystem. *Proceedings of the First International Congress of Ecology, The Hague, The Netherlands, 8–14 September 1974* (Centre for Agricultural Publications and Documentation, Wageningen), 22–8.

ART, H.W., MARKS, P.L. and SCOTT, J.T. 1971: Productivity profile of New York. *Eastern Deciduous Forest Biome US-IBP Memo*, report no. 71–12.

BAKER, J.N.L. 1963: *The history of geography* (Oxford).

BAZILEVICH, N.I. and RODIN, L.E. 1968: World distribution of plant biomass. In ECKHARDT, F.E., editor, *Functioning of terrestrial ecosystems at the primary production level* (UNESCO, Paris), 45–52.

1971: Geographical regularities in productivity and circulation of chemical elements in the earth's main vegetation types. *Soviet Geography — Review and Translation* **12**, 24–53.

BLISS, L.C. 1970: Primary production within arctic tundra ecosystems. *Proceedings of the Conference on Productivity and Conservation in Northern Circumpolar Lands, Edmonton, 1969*, FULLER, W.A. and KEVAN, P.G. editors, IUCN publication, new series, **16** (Morges, Switzerland), 75–85.

BOGAROV, V.G. 1967: Problems concerning the productivity of the ocean. *Gidrobiologicheskiy Zhurnal* **3**, 12–21 (in Russian).

BORGSTROM, G. 1973: *World food resources* (Aylesbury, Bucks).

BOURLIERE, F. and HADLEY, M. 1970: The ecology of tropical savannas. *Annual Revue of Ecology and Systematics* **1**, 125–52.

BP 1973: *Statistical Review of the World Oil Industry* (London).

BURR, G.O. 1957: The sugarcane plant. *Annual Revue of Plant Physiology* **8**, 275–308.

CABINET OFFICE 1976: *Future world trends* (HMSO, London).

CARSON, RACHEL 1962: *Silent spring* (London).

CHEW, R.M. and CHEW, A.E. 1965: The primary productivity of a desert shrub (*Larrea tridentata*) community. *Ecological Monographs* **35**, 355–75.

CLARK, C. 1967: *Population growth and land use* (London).

CLOUD, PRESTON 1969: Mineral resources from the sea. In *Resources and man* (National Academy of Sciences, Washington) 135–55.

COOPER, J.P., editor, 1975: *Photosynthesis and productivity in different environments* (IBP, London).

COTTRELL, SIR ALAN 1973: Problems of predicting world trends. *Nature* **245**, 280–81.

COUPLAND, R.T. 1973: Productivity of the Matador grassland site. *Proceedings of the Canadian IBP/PP Synthesis Meeting, Guelph, December 1972.*

CURRY-LINDAHL, K. 1974: Conservation problems and progress in northern and southern Africa. *Environmental Conservation* **1**, 263–70.

DANIELS, F. 1964: *Direct use of the sun's energy* (New Haven, Conn.).

DAUBENMIRE, R. 1972: Standing crops and production in savanna derived from semi-deciduous forest in Costa Rica. *Botanical Gazette* **133**, 395–401.

DEEVEY, E.S. 1960: The human population. *Scientific American* **203** (3).

DENEVAN, W.M. 1973: Development and the imminent demise of the Amazon rain forest. In HILL, A.D., editor, *Latin American Development Issues* (East Lansing Mich.), 80–85.

DENNIS, J.G. and JOHNSON, P.L. 1970: Shoot and rhizome-root standing crop of tundra vegetation at Barrow, Alaska. *Arctic and Alpine Research* **2**, 253–66.

DE SELM, H.R. 1971: Tennessee productivity profiles. *Eastern Deciduous Forest Biome US-IBP Memo*, report no. 71–13.

DE VRIES, C.A., FERWERDA, J.D. and FLACH, M. 1967: Choice of food crops in relation to actual and potential production in the tropics. *Netherlands Journal of Agricultural Science* **15**, 241–8.

DUNCAN, D.C. and SWANSON, V.E. 1965: *Organic-rich shales of the United States and world land areas.* US Geological Survey Circular 523.

DUVIGNEAUD, P. and DENAEYER-DESMET, S. 1970: Biological cycling of minerals in temperate deciduous forests. *Ecology Studies* **1**, 199–225.

EADIE, J. and CUNNINGHAM, J.M.M. 1971: Efficiency of hill sheep production systems. In WAREING, P.F. and COOPER, J.P., editors, *Potential crop production* (london).

EHRLICH, P.R. and EHRLICH, A.H. 1972: *Population, resources, environment: issues in human ecology.* (San Francisco).

EYRE, S.R. 1966: The vegetation of a south Pennine upland. In EYRE, S.R. and JONES, G.R.J., editors, *Geography as human ecology* (London).

1968: *Vegetation and soils — a world picture* (2nd edition, London).

EYRE, S.R. and JONES, G.R.J., editors, 1966: Introduction to *Geography as human ecology* (London).

EYRE, S.R. and PALMER, J. 1973: *The face of northeast Yorkshire* (Clapham, Yorks).

FISHER, C.A. 1959: The compleat geographer. Inaugural address, University of London.

FLAWN, P.T. 1966: *Mineral resources* (New York).

FAO 1966: *Yearbook of fishery statistics* **22, 23** (Rome).

1970: *Yearbook* **24** (Rome).

1973: *Commodity review and outlook, 1972–73* (Rome).

FORESTRY COMMISSION 1976: Statistical review (unpublished), Table 47 : volume of imports, exports, home production and apparent consumption of wood products for the United Kingdom (P and E Branch).

FORREST, W.G. and OVINGTON, J.D. 1970: Organic matter changes in an age series of *Pinus radiata* plantations. *Journal of Applied Ecology* **7**, 177–86.

FORRESTER, J.W. 1971: *World dynamics* (Cambridge, Mass.).

GOLDMAN, M.I. 1972: *The spoils of progress: environmental pollution in the Soviet Union* (Cambridge, Mass.).

HERBICHOWA, MARIA 1969: Primary production of a ryefield. *Ekologia Polska*, seria A **17** (18), 343–50.

HOLE, F., FLANNERY, K.V. and NEELY, J.A. 1969: *Prehistory and human ecology of the Deh Luran Plain* (Ann Arbor, Mich).

HOLMES, W. 1971: Efficiency of food production by animal industries. In WAREING, P.F. and COOPER, J.P., editors, *Potential crop production*, (London).

HUBBERT, M.K. 1969: Energy resources. In *Resources and man*, (National Academy of Sciences, Washington), 157–242.

HUMBOLDT, ALEXANDER VON 1842: *Kosmos* (English translation, London, 1848–58).

HUNTINGTON, E. 1907: *The pulse of Asia* (Boston).

1915: *Civilization and climate* (New Haven).

HUXLEY, T.H. 1877: *Physiography: an introduction to the study of nature* (London).

INSTITUTE OF PETROLEUM 1972: *Oil — world statistics* (London).

IBP 1965: *IBP News*, no. 2.

IUCN 1975: *IUCN Bulletin* **6** (6).

IWAKI, H. 1974: Comparative productivity of terrestrial ecosystems in Japan, with emphasis on the comparison between natural and agricultural systems. *Proceedings of the first International Congress of Ecology, The Hague, The Netherlands, 8–14 September 1974* (Centre for Agricultural Publications and Documentation, Wageningen).

JOHNSON, E.A.J. 1937: *Predecessors of Adam Smith* (New York).

JOHNSON, S. 1970: *Life without birth — a journey throughout the Third World in search of the population explosion* (London).

JORDAN, C.F. 1971: Productivity of a tropical rain forest and its relation to a world pattern of energy storage. *Journal of Ecology* **59**, 127–42.

KIMURA, M. 1960: Primary production of warm temperate laurel forest in southern part of Osumi Peninsula, Kyushu, Japan. *Miscellaneous Report of the Research Institute of National Resources* (Japan) **52**, 36–47.

KIRA, T., OGAWA, H., GODA, K. and OGINA, K. 1967: Comparative ecological studies in three main types of forest region in Thailand. IV. Dry matter production with special reference to the Khao Chong rain forest. *Nature and life in Southeast Asia* **6**, 149–74.

KJELVIC, S. 1973: Biomass production of trees and bushes at two IBP sites at Hardangervidda, Norway. In BLISS, L.C. and WIELGOLASKI, F.E., editors, *Primary production and production processes, Tundra Biome* IBP Tundra Biome Steering Committee, Edmonton and Oslo.

KOBLENZ-MISHKE, O.I. 1965: The magnitude of the primary production of the Pacific Ocean. *Okeanologiya* **5**, 325–37 (in Russian).

KÖPPEN, W. 1931: *Grundriss der Klimakunda* (Berlin, 2nd edition).

KUCERA, C.L., DAHLMAN, R.C. and KOELLING, M.R. 1967: Total new productivity and turnover on an energy basis for tall grass prairie. *Ecology* **48**, 536–41.

LAMOTTE, M. 1972: Productivité des communautés terrestres en zones tropicales. In MONOD, TH., editor, *Compte-rendue d'activité des la participation française* (Progrès Biologie Internationale, Paris), 45–65.

LASKY, S.G. 1950: How tonnage-grade relations help predict ore reserves. *Engineering and Mining Journal* **151**, 81–5.

LEAKEY, L.S.B. 1965: *Olduvai Gorge 1951–61* **1**.

LEITCH, I. and GODDEN, W. 1953: The efficiency of farm animals in the conversion of feeding stuffs to food for man. *Commonwealth Bureau of Animal Nutrition*, Technical Communication no. 14.

LEMON, E., ALLEN., L.H. and MULLER, L. 1970: Carbon dioxide exchange of a tropical rain forest. Part II. *Bioscience* **20**, 1054–9.

LEWIS, R.W. 1965: Phosphate rock. In *Mineral facts and problems (US Bureau of Mines), 630.*

LIETH, H. 1972: Modelling the primary productivity of the world. *Nature and Resources* **8** (2), 5–10.

1973: Primary production: terrestrial ecosystems. *Human Ecology* **1** (4), 303–32.

LIETH, H. and WHITTAKER, R.H., editors, 1975: *The primary productivity of the biosphere (New York).*

LILIENTHAL, D.E. 1944: *Tennessee Valley Authority* (New York).

LOVERING, T.S. 1969: Mineral resources from the land. In *Resources and man* (National Academy of Sciences, Washington D.C.), 109–34.

LOVINS, A. 1975: *World energy strategies* (London, 2nd edition).

MACKINDER, H.J. 1887: On the scope and methods of geography. *Proceedings of the Royal Geographical Society* (new series) **9**, 141–6 and 698-701.

MALTHUS, T.R. 1798: An essay on the principles of population as it affects the future of society.

1803: *An essay on the principles of population or a view of its past and present effects on human happiness with an inquiry into our prospects respecting the future removal or mitigation of the evils it occasions* (reprinted for the Royal Economic Society, London, 1926).

MARSH, G.P. 1864: *Man and nature, or physical geography as modified by human action* (reprinted 1965, Harvard).

MARUYAMA, K. 1971: Effect of altitude on dry matter production of primeval Japanese beech forest communities in Naeba Mountains. *Memoirs of the Facilty of Agriculture, Niigata University* **9**, 87–171.

MASON, B. 1952: *Principles of geochemistry* (New York).

MCKEOWN, THOMAS 1976: The modern rise of population (London).

MCNAUGHTON, S.J. and WOLF, L.L. 1973: *General ecology* (New York).

MEADOWS, D.H., MEADOWS, D.L., RANDERS, J. and BEHRENS, W.W. 1972: *The limits to growth: a global challenge* (Washington, D.C.).

MILL, JOHN STUART 1857: *Principles of political economy* (London).

MINISTRY OF AGRICULTURE, FISHERIES AND FOOD 1968: *A century of agricultural statistics, Great Britain, 1866–1966* (London).

1970: *Modern farming and the soil* (London).

1974: *Household food consumption and expenditure and food facts*, no. 14.

MISRA, R. 1972: A comparative study of net primary productivity of dry deciduous forest and grassland of Varanasi, India. In GOLLEY, P.M. and GOLLEY F.B., editors, *Tropical ecology with an emphasis on organic production* (Athens Ga.), 279–93.

MUE, M. 1973: Primary production of plant communities of the Truelove Lowland, Devon Island, Canada — sedge meadows. In BLISS, L.C. and WIELGOLASKI, F.E., editors, *IBP Tundra Biome; Proceedings of the Conference on Primary Productivity and Production Processes, Tundra Biome, Dublin, April 1973* (Swedish IBP Committee, Stockholm).

MULLER, D. and NIELSEN, J. 1965: Production brute, pertes par respiration et production nette dans la forêt ombrophile tropicale. *Det forstlige Forsögsvaesen i Danmark* **29**, 69–110.

NATIONAL FARMERS' UNION 1975: *Insight*, Special issue, March.

ODUM, H.T. 1970: An emerging view of the ecological system at El Verde. In ODUM, H.T. and PIGEON, R.F., editors, *A tropical rain forest*, (US Atomic Energy Commission, Division of Technical Information, Oak Ridge Tennessee I–191 to I–281.

OGINO, K., RATANAWONGS, D., TSUTSUMI, T. and SHIDEI, T. 1967: The primary production of tropical forests in Thailand. *The South-East Asian Studies, Kyoto* **5**, 121–54.

POPULATION REFERENCE BUREAU 1968 and 1971: *World population data sheet.* (Washington D.C.).

RICKER, W.E. 1969: Food from the sea. In *Resources and man* (National Academy of Sciences, Washington), 87–108.

RODIN, L.E., BAZILEVICH, N.I. and ROZOV, N.N. 1974: Primary productivity of the main world ecosystems. *Proceedings of the First International Congress of Ecology, The Hague, The Netherlands, 8–14 September 1974* (Centre for Agricultural Publications and Documentation, Wageningen).

ROSCOE, S.M. 1965: Atomic energy developments and future uranium requirements as envisaged at the Third International Conference on the peaceful uses of atomic energy, Geneva, September 1964. *Geological Survey of Canada,* Paper 65–33.

SCHIMPER, A.F.W. 1903: *Plant geography upon a physiological basis* (translated by W.R. FISHER, Hitchin, Herts., 1960).

SCHUMACHER, E.F. 1973: *Small is beautiful: a study of economics as if people mattered* (London).

SHAW, M. 1968: *The US fast breeder reactor program*, US Atomic Energy Commission, press release of 1 May 1968.

SILK, L. 1976: Economic profession debates its role. In MERMELSTEIN, DAVID, editor, *Economics: mainstream readings and radical critiques* (New York, 3rd edition).

SIMS, P.L. and SINGH, J.S. 1971: Herbage dynamics and net primary production in certain ungrazed and grazed grasslands in North America. In *Preliminary analysis of structure and function of grasslands*, Range Science Department Science Series no. 10 (Colorado State University) 59–113.

SMITH, ADAM 1776: *An inquiry into the nature and causes of the wealth of nations* (reprint of 1812, London).

SMITH, C.S. 1965: Materials and the development of civilization and science. *Science* **148**, 908–17.

SOMERVILLE, MARY 1848: *Physical geography* (London).

STAMP, L.D. 1962: *Land of Britain* (London, 3rd edition).

STATESMAN'S YEARBOOK 1972–3: London.

STEARNS, F., KOBRIGER, N., COTTAM, G. and HOWELL, E. 1971: Productivity profile of Wisconsin. *Eastern Deciduous Forest Biome US-IBP Memo*, report no. 71–14.

SVOBODA, J. 1973: Primary production of plant communities of the Truelove Lowland, Devon Island, Canada — beach ridges. In BLISS, L.G. and WIELGOLASKI, F.E., editors *IBP Tundra Biome, Proceedings of the Conference on Primary Productivity and Production Processes, Tundra Biome, Dublin, April 1973* (Swedish IBP Committee, Stockholm).

TADAKI, Y. and HATIYA, K. 1968: *The forest ecosystem and its dry matter production* (Tokyo).

TAYLOR, G.R. 1970: *The doomsday book* (London).

THE ECOLOGIST 1972: *Blueprint for survival.*

UN 1967: *Demographic Yearbook.*

1969: *World population prospects, 1965–85, as assessed in 1968.* Population Division Working Paper no. 30.

1970a: *Natural resources of developing countries. Investigation, development and rational utilization.*

1970b: *Total population estimates for world, regions and countries, each year, 1950–1985.* Population Division Working Paper no. 34.

1971: *Population and vital statistics report,* series A **23**(1).

1973a; 1974a; 1975: *Commodity Trade Statistics.*
1973b; 1974b: *Statistical Yearbook.*
1974c: *Yearbook of International Trade Statistics.*
US BUREAU OF MINES 1965: *Minerals Yearbook.*
1966: *Minerals Yearbook.*
1970a: *Mineral facts and problems.*
1970b: *Minerals Yearbook* 3.
VINCENTE-CHANDLER, J., SILVA, S. and FIGARELLA, J. 1959: The effect of nitrogen fertilization and frequency of cutting on the yield and composition of three tropical grasses. *Agronomy Journal* **51**, 202–6.
WARREN WILSON, J. 1957: Arctic plant growth. *Advancement of Science* **13**, 383–8.
WATKINS, J.M. and LEWY-VAN SEVEREN, M. 1951: Effect of frequency and height of cutting on the yield, stand and protein content of some forages in El Salvador. *Agronomy Journal* **43**, 291–6.
WATT, K.E.F. 1974: *The Titanic effect* (Stamford, Conn.).
WESTLAKE, D.F. 1963: Comparisons of plant productivity. *Biological Revues* **38**, 385–425.
WHIGHAM, D., LIETH, H., NOGGLE, R. and GROSS, D. 1971: Productivity profile of North Carolina; preliminary results. *Eastern Deciduous Forest Biome, US-IBP Memo*, report no. 71–9.
WHITE, D.E. 1965: *Geothermal energy*. US Geological Survey Circular 519.
WOOLDRIDGE, S.W. 1950: Reflections on regional geography in teaching and research. *Institute of British Geographers, Transactions and Papers.*
WORKER, G.F. and MARBLE, V.L. 1968: Comparison of sorghum forage types as to yield and chemical composition. *Agronomy Journal* **60**, 669–72.

Index